W9-BLG-908

18,813

LC
111   Boles
.B55   The Bible, religion, and
1965   the public schools

DATE DUE

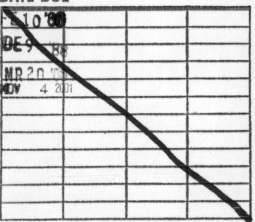

The Bible, religion, and the public scho
LC111.B55 1965   18813

Boles, Donald Edward
VRJC/WRIGHT LIBRARY

The Bible, Religion, and the Public Schools

DONALD E. BOLES

The Bible,
Religion,
and the
Public Schools

IOWA STATE UNIVERSITY PRESS, AMES, IOWA

1965

The Author

DONALD E. BOLES, professor of government, Iowa State University, is a widely known political scientist whose field of special interest is public law. He has been Chairman of the Iowa Governor's Commission on Human Rights, and Chairman of the Federal Advisory Committee on Civil Rights for Iowa, an advisory committee appointed by the U.S. Commission on Civil Rights to examine infringement of civil rights in each state. During the 1961–62 academic year, he was Visiting Professor at the Bologna Center of the John Hopkins University School of Advanced International Studies, Bologna, Italy. Besides this book, his publications include articles in *World Affairs Quarterly*, *The American Review*, and other law, political science, and education journals. He is coauthor of *An Evaluation of Iowa County Government* and *Welfare and Highway Functions of Iowa Counties: A Quantitative Analysis*. He served in 1964 as a member of the Commission on Religion and the Schools of the American Association of School Administrators which issued the report, *Religion and the Schools*.

© 1961, 1963, 1965 The Iowa State University Press
All rights reserved. Printed in the U.S.A.

FIRST EDITION, 1961
SECOND EDITION, 1963
THIRD EDITION, 1965

Second Printing, 1966

Library of Congress Catalog Card Number: 65–16369

FOR ROSEMARY

whose piano lessons suffered

Contents

Preface

Amendments to
THE CONSTITUTION OF THE
UNITED STATES

Article I. Congress shall make no law respecting an establishment of religion, or prohibiting the free exercise thereof; or abridging the freedom of speech, or of the press; or the right of the people peaceably to assemble, and to petition the Government for a redress of grievances. December 15, 1791.

Article XIV, Section I. All persons born or naturalized in the United States, and subject to the jurisdiction thereof, are citizens of the United States and of the State wherein they reside. No state shall make or enforce any law which shall abridge the privileges or immunities of citizens of the United States; nor shall any state deprive any person of life, liberty, or property without due process of law; nor deny to any person within its jurisdiction the equal protection of the laws. July 21, 1868.

THE 1960's MAY WELL BE REMEMBERED as the years when the United States Supreme Court began to look religion and the Constitution squarely in the eye. After years of being a bit gun-shy about getting to the heart of some of the fundamental questions of practice that were causing debates over the meaning of the "Establishment of Religion Clause" and the "Free Exercise of Religion Clause," the court moved dramatically in 1961, 1962, and 1963 to clarify a number of points.

In this short time span, the court upheld the validity of Sunday "Blue Laws," struck down a state regulation requiring a profession of the belief in the existence of God before one could hold public office, and, in probably the most far-reaching and controversial areas, held unconstitutional a state-authorized program of compulsory prayer in the public schools and two state-authorized programs of compulsory Bible reading in the public schools.

And the debate over the relationship between church and state was not restricted to the quiet confines of the judicial chambers during these years. A Roman Catholic was elected President of the United States, stirring in some areas old feelings not noticed since the presidential election of 1928. The proposed Federal Aid to Education Bill raised anew the long-smoldering controversy over public aid to parochial schools. In some parts of the United States this has become the crucial issue upon which congressional elections may turn, as pressure groups such as the "Citizens for Educational Freedom" pledge themselves to oppose any candidate who refuses to support federal aid to parochial schools.

Following the three Supreme Court decisions of 1962–1963, proposals to change drastically the Bill of Rights attracted wide attention. The most publicized and seriously considered was the Becker Amendment that would permit such religious observances as prayers and Bible reading on a voluntary basis (see Chapter 8). However, it was only one of at least one hundred and forty-seven bills and resolutions that took thirty-four different approaches to cancel the effect of the Supreme Court rulings.

Controversies over the relationship between church and state have shaken society to the roots from the earliest moments of recorded history. Unlike most of the nations in the Western World, the United States, while troubled to some extent by these disputes, has escaped the extremes that have plagued other nations. This has been traceable in large measure to the First Amendment to the United States Constitution and its interpretation by the United States Supreme Court.

Through its founding fathers, the United States has made two great contributions to Western civilization — the concept of the separation of church and state, and the secular public school system. True, the integrity of these two principles is often compromised while their virtues are being extolled, and they are frequently honored more in breach than in fulfillment. But the fact cannot be denied that they are important planks in the platform of American political philosophy.

Historically, those who oppose the theory of separation of church and state have centered their attack on the public school system. This method of attack is still being used, as is apparent to all who keep abreast of the news and who follow, even superficially, the activities of the Supreme Court.

Two fundamental propositions basic to our public school system are: public funds shall not be granted to sectarian schools, and sectarian instruction shall not be given in public schools. Most Americans agree with these principles in theory, but cannot agree as to how they shall be practiced. Because of this disagreement on the part of those who sincerely believe in the separation principle, those who oppose it have frequently been able to take advantage of the resulting confusion. In this way they have been able to syphon off public funds to parochial schools, and to introduce into the public schools Bible reading, prayers, and other exercises.

We propose here to look more closely at the second principle — that sectarian instruction not be given in our public schools — and in so doing to recognize it as one of the most persistent problems in United States Constitutional history involving the scope and interpretation of the First and Fourteenth Amendments.

To do this we must look not only at the various state constitutions, statutes, and court decisions, but also at the historic past from which all of our customs and theories spring.

In an area such as this, where controversies are frequently characterized by more heat than enlightenment, it might be well to begin this book with the admonition of the late Harry P. Judson, President of the University of Chicago.

> We should discuss the question without bitterness. It is not wise on the one hand for those who disapprove of the present system to stigmatize our public institutions as Godless schools; it is not wise, on the other hand, for those who believe in the advisability of maintaining this secular character of public education to assail others as bigoted religionists. There can be no doubt that each side embraces people of the utmost integrity of thought and of earnest moral purpose. The question should be discussed solely on its merits, and we should try to reach conclusions as a body of American citizens, respecting one another, recognizing the weight of opposing convictions, and seeking only the highest good of the young intrusted to our charge.

1

Historical Backgrounds

THE EIGHTH GRADE PUPILS of P.S. 7 gradually quiet down after the morning tardy bell has finished ringing. The teacher picks up a copy of the King James Version of the Bible from her desk and announces, "We will begin the school day by reading five verses of the Scriptures as is required by state law." She opens the book and starts reading the Beatitudes from the Book of Matthew in a flat voice. (The state law also requires that the Bible be read without note or comment to avoid sectarian bias.) Harold, the Jewish rabbi's son, squirms uncomfortably as he listens to the words of the New Testament. Mickey wonders uneasily about his parish priest's remarks regarding the King James Bible of the Protestants. George, son of "Freethinkers," sits scowling impatiently. Ann, listening intently, finds several things that puzzle her in the reading, but knows she cannot ask questions, since the teacher is prohibited from commenting. The reading finished, the teacher replaces the book, and the atmosphere of the classroom is cleared. But is it?

This is, of course, an extreme illustration of a practice dating back to Colonial days, and common to many public schools of the land before being declared unconstitutional by the Supreme Court in 1963. It is extreme — but it demonstrates some of the basic problems of religious freedom involved in such programs of Bible reading in the public schools.

It has been conjectured that two fortunate historical coincidences are responsible for our American tradition of religious freedom and disestablished religion. First, this country was colonized during a period of religious revolutions and counter-revolutions. Secondly, the United States Constitution was adopted during a period of intellectual rationalism and skeptical enlightment. "Neither by itself would suffice, but together they resulted in the First Amendment."[1] It is important to keep these two observations in mind during an investigation that attempts to determine the efficacy of Bible-reading programs, as well as their conformity to American conceptions regarding the relationship between church and state.

COLONIAL CONCEPTS

It is commonly known that religious controversies in England during the late sixteenth and early seventeenth centuries had destroyed the unity of the English people and reduced them to a series of warring sects. The Protestants presented a united front in opposing Roman Catholics, but their unity ended there. Anglicans fought with Calvinists and Methodists, while all opposed the Quakers and Anabaptists. To escape this unceasing and many-sided antagonism, dissenters of one sect or another sought refuge in the new world.

But once these people established themselves here, they

were not at all ready or willing to accord religious freedom to others who settled in their area and who held dissimilar views. Most of those who came to the Colonies were attempting to escape the Established Church of England. But they could not have been opposed to the theory of "establishment" as such, for almost immediately they created established churches of their own in most of the Colonies.

The Puritan states of New England during the early seventeenth century provide the best example of the single establishment principle. Here, not only was suffrage limited to church members (with the clergy deciding who qualified for membership), but the most vigorous methods were used to discourage dissenters from making known their views. The attitudes current in these Colonies were summed up by Nathaniel Ward in *The Simple Cobler of Aggawam:*

> I dare take upon me to be the Herald of New England so far as to proclaim to the world in the name of our colony that all Familists, Antinomians, Anabaptists and other Enthusiasts shall have free liberty to keep away from us and such as will come be gone as fast as they can, the sooner the better. . . . He that is willing to tolerate any religion . . . either doubts his own, or is not sincere in it.[2]

It is obvious from this that there could be no free exercise of religion in Colonial New England.

The militant Calvinism of the Puritans was concomitant with a great interest in education. This was partially because most of the founders of the Puritan Commonwealth were educated men and were more conscious of the benefits of education than was the average person of that day. A second and more compelling reason was that Calvinist theology demanded that each individual read, evaluate, and interpret the Bible, as well as Calvin's works. To do this, of course, it was necessary that every church member be able to read. And, it might be facetiously added, to read Calvin, one must read well. Furthermore, the Puritans were also humanists. Particularly in the early stages of their settlement, they were interested in the literature and thought of the Renaissance as well as that of the Reformation.

Development of the Colonial School System

Because of this element of the Puritans' belief it was necessary for them to establish some sort of school system. To enable all members of the congregation to send their children to school, they developed a system of public schools. These were sectarian public schools, where the public supported a single established religion and where dissenters' schools were not allowed to function.[3]

Puritanism was characterized by a learned clergy. And, as Professor Curti has pointed out, "The conception of a learned clergy capable of expounding the Bible in the light of scholarship and reason implies a sufficiently well educated laity to follow theological discussions."[4] While the clergy not only supported higher learning but also aided in the dissemination of knowledge, he goes on to explain, no function of the trained clergy was equally as important as the exposition of God's word. During this period each denomination relied on revelation as the only certain path to truth and knowledge. It is in this respect that the Bible was all-important, for "God had spoken and His word, contained in the Bible, was holy, absolute and final."

These factors, Curti states, help to explain why Puritan New England led in compulsory secondary education. As the local school systems developed, ministers usually continued to supervise the town schools, and when the town did not or could not support a Latin grammar school, it was they who prepared ambitious and studious youths for college. The important role played by clergymen in the development and functioning of public school systems in the United States was not, however, confined to Puritans.

> In New York the Dutch Reformed Church continued its early interest in schools, and among the German Pennsylvanians both Henry Melchior Muglenberg, the Lutheran leader and Michael Schlatter, the Swiss born patriarch of the German Reformed sect devoted much time to establishing and improving church schools. The Moravian Bishops at Bethlehem and Nazareth enjoyed wide renown for the excellence of their schools. Nor was the Scotch-Irish Presbyterian clergy negligent in regard to education; in Pennsylvania, New Jersey, and the Carolinas they too were leaders in founding and maintaining elementary and secondary schools.[5]

Frequently Anglican ministers in both Maryland and Virginia conducted schools or taught boys in the rectory. The Quakers alone among the Colonial denominations placed less emphasis on secondary education. They were relatively unique during this period also because they had no specially trained clergy. The Quakers insisted that any soul, however ignorant and unlearned, could commune directly with the Holy Spirit. But while this group de-emphasized secondary education, they did not ignore it, and they actively supported elementary schools.

Possibly it is due to this "respectable" beginning that the public schools in the United States have been able to maintain a status seldom accorded the state-supported schools of England until recently. In explaining this, and dealing with the sectarian nature of the first public schools, Pfeffer concludes that, "The origin of public education in the United States not merely antedates separation of Church and State. To a considerable extent, it owes its very existence to the fact that it antedated separation." [6]

Early School Laws

A look at various statutes and state constitutions bears out the fact that the motivating force behind public education in the American Colonies was to enable the students to read the Bible and to become better versed in Protestant religious dogma. The first school law emphasized this aspect of education. In 1642 Massachusetts invested local school boards with power to ". . . take account from time to time of all parents and masters, and of their children, concerning their calling and implyment of their children, *especially of their ability to read and understand the principle of religion and the capitall lawes of this country*."[7] [Italics mine]

Five years later, Massachusetts was even more specific. The school law of 1647 stated that every town with more than fifty householders must provide a schoolmaster, so that the children might learn to read the Scripture. The law quaintly explained:

> It being one chiefe project of ye ould deluder, Satin, to keepe men from the knowledge of ye Scripture, as in formr times by keeping ym in an unknowne tongue, so in these lattr times by perswading from ye use of tongues, yt so at least ye true sence and meaning of ye originall might be clouded by false glosses of saint seeming deceivers, yt learning may not be buried in ye grave of o[u]r fathrs in ye church and commonwealth . . .[8]

The first Massachusetts Constitution of 1780 took explicit notice of the important role religion must play in public education. It stated:

> As the happiness of a people, and the good order and preservation of civil government, essentially depend on piety,

religion, and morality; and as these cannot be generally defused through a community but by the institution of public worship of God, and of public instructions in piety, their happiness, and to secure the good order and preservation of their government, the people of this commonwealth have a right to invest their legislature with power to authorize and require and the legislature shall, from time to time, authorize and require, the several towns, parishes, precincts, and other bodies politic, or religious societies, to make suitable provision at their own expense, for the institution of the public worship of God, and for the support and maintainance of public Protestant teachers of piety, religion, and morality, in all cases where such provision shall not be made voluntarily.

And the people of this commonwealth have also a right to, and do, invest their legislature with the authority to enjoin upon all the subjects an attendance upon the instructions of the public teachers aforesaid, at stated time and seasons, if there be any on whose instructions they can conscientiously attend.[9]

The Bible played an important part in Colonial public schools, both for reading exercises and for moral instruction. E. P. Cubberley, when discussing Colonial education, has explained, "The most prominent characteristic of all the early Colonial schooling was the predominance of the religious purpose in instruction. One learned chiefly to be able to read the catechism and the Bible. . . . There was scarcely any other purpose in the maintenance of elementary education."[10]

Colonial Textbooks

The great differences in dogma separating the various sects during this period were overshadowed by the importance each denomination attached to the Bible. Anglicans and Catholics placed less emphasis on Bible reading by individuals than did the other groups, but the Bible was their ultimate authority on matters of dogma, and the highest source of God's revelation. By this time the early Puritan prejudice against reading the Bible in church services because it closely resembled the Catholic and Anglican liturgy had begun to disappear. But regardless of how they might feel about the Scripture's place in the church service:

> The Bible was to be found in almost every Calvinist household that possessed any books at all, and it was read not only once but over and over again. The obligation to read it was the chief reason for universal elementary education in communities dominated by Calvinism. Children sometimes learned their first letters from its pages; and even when they got their start in a catechism, a book of piety, or the highly Biblical *New England Primer,* they were soon graduated to the Testaments.[11]

It is important to note that even when the textbook used in elementary schools was not the Bible, it was usually a handbook closely paralleling biblical teaching and drawing heavily upon the Scriptures for its moral lessons. The *Hornbook,* one of the first texts, had at least half of its contents taken up with the Lord's Prayer. The *New England Primer* (*ca.* 1690), mentioned above, was noted for its religious flavor in both its rhyming alphabet and its catechism which was called "Spiritual Milk for American Babes Drawn Out of the Breasts of Both Testaments for Their Soul's Nourishment."[12]

The New England states were not alone in their belief that religion and the Bible constituted the core of education. The Bible was the chief reading matter in the German schools which the German Reformed and Lutheran bodies maintained in the Middle Colonies. The children of many of these households could repeat by heart a truly impressive number of Scripture verses. The Bible or Pastorius's *New Primer,* a thoroughly scriptural handbook, was used as a mainstay in instructing youthful readers among Quakers and Mennonites. Anglo-Americans had to depend upon imported Bibles until 1777, when the first American edition of the New Testament in English was printed. The German population as early as 1743 could read the Bibles which began to issue from the press of the Pennsylvania Dunker Christopher Saur.[13]

Early laws in a number of southern states also stressed the important role religion must play in education. A South Carolina statute of 1710 provided:

> . . . [I]t is necessary that a free school be erected for the instruction of the youth of this province in Grammar, and other arts and sciences and useful learning and also in the principles of the Christian religion.[14]

Its sister state North Carolina, as late as 1766, stated in the preamble of its constitution:

> Whereas a number of well-disposed persons, taking into consideration the great necessity of having a proper school of learning established whereby the rising generation may be brought up and instructed in the principles of the Christian religion . . .[15]

In spite of the fact that all denominations in Colonial America put great emphasis upon Bible reading in home, church, and school, there were wide differences in interpretation of the Bible. The vindictive form which these differences over scriptural interpretation took was particularly noticeable concerning the most effective way to achieve salvation. Such differences over biblical interpretation were at the heart of most of the sectarian disputes of the time, and each sect used different portions of the Scriptures to enforce its own beliefs. When discussing this point, Curti notes in *The Growth of American Thought*:

The Protestant churches, thus held apart by class as well as by doctrinal differences, believed firmly in the absolute correctness of their own interpretation of Scripture. Sectarianism was bitter, and this fact had and continued to have a marked effect on education. It meant that sects regarded education as of first importance in the maintenance of sectarianism: the education of children was to be controlled either in sectarian schools or, as in New England, in public schools whose policies and practices were determined by the orthodox in the community.[16]

From this it is difficult to escape the conclusion that during the Colonial period the Bible played an important role in sectarian religion and various portions of it were used by the different sects to enforce their beliefs both in and out the schools. The impetus behind the public school movement was to maintain the status quo of the established church. And one of the best ways to do this, it was believed, was to have pupils study the Bible. So pervasive and deepseated was this view that as late as 1846, the majority of Connecticut public schools, for example, still used the Bible as a reading book, despite the fact that the Connecticut Constitution of 1818 attempted to divorce the public schools from the influence of the Congregational church.

The Decline of Orthodoxy

Our system of public schools today owes much to the Puritan schools, minus, of course, the theory of sectarian instruction in the dogmas of the single established church. But even in the waning days of the Puritan theocracy, it is possible to discern a slight movement away from the teaching of sectarian religion. There were a number of reasons for this, although in this context giving a few will suffice.

The system of thought-control essential to the Puritan

commonwealth flourishes only in isolation. The New England states, however, became actively engaged in commerce and business, which by their very nature prevent an area from remaining isolated. This growth of commerce saw a corresponding growth of villages into cities, and in cities people of diverse religions sought employment. This influx of city workers, coupled with the policy of the states to grant agricultural land in fee simple to farmers, made the orthodox Puritans a minority group in many areas. It seems reasonable to assume that when the majority found that their children were subject in school to the indoctrination of Puritan religious views (that in many cases ran contrary to the parents' beliefs), a public outcry to eliminate such practices resulted. Since a great variety of sects existed in the United States at that time, no common denominator could be found which would allow any religious instruction and still not antagonize some group. As a result, the logical alternative was to eliminate all sectarian instruction. This did occur in the early days of the nineteenth century.

While it is certainly true that vestiges of sectarian instruction remained in the public schools (particularly in New England) well into the nineteenth century, James Lowell in his tribute to the village schools of Massachusetts foresaw the eventual trend toward secular instruction.

> Now this little building, and others like it, were an original kind of fortification invented by the founders of New England. They are the martello towers that protect our coast. *This was the great discovery of our Puritan forefathers. They were the first law givers who clearly saw and enforced practically the simple moral and political truth, that knowledge was not an alms to be dependent on the chance charity of private men or the precarious pittance of a trust fund, but a sacred debt which the commonwealth owed to every one of her children.* The open-

ing of the first grammar school was the opening of the first trench against monopoly of Church and State; the first row of trammels and pothooks which the little Shear-fashobs and Elkanahs blotted and blubbered across their copy-books, was the preamble to the Declaration of Independence . . . What made our Revolution a foregone conclusion was the act of the General Court passed May, 1647, which established the system of common schools.[17]

POST REVOLUTIONARY WAR CONCEPTS

During the last years of the Colonial period and during the early period of independence, the church-state separation movement advanced steadily. This is seen by the fact that when the Constitutional Convention met in 1787 only five of the thirteen states still retained some form of an established church. Toleration of a limited kind (excluding Catholics, Jews, Unitarians, and Deists) was fairly widespread through all the states when they adopted their constitutions during the Revolutionary War. While this period saw an increase in the influence of deism, particularly among the educated classes, religion and the Bible were not ignored.

An early act of Congress under the Articles of Confederation was directed toward procuring an American edition of the Bible. This seeking of federal aid to meet the lack of Bibles in the colonies materialized in 1777, when a resolution was passed, on September 11, instructing the Committee on Commerce "to import 20,000 copies." This proposal replaced an earlier one which sought to have the Bibles printed in this country, in order to save money. This plan was abandoned when it was found it would cost £10, 272 10s to buy type and paper abroad for the 30,000 copies originally considered. The proposal was argued for on moral and patriotic grounds.[18]

The *Journals* of Congress specifically note that Dr.

Patrick Allison (1740–1802), pastor of the First Presbyterian Church in Baltimore, and others were active in pushing this proposal. The Committee on Commerce reported
on September 11, 1777:

> The committee to whom the memorial of Dr. Allison and
> others was referred, report, 'That they have conferred
> fully with the printers, etc., in this city, and are of the
> opinion, that the proper types for printing the Bible are
> not to be had in this country, and that the paper cannot
> be procured, but with such difficulties and subject to
> such casualties, as render any dependence on it alto-
> gether improper: that to import types for the purpose of
> setting up an entire edition of the Bible, and to strike off
> 30,000 copies, with paper, binding, etc., will cost £10,272
> 10s, which must be advanced by Congress, to be reimbursed
> by the sale of the books: that, in the opinion of the com-
> mittee, considerable difficulties will attend the procuring
> the types and paper; that afterwards, the risque of import-
> ing them will considerably enhance the cost, and that the
> calculations are subject to such uncertainty in the present
> state of affairs, that Congress cannot much rely on them:
> that the use of the Bible is so universal, and its importance
> so great, that your committee refer the above to the con-
> sideration of Congress, and if Congress shall not think it
> expedient to order the importation of types and paper, the
> committee recommends that Congress will order the com-
> mittee of commerce to import 20,000 Bibles from Holland,
> Scotland, or elsewhere, into the different ports of the
> states of the Union.'[19]

Seven states, New Hampshire, Massachusetts, Rhode Island,
Connecticut, New Jersey, Pennsylvania, and Georgia voted
that the Committee of Commerce be directed to import the
20,000 copies of the Bible. Six states, New York, Delaware,
Maryland, Virginia, North Carolina, and South Carolina
opposed this suggestion. But while the motion was "re-
solved in the affirmative," the one-vote margin of victory
was so small that it was deemed wise to reconsider the matter. The result was that no final action was taken on this

proposal. Since no action had been taken in this direction by 1780, Congress adopted a resolution recommending that the states take action to procure one or more editions of the Testaments to be printed within their boundaries. It was also recommended that the states pass laws regulating their printers to insure that the Scriptures would not be misprinted.[20]

The First Amendment

The adoption of the First Amendment to the United States Constitution insured that the Federal Government could not violate religious freedom (within reasonable limits) and also prohibited that government from establishing a religion. Within recent years and partially because of the United States Supreme Court's decisions in the Everson and McCollum cases (discussed in Chapter 5) a great controversy has arisen over the intent of the founding fathers when they framed the First Amendment.

Some have maintained that James Madison and the others responsible for the wording of the Amendment desired to erect an insurmountable "wall of separation" between church and state. This would prevent any form of single or multiple establishment as well as prohibit all forms of governmental cooperation and indirect aids to religious groups.[21] Others stoutly maintain that this is not the case. They believe that the men responsible for the Amendment did not expect the state to be wholly neutral in matters of religion. Rather, the Amendment was for preventing the establishment of a single state church, and carried no injunction against incidental or indirect aid to all religions.[22]

We point out this controversy simply to illustrate the complete lack of agreement surrounding the historical antecedents of the American tradition of church-state separation. Moreover, an additional factor is involved in trying to determine the relationship of Bible-reading exercises in public schools to the American attitudes toward church and state. While proponents of such programs might agree that the First Amendment prohibits even indirect aids to religion, and while they might further agree that most state constitutions and statutes forbid sectarian instruction, they would not agree that Bible-reading exercises would be included in this ban. They argue that a program of Bible reading without comment is not sectarian. Others go so far as to state that it is not religious instruction, but merely instruction in morals and the American heritage.

An illustration of this may be seen in noting the practices in several of the states during the early nineteenth century. In Massachusetts, for example, sectarian instruction existed in many schools until 1827. The education law of that year gave school committees power over textbooks, and prohibited the introduction of books of a sectarian nature. The law read in part, "Provided also that said committee shall never direct any school books to be purchased or used in any of the schools under their superintendence, which are calculated to favor any particular religious sect or tenet."[23]

Sherman Smith points out, however, that even after the law of 1827 was passed, the Bible or the New Testament was still used as a reader in most schools in Massachusetts, although religion was taught incidentally rather than directly.[24] It has been previously noted that in spite of the

Connecticut Constitution of 1818 which attempted to divorce the public schools from church influence, a majority of public schools as late as 1846 still used the Bible as a reading book. Here in a nutshell, is the basic problem inherent in a discussion of Bible reading in public schools: namely, is the Bible a sectarian book? The educators of Massachusetts and Connecticut obviously felt it was not, and, hence, they were violating neither constitutional nor statutory prohibitions against sectarian instruction.

ATTITUDES OF THE FOUNDING FATHERS

The attitudes expressed by the founding fathers regarding religion and education are distinct and interesting. Since several of these men were extremely active in the religious disputes of the day, no definitive summary of all their statements on religion can be given. An attempt is made here simply to present some of their more characteristic views.

Stokes believes that George Washington's major contribution to religious liberty was his "Farewell Address," and that he should be considered a supporter of the movement for religious freedom rather than one who played an important part in initiating it.[25] In fact, at an earlier date he had supported the assessment plan in Virginia by which the state would contribute funds to the various Christian denominations. Washington, however, gave this up when he found that it had become a source of friction and bitter debate. Several points in the "Farewell Address" are of interest here. He stated:

> Of all the dispositions and habits which lead to political prosperity, Religion and Morality are indispensable supports. . . . In vain would that man claim the tribute of Patriotism, who should labour to subvert these great

pillars of human happiness, these firmest props of the duties of Men and Citizens. The mere Politician, equally with the pious man ought to respect and to cherish them . . . And let us with caution indulge the supposition, that morality can be maintained without religion. Whatever may be conceded to the influence of refined education on the minds of peculiar structure; reason and experience both forbid us to expect that national morality can prevail in exclusion of religious principle.[26]

The question whether moral instruction can be imparted without religious instruction is one of the main points in the debate over Bible-reading programs in the schools.

On the other hand, the treaty with Tripoli signed in 1796 during the presidency of George Washington, casts some doubt on the validity of the often-heard statement that the United States is a Christian nation. It said, in part:

As the Government of the United States of America is not in any sense founded upon the Christian Religion—as it has in itself, no character of enmity against the laws, religion or tranquility of Musselmen—it is declared by the parties, that no pretext arising from religious opinions shall ever produce an interruption of the harmony existing between the two countries.[27]

An interesting account is told of Benjamin Franklin's attitudes on this subject, and while it does not deal specifically with Bible reading, it illustrates his views on the efficacy of prayer in general. When the proceedings of the Constitutional Convention bogged down and it seemed likely that no formula could be worked out which would be satisfactory to a substantial majority of the delegates, Franklin moved that, "henceforth prayers imploring the assistance of heaven and its blessings on our deliberations be held in this assembly every morning before we proceed to business." The Convention, with the exception of three or four persons, however, felt that prayers were unnecessary, and adjournment was taken without any vote on the motion.[28]

The Views of Jefferson

Thomas Jefferson was extremely active in the movement to guarantee religious freedom and he opposed the creation of an established church in Virginia. It was his "Bill for Establishing Religious Freedom," which he and James Madison successfully piloted through the Virginia Legislature, that replaced Patrick Henry's "Bill Establishing a Provision for Teachers of the Christian Religion." The latter bill would have used public funds for sectarian religious purposes. But of particular interest to us here are his views on Bible reading and religious instruction in the schools.

When commenting on the elementary curriculum of the proposed Education Bill of 1779 in Virginia, he wrote, "Instead, therefore, of putting the Bible and the Testaments into the hands of children at an age when their judgments are not sufficiently mature for religious inquiries, their memories may be stored with the useful facts from Grecian, Roman, European and American history."[29] It may be seen from this that Jefferson clearly regarded Bible reading as, at least, *religious inquiry,* if not instruction.

The Bill of 1779 was not passed by the legislature, but in 1817 Jefferson tried again. The Education Bill of 1817, which he drew up, contained most of the provisions of the earlier bill, but was even more specific regarding religion. Essentially he was attempting to prohibit all religious influence or control in the schools. The Eleventh Article specifically attempted to rule out all religious instruction by providing that:

> . . . [N]o religious reading, instruction or exercise, shall be prescribed or practiced inconsistent with the tenets of any religious sect or denomination.[30]

Had this bill been passed, it surely would have prohibited Bible reading in the public schools of Virginia, for as Jefferson and Madison understood the meaning of the words "sectarian religion" they referred to Jewish, Mohammedan, and Hindu religions as well as to Christianity.

Another example of Jefferson's attitude toward the teaching of religion in schools may be seen by noting his proposal to amend the constitution of William and Mary College. "His major proposal for curriculum reforms was to remove the six professors established by the original Charter (two of whom were to teach theology) and to establish in their place eight professors, (none of whom were to teach theology)."[31] This proposal would have brought the college more in line with the aims of the democratic state by in effect making it a state university.

Finally, we need only to look at Jefferson's influence on the University of Virginia from the time of its origin, to be convinced of his antagonism toward religious instruction in public schools. Jefferson's report, which was accepted by the Board of Commissioners and passed by the state legislature, established the University on a purely secular basis. There were no professors of religion or theology in the new school; instead, the instruction of moral philosophy was left to a professor of ethics. Instruction was also in Latin, Greek, and Hebrew, so that if a student so desired he might read the original religious writings. Jefferson summed up his position by concluding:

> Proceeding thus far without offense to the Constitution, we have thought it proper at this point to leave every sect to provide, as they think fittest, the means of further instruction in their own peculiar tenets.[32]

There were those who objected to the secular nature of the University, and called it an atheistic school. In an

VERNON REGIONAL
JUNIOR COLLEGE LIBRARY

attempt to mollify the critics, Jefferson and the Board of Commissioners worked out a plan allowing the various sects, if they wished, to set up seminaries on the boundaries of the University of Virginia. In this way they might enjoy its facilities, but still be kept separate. Butts feels that this form of cooperation was a compromise for expediency's sake, worked out by Jefferson to gain the religious groups' support for the infant University, and yet not sacrifice any of its independence.[33]

In line with these views, it is not surprising to find that a chaplain was not appointed to the University of Virginia until 1829. This was done only after Madison, who followed Jefferson as Rector, had written that support of such a chaplain should be entirely voluntary. In 1828, he wrote:

> I have indulged the hope that provisions for religious instruction and observance among the students would be made by themselves or their parents and guardians, each contributing to a fund to be applied in remunerating the services of clergymen of denominations corresponding with the preferences of the contributors. *Being altogether voluntary, it would interfere neither with the characteristic peculiarity of the University, with the consecrated principle of law, nor the spirit of the country.*[34]

Madison, like Jefferson, was an active champion of religious freedom, and like the latter he was strongly opposed to all religious programs which received even the most indirect public aid. When speaking of the First Amendment which Madison fathered, Brant, one of his leading biographers, states, "His aim was to strike down financial aid to religious institutions out of the public purse. . . . Not by the most microscopic concession would he deviate from absolute separation between 'the authority of human laws and the natural rights of Man!' "[35]

An example of this may be seen by his action while President of the United States in vetoing a bill to incorporate the Protestant Episcopal Church in the District of Columbia. He noted that the bill, "violates in particular the article of the Constitution of the United States which declares that 'Congress shall make no laws respecting a religious establishment.' " Of more immediate interest to us here was his objection to the bill's provision for the education of the poor children of the church. He feared this as "establishing" a precedent for giving religious societies, as such, a legal agency in carrying into effect a public and civic duty.[36] Some argue from this that Madison would object to allowing parochial schools to qualify for the public and civic duty of educating the youth of our land.[37]

EARLY NINETEENTH CENTURY LEGAL ASPECTS

It is generally agreed that education is a state matter, and the rule of *Barron* v. *Baltimore*[38] and *Permoli* v. *New Orleans*[39] states the federal principle of dual citizenship, which held that the Bill of Rights of the United States Constitution applied only to national rights and privileges, and was not binding on the states. The Permoli case dealt specifically with the religious liberty section of the First Amendment. Until fairly recently, questions of educational policy, such as Bible reading, or state laws restricting religious freedom, such as were involved in the Permoli case, were not regarded as coming within the scope of the First Amendment or the remaining portions of the Bill of Rights.

The modern Supreme Court, however, has interpreted the Fourteenth Amendment broadly enough so as to include the entire First Amendment. The religious liberty section of the First Amendment was read into the Fourteenth Amendment by the Cantwell[40] decision, and the disestablishment principle was incorporated by the McCollum[41] case holding. Thus credence is given to Pfeffer's statement that the evolution of the First Amendment "is a continuous evolution, and each generation must interpret the meaning of separation [of church and state] for itself in the light of its conception of American democracy and the enlightened political thinking of the day."[42] Surely such an interpretation cannot help but be influenced by the firm attitudes of men like Madison and Jefferson who were so greatly responsible for the First Amendment.

THE ANTE BELLUM PERIOD
AND THE SECULAR PUBLIC SCHOOL

During the Jacksonian period and the period of the great awakening, the Democrats remained true to the principles of Jefferson and Madison. Schlesinger has pointed out that in place of the Whig or Federalist theory of a "national religion," the Democrats set up a theory of religious nonintervention. This was their version of the Jeffersonian theory of complete separation of church and state. The Whigs had long charged that the Democratic party was the party of irreligion, and Tom Paine, who was a Democratic hero, was to the Whigs a "filthy little Atheist." It is apparent that the arch-conservatism of much of the clergy had alienated many liberals. "Samuel Clesson Allen put it, 'The clergy as a class has always been ready to come in for a share in the advantages of the privileged classes, and in return for the ease and convenience accorded to them by these classes, to spread their broad mantle over them.' "[43]

Another characteristic of the Jacksonian era was the

broadening of the franchise. This, a number of writers believe, is the major cause for the great development of true public schools during and immediately following this period. At least one writer thinks that the broadened franchise coupled with the more liberal attitude of the Democrats toward religion, in a sense encouraged the development of many dissenting religious sects; for by this time the churches established or supported by the state had disappeared.[44] Once these sects could worship freely, they began to promote their own religious schools. Thus, along with the enlargement of the public school system during this period came a corresponding increase in a varied assortment of parochial schools.

The period from 1830 through the 1840's saw not only an increase in the number of Protestant sects, but an enormous influx of Roman Catholic immigrants. The fear that early Catholic opposition to Bible reading and other Protestant practices in the public schools would lead to Catholic domination led to open and at times violent hostility toward Roman Catholics. Debates over the efficacy of Bible reading became increasingly common during this time, and the extreme Protestant opposition to the Catholic viewpoint finally crystallized in the Know-Nothing political movement which was organized officially as a party in 1853.[45] During this period of strife, Horace Mann, the father of the public school system in America, emerged as the great crusader against sectarianism in the public schools.

Horace Mann and Sectarianism

The increase in the number of Protestant sects and the growth of a significant Roman Catholic minority made it clear to Mann that the narrow sectarianism which was still a part of many school curricula was an undue handicap on the public school system. His critics have often accused him of being irreligious because of his militant opposition to sectarian instruction. But Mann's dilemma is best expressed by Blau:

> Horace Mann could not but reject the view that government should concern itself with the fixing of religious truth. On the other hand he could not accept the view that abjured all religion and was a reaction to it. He accepted the view that 'Government should do all that it can to facilitate the acquisition of religious truth, but shall leave the decision of the question what religious truth is, to the arbitrament, without human appeal, of each man's reason and conscience.'[46]

He pointed out to his critics that they would not suggest teaching one set of political beliefs in school. It would be just as absurd to teach one religious viewpoint. On the other hand he was cognizant of the need for the schools to contain some form of moral instruction. His solution was for the schools to teach the *common* elements of Christianity contained in the Bible. Some of these are honesty, fairness, and truth. In teaching these, he felt that it would be possible to use the Bible as a reader, but to distinguish his plan from those then in use, he insisted that no remarks or comments should be made on the reading. When the Bible spoke for itself, Mann believed that it was not sectarian.

Besides the Bible, a multitude of other books that had a sectarian slant were used in the public schools. The extent of this use is illustrated in Mann's speech (regarding the Education Statute of 1826 that prohibited sectarian instruction) contained in his *First Report* to the Massachusetts Board of Education, January 1, 1838. He stated:

The consequence of the enactment, however, has been, that among the vast libraries of books, expository of the doctrines of revealed religion, none have been found free from that advocacy of particular 'tenets' or 'sects' which includes them within the scope of the legal prohibition; or, at least, no such books have been approved by the committees and introduced into the schools. Independently, therefore, of the immeasurable importance of moral teaching in itself considered, this entire exclusion of religious teaching, though justifiable under the circumstances, enhances and magnifies a thousand fold, the indispensableness of moral instruction and training. Entirely to discard the inculcation of the great doctrines of morality and of natural theology has a vehement tendency to drive mankind into opposite extremes; to make them devotees on one side, or profligates on the other; each about equally regardless of the true constituents of human welfare.[47]

While Mann would not go as far as Jefferson and Madison in granting the freedom of conscience to those outside the Christian religion, he went further than most people of that day in his willingness to grant it to unpopular or minority Christian groups. For example, Mann disputed with the Sunday School Union over having its book *The Child at Home* accepted in the Massachusetts public schools while he was secretary of the State Board of Education. He objected to the book as being sectarian since its doctrinal basis regarding the last judgment, sin, and other matters, represented orthodox doctrines not accepted by such groups as the Unitarians and the Universalists.[48] Although Mann won the battle to exclude this book from the public schools, it was done only after bitter attacks upon him by the newspapers, instigated by Fredrick A. Packard, recording secretary of the Sunday School Union. Packard was so incensed by his failure that he anonymously wrote a scurrilous attack upon Mann, after the great educator had died.

There is little doubt regarding Mann's views on Bible reading. On September 1, 1844, he wrote:

> I believe it is their wish, as it is mine, that the Bible should continue to be used in our schools; but still, that it shall be left with the local authorities,—where the law now leaves it,—to say, in what manner, in what classes, etc., it shall be used. I suppose it to be their belief, as it is mine, that the Bible makes known to us the rule of life and the means of salvation; and that, in the language of the apostle, it is a 'faithful saying, and worthy of all acceptance, that Christ Jesus came into the world to save sinners'; but still, that it would be a flagrant transgression of our duty to select any one of those innumerable guide boards—whether pointing forward, right, left, or backward—which fallible men have set up along the way, and to proclaim that the kingdom of heaven is only to be sought for in that particular direction.[49]

Mann's belief that it was possible to use the Bible as a nonsectarian text was also enunciated in a Fourth of July oration he gave. He said, "In every course of studies, all the practical and preceptive parts of the Gospel should be sacredly included, and all dogmatical theology and sectarianism sacredly excluded. In no school should the Bible have been opened to reveal the sword of Polemic, but to unloose the dove of peace."[50]

He phrased his argument a little differently in his Eleventh Annual Report of the State Board of Education, and also gave some indication of the prevalency of Bible reading in Massachusetts' schools. He wrote:

> The use of the Bible in schools is not expressly enjoined by law, but both its letter and spirit are in consonance with that use; and as a matter of fact, I suppose there is not, at the present time, a single town in the Commonwealth in whose schools it is not read. . . . The administration of this law is entrusted to the local authorities in the respective towns. By introducing it, they introduce what all believers hold to be the rule of faith and prac-

tice; and although by excluding theological systems of human origin they may exclude a peculiarity which one denomination believes to be true, they do but exclude what other denominations believe to be erroneous.[51]

In his final report all of these sentiments are summed up in an eloquent plea for schools free from sectarian influence.

> Our system earnestly inculcates all Christian morals; it founds its morals on the basis of religion, it welcomes the religion of the Bible, and in receiving the Bible, it allows it to do what it is allowed to do in no other system—to speak for itself . . . if a man is taxed to support a school where religious doctrines are inculcated which he believes to be false, and which he believes God condemns, he is excluded from the school by divine law at the same time that he is compelled to support it by human law. This is a double wrong.[52]

Horace Mann, then, was the originator of the theory which approved of Bible reading when done without comment. If the Bible was allowed to speak for itself, Mann believed, it was not sectarian instruction. This is essentially the argument used by most proponents of Bible reading today. There are, however, several factors to consider to understand his motivation in this direction. He was a deeply religious man with an extremely sensitive nature. And while he consistently opposed orthodoxy,[53] he could never completely ignore the compelling power of the Christian religion generally. This perhaps explains his somewhat inconsistent stand on religion. To paraphrase Mr. Dooley, on the one hand he would banish religion from the schools, but on the other — not so fast.

Effects of the Roman Catholic Influx

Another factor to be noted here is that Mann formulated his views on Bible reading before the full impact and consequence of the vast Roman Catholic migration was known. Had the United States remained a Protestant country it is possible Mann's theory would have worked. But when Irish and German Roman Catholics flocked to this country in the 1840's, they almost immediately raised objections to the use of the Protestant Bible as required reading in the public schools. Mann, it will be remembered, would be the first to admit that to teach something in school which is opposed to a man's conscience and yet force him to attend the instruction is a "double wrong." The question which still remains unanswered in spite of his novel plan, is not "Shall the Bible be read in school," but "Which version of the Bible shall be read?"

Some idea as to the manner of attack by the Roman Catholics on Protestant influence in the public schools may be gained by studying the fight which occurred in New York during the early 1840's. In 1805, the Protestant groups had founded the Free School Society, which had as its goal the education of the city's poor children. As the organization gained prestige, it was able, after a time, to win public financial support and finally it evolved into the public school system of New York City, still retaining many of the vestiges of the Protestant religion.

In 1840, the Roman Catholics had become an important enough group in the city to challenge seriously the Protestant coloration of the public schools. This led to a heated political fight during the years 1840–41 to establish the right of conscience of the Catholic student. The Catholics argued that while the form of cooperation between the state and the church which existed in New York State was acceptable to them in theory, they would prefer that in practice it take the form of dividing the public funds in such a way that they could be used to support Roman Catholic schools apart from the existing public school system.[54]

As a result of this controversy, a law was passed by the New York legislature in 1842, which brought the New York City schools into the state public school system, and prohibited the teaching of sectarian religious doctrines.[55] The latter portion of the statute read:

> No school above mentioned, or which shall be organized under this act in which any religious, sectarian doctrine or tenet shall be taught, inculcated or practiced, shall receive any portion of the school moneys to be distributed by this act . . .

In 1853, the State Superintendent of Schools of New York, in line with the law of 1842, ruled that prayers could not be required as part of school activities; and where the King James Version of the Bible was read in the schools, Catholic pupils could not be required to attend.[56] In a fairly recent decision[57] the State of New York's Supreme Court reaffirmed this view. The theory of this compromise closely resembles Horace Mann's views on such programs in the public schools. It was at this point that the Civil War intervened temporarily to unify state factions during the great battle of sectionalism.

POST CIVIL WAR CONCEPTS

Before the Civil War, the political movement to gain public support of sectarian education had taken place on a state level, but after the war it took on national importance. The Roman Catholic minority in the United States had continued to grow, and their opposition to Bible reading and other exercises which they considered to be Protestant-inspired became more and more vocal. Fear of Catholic domination and public concern over the rumor that the Pope might move the papal see to the United States because of Garibaldi's encroachments on papal authority in the early 1870's caused a wave of anti-Catholicism which swept the nation.[58]

Even the eminent cartoonist Thomas Nast was drawn into the debate. He produced a series of biting caricatures attacking papal influence in the United States and criticizing Catholic opposition to the public schools, particularly their stand on Bible reading.[59] It is not surprising that before long the two major political parties became partisans in the dispute. Rightly or not, the Democratic Party came to be associated with the Roman Catholic cause, which in the public mind stood for state support of parochial schools, opposition to Bible reading in the public schools, and a hostility to public schools in general. As might be assumed, the Republican Party took the opposite view.

This helps explain Grant's famous speech to the Army of Tennessee at Des Moines in September, 1875. He said in part:

> Let us all labor to add all needful guarantees for the security of free thought, free speech, a free press, pure morals, unfettered religious sentiments, and of equal rights and privileges to all men, irrespective of nationality, color, or religion. Encourage free schools, and resolve that not one dollar appropriated for their support shall be appropriated to the support of any sectarian schools. Resolve that neither the state nor the nation, nor both combined, shall support institutions of learning other than those sufficient to afford every child growing up in the land the opportunity of a good common-school education, unmixed with sectarian, pagan, or atheistical dogmas. *Leave the matter of religion to the family altar, the church, and*

the private school, supported entirely by private contributions. Keep the church and state forever separated.[60]

In his annual message to Congress in 1875, Grant recommended a constitutional amendment forbidding the teaching in the public schools of any sectarian religious tenets and further prohibiting "the granting of any school funds or school taxes or part thereof, either by the legislative, municipal or other authority, for the benefit or aid, directly or indirectly, of any religious sect or denomination."[61]

The Blaine Amendment

Acting on Grant's suggestion, James G. Blaine proposed the following amendment to the United States Constitution in 1876.

> No state shall make any laws respecting an establishment of religion or the free exercise thereof; and no money raised by taxation in any state for the support of public schools, or derived from any public funds thereof, nor any public lands devoted thereto, shall ever be under the control of any religious sect or denomination, nor shall any money so raised or lands so devoted be divided between religious sects and denominations.[62]

The amendment, in a form considerably stronger than that proposed by Blaine — it carried additional provisions prohibiting teaching of religion in publicly supported schools — was overwhelmingly passed by the House (180–7). However, it failed to obtain a two-thirds majority vote in the Senate (28–16). The vote followed straight party lines, with the Republicans voting for it and the Democrats opposing it. One writer believes that an explanation for the failure of the amendment was the feeling among many legislators that the state constitutions were adequately equipped to handle this question.[63]

However, a number of legislators could not have been absolutely convinced of the states' ability to handle this problem. Despite the failure of the Blaine Amendment, Congress required that all new states admitted to the Union after 1876, must adopt irrevocable ordinances that not only guaranteed religious freedom, but also required the state to include a provision "for the establishment and maintenance of a system of public schools which shall be open to all the children of said state and free from sectarian control."[64]

Additional evidence of the deep concern felt by men over sectarian instruction in public schools and public support of sectarian schools may be seen by noting a plank in the Republican national platform of 1876 and 1880. It read:

> The public school system of the several States is the bulwark of the American Republic; and with a view to its security and permanence, we recommend an amendment to the Constitution of the United States forbidding the application of any public funds or property for the benefit of any school or institution under sectarian control.[65]

It is clear from all of this that a significant number of people in the United States during this period were opposed to sectarian instruction in the public schools. The big question left unanswered, however, is, "Did they regard Bible reading as an example of sectarian instruction?" It would appear that many Protestants did not see the Bible as a sectarian book, and could not conceive of Bible reading in the public schools as sectarian instruction. But from the 1870's through the turn of the century Roman Catholics and Jews in their sincere opposition to the use of the King James Bible in the public schools were gaining adherents from a variety of other groups.

Growing Resistance to Sectarianism

In the late 1870's Roman Catholics and Jews were joined by the so-called liberal movement which vehemently attacked all traces of religion in American life. This group attempted to exclude from public place not only the Bible but all references to the Deity.[66] Shortly after this, Roman Catholics and Jews picked up support from a group of ministers whose theological beliefs had been shaken by the disproving of many tenets which the authoritarian religion of their youth had insisted must be accepted without question. This resulted in their conclusion that nothing could be gained by forcing religion on pupils and teachers. A required exercise, they stressed, did not best serve the interests of religion itself.[67] Thus, by the end of the nineteenth century an increasing number of people from all sects and with all intellectual leanings had come to regard the practice of Bible reading as sectarian instruction in the public school.

This period saw a number of court actions in the state courts seeking to prohibit Bible reading in the schools.[68] Not all were successful, but the rationale of the Wisconsin Supreme Court in outlawing Bible reading has come to be used as the standard line of reasoning used by the courts that have ruled against such practices. But, as will be seen later, the courts that heard these cases showed no agreement as to whether Bible reading in the schools is a sectarian practice.

During the last half of the nineteenth century then, it became clear to most Americans that a definite need existed to keep public schools free from sectarian instruction and to divorce parochial schools of all types from public funds.

The major reason for this was the vast increase and diversity of religious sects in this country. It had become increasingly apparent that the only way to keep the local, state, and federal governments from becoming embroiled in religious controversies, which had a habit of centering around the schools, was to keep government as aloof as possible from religion.

This tendency is reflected in specific constitutional provisions incorporated into the constitutions of many of the states entering the Union from around the middle of the nineteenth century to its end, as well as additions or revisions to the then existing state constitutions and statutes. In 1896 and 1897 the federal government took notice of the prevailing climate of opinion in the nation. It announced in the Appropriation Acts for the District of Columbia for those years a national policy which conformed with the constitutional provisions in the vast majority of states. The act read in part:

> And it is hereby declared to be the policy of the government of the United States to make no appropriations of money or property for the purpose of founding or maintaining, or adding by payment for services, expenses or otherwise, any church or religious denomination, or any institution or society which is under sectarian or ecclesiastical control.[69]

This avowal of principles, however, was not interpreted by the schoolmen to prohibit the reading of the Bible in the District of Columbia public school system, for Bible reading has for long been the rule rather than the exception there.[70]

This brings us then to the twentieth century attitudes on such exercises with which the remainder of this book will deal.

Summary

Before moving on, however, several important points should be summarized. During the heyday of the Puritan Commonwealth and its single established church, the primary purpose behind public education was to enable the student to read and understand the Bible. Bible reading in the public schools was universal during this period. In the early days of our independence, it became apparent to thoughtful men that the multiplicity of sects arising in the United States required some form of divorce between church and state — for the good of both. This theory became national policy with the inauguration of the First Amendment. Jefferson and Madison, two of the leaders in the fight to achieve religious liberty in the United States, both were critical of religious exercises in public-supported schools. Jefferson, in particular, objected to programs of Bible study in these schools.

Despite the attitudes of men like Jefferson and Madison, Bible reading was quite common during the ante bellum period. This period saw increased attacks upon sectarianism in the public schools by newly arrived Roman Catholic and Jewish immigrants, and they included Bible reading in their list of sectarian influences. Horace Mann, who played such an important part in the development of our true public schools, felt, however, that it was possible to study the Bible in a way that would not be sectarian. He believed the Bible read without comment in order to study the common elements of Christianity, could not possibly injure the religious sensibilities of anyone.

Following the Civil War the debate over sectarian instruction and Bible reading in the public schools grew especially heated, and took on national scope. It became a lively issue in the political campaigns of the day with the major parties aligning themselves on opposite sides. During the process of the dispute the Roman Catholics and Jews who had consistently opposed such exercises found themselves joined by "liberal intellectuals" and some important Protestant clergymen who objected to any type of compulsory religious service. Thus, the attitudes regarding such programs were no longer crystallized along denominational lines. By the end of the century several courts had declared Bible reading in the schools illegal.

The issues involved in this problem which appeared relatively simple to an observer in the mid-nineteenth century have become, as we shall see, increasingly cloudy in the twentieth. Today it is no longer possible to predict a person's attitudes on Bible reading simply by knowing his religious affiliation. Now legislatures, courts, and pressure groups tack and twist tortuously in an attempt to fathom the public's opinion.

2

State Constitutions
and Statutes

DESPITE THE SENATE DEFEAT in 1876 of the Blaine Amendment, the movement for prohibiting sectarian instruction in the public schools and forbidding state support of parochial schools was too powerful to be ignored. During the period just prior to and following the Civil War, most states were including in their constitutions prohibitions concerning the use of tax revenue for sectarian purposes in both public and parochial schools. In 1876, the Congress of the United States passed a law requiring all states admitted to the Union after that date to have irrevocable provisions in their constitutions that guaranteed religious freedom and the establishment of a public school system free from sectarian control.[1]

It would appear, however, that the United States Supreme Court's ruling in *Coyle* v. *Smith* would make such a provision unenforceable by Congress once the state has has been officially admitted.[2] There, the court held that states, after being admitted to the Union, were on a basis of equality with all other states, and that restrictions placed upon them by Congress as conditions for admission, could not include matters normally considered to be completely under a state's jurisdiction.

Even before the 1876 federal requirement, states entering the Union around the middle of the nineteenth century had anticipated the need for such provisions and included them in their constitutions. Wisconsin, which became a state in 1848, has provisions covering these subjects which are fairly representative of this voluntary tendency:

> The right of every man to worship almighty God according to the dictates of his own conscience shall never be infringed; nor shall any man be compelled to attend, erect, or support any place of worship . . . nor shall any control of or interference with the rights of conscience be permitted, or any preference be given by law to any religious establishment or modes of worship.[3]

Another section provides that the legislature shall set up common schools, "and no sectarian instruction shall be allowed therein."[4]

EARLY STATE CONSTITUTIONS

The Revolutionary War constitutions of the original thirteen states illustrate the close affiliation and cooperation between church and state which existed at that time. Some of their more outstanding features are noteworthy here as demonstrating no real antagonism, for the most part, toward the use of public funds for sectarian education.[5]

The Delaware Constitution of 1776 required an officeholder to profess his faith in Christianity and a belief in the validity of the Old and New Testaments. While it did not exclude Roman Catholics it did exclude Jews and other non-Christians. At the same time it provided that the state could not establish one religious sect in preference to another.

The Georgia Constitution of 1777 also required that members of the state legislature be of the Protestant religion. It did, however, provide that all persons should have free exercise of religion, and need not support any teachers, "except those of their own profession."

The New Hampshire Constitution of 1776 said nothing about religion, but the one which went into operation in 1784 required officeholders to be of the Protestant faith. It also empowered the legislature to authorize the municipalities to provide at their own expense for the support of Protestant teachers of "piety, religion and morality."[6] At the same time it provided that no Christian sect would be established by law.

The New Jersey Constitution of 1776 excluded Roman Catholics from elective offices, but required that there be no establishment of religion, and no preference shown to any Protestant sect by the State.

The constitution adopted by North Carolina in 1776 also required officeholders to be Protestants. It prohibited the establishment of religion and the compulsory attendance or support of the "building of any house of worship."

The Massachusetts Constitution of 1780 contained a Declaration of Rights which was largely the work of John Adams.[7] While it prohibited the establishment of any sect and granted all Christians equal protection under the law, it also provided for the public support of Protestant teachers of "piety, religion and morality, in all cases where such provision shall not be made voluntarily."[8]

The New York Constitution of 1777 after making some barbed remarks about the "spiritual aggression and intolerance" of "wicked priests," goes on to grant the "free exercise and enjoyment of religious profession and worship without discrimination or preference." In spite of this, the Episcopal church still retained special privileges until a legislative act of 1784 put an end to them.

The constitution adopted by Pennsylvania in 1776 required a Christian oath and belief in both Testaments as prerequisites for holding public office. However, it stressed religious freedom, and placed Christian sects on an even footing by forbidding the compulsory support of any place of worship.

The state of Rhode Island did not immediately adopt a constitution during the Revolutionary era, but remained under its Colonial charter of 1663. This prohibited an establishment of religion and granted religious freedom to all Christians. It was this that made Rhode Island the most tolerant of the original thirteen states toward religious diversities, but here too, the religious freedom of Jews and non-Christians was restricted.

South Carolina's first constitution of 1776 contains no Bill of Rights and makes no reference to religion or religious freedom. But the Constitution of 1778 is exceptionally clear-cut in providing for the establishment of the Protestant religion. However, it refers to no specific denomination. Only Protestants could hold seats in the state legislature, and a belief in God was required of all voters. Article XXVIII contains the most detailed provisions to insure a Protestant state of any constitution in the history of the United States.[9]

The Vermont Constitution of 1777 contains a Bill of Rights which is devoted to religion and which closely resembles the Pennsylvania Constitution of 1776. It provides that no one can be compelled to support a place of worship against his will, and unlike the previously mentioned constitution of Pennsylvania states that no Protestant can be deprived of his civil rights due to his religious sentiments. (The Pennsylvania constitution made no reference to Protestantism.) Section XLI of this Vermont document also provided for the public encouragement and protection of religious societies incorporated for the advancement of religion and learning.

Furthermore, the Vermont Supreme Court held in 1961 that merely because public funds were expended to an institution operated by a religious enterprise, this did not establish the fact that the proceeds were used to support the religion professed by the recipients.[10]

The struggle for religious freedom and disestablishment in Virginia is too complex to be covered in this cursory review. It must suffice to say that the Anglican church was the established church here in 1776, and continued to be preferred until the active opposition of men such as Madison and Jefferson in 1785 resulted in the "Bill for Establishing Religious Freedom" which prohibited such public aid to religion.[11]

The Congregational church was the established church in Connecticut until the beginning of the nineteenth century. During this period it was extremely influential and received many special privileges. The Constitution of 1818 put an end to all this and stands somewhat as a guidepost in the drive that later was to influence all the states in restricting the use of public funds to sectarian schools. Following the adoption of this constitution a strong movement to divorce the public schools from the influence of the Congregational church developed in Connecticut. The article of particular importance to this study states in part:

It being the right and duty of all men to worship the Supreme Being, the Great Creator and Preserver of the Universe, in the mode most consistent with the dictates of their consciences; no person shall be compelled to join or support, nor by law be classed with, or associated to any congregation, church or religious association. . . . And each and every society or denomination of Christians in this State, shall have and enjoy the same and equal powers, rights and privileges; and shall have power and authority to support and maintain the Ministers or Teachers of their respective denominations, and to build and repair houses of public worship, by a tax on the members of their respective societies only . . .[12]

While Kentucky did not become a state until 1792, its constitution is notable for a Bill of Rights (Article XII) drafted by Thomas Jefferson, which is illustrative of the tendency of all the states in the nineteenth century to prohibit the use of public funds for sectarian purposes. It states:

3. That all men have a natural and indefeasible right to worship Almighty God according to the dictates of their consciences; that no man of right can be compelled to attend, erect, or support any place of worship, or to maintain any ministry against his consent; that no human authority can in any case whatever control or interfere with the rights of conscience; and and that no preference shall ever be given by law to any religious societies or modes of worship.
4. That the civil rights, privileges, or capacities of any citizen shall in no ways be diminished or enlarged on account of his religion.[13]

Formalizing the Principle of Church-State Separation

In his monumental study of church-state relations in the United States, Stokes dates the constitutional guarantees of religious freedom in the United States from 1833. From this date on, he believes, the complete legal separation between church and state had been won. However, the National Educational Association in its study of sectarian influences in the public schools, has concluded that prior to the Civil War, few states specifically prohibited the use of public funds for sectarian education.[14] It would appear that the great drive by the states to stop the use of public funds for sectarian purposes by constitutional and statutory provisions reached its crest following the Civil War.

New states entering the Union after 1870, when touching on religious liberty and public support of sectarian instruction in their constitutions, usually adopted a form similar to those of Connecticut or Kentucky mentioned above. The theory of those constitutional enactments was summed up by Cooley, in his five conditions for religious liberty. He pointed out that constitutions should prohibit the passage of laws:

(1) respecting the establishment of religion.
(2) compelling support by taxation or otherwise of religious instructions.
(3) compelling attendance upon religious worship.
(4) restraining the free exercise of religion according to the dictates of one's conscience.
(5) restraining the expression of religious beliefs.[15]

PRESENT CONSTITUTIONAL PROVISIONS

Today, all states but Vermont[16] have constitutional provisions prohibiting the expenditure of public funds, or at least school funds for sectarian purposes.[17] While there is considerable variation in the phraseology of these provisions, they are capable of being arranged in a rough categorical order according to their decreasing order of scope.[18] First, there are the provisions which prohibit the use of public funds for any sectarian purpose or institution.[19] Secondly, there are the state constitutional provisions which prohibit the use of public funds for sectarian[20] or non-state-controlled schools.[21] Finally, there are provisions which prohibit the use of *public school* funds for sectarian[22] or other than public school purposes.[23]

A more specific breakdown of state constitutional provisions prohibiting the use of public and school funds for sectarian purposes is possible and establishes seven generic types. They are: (1) public school funds may not be used for any purpose other than for the support of common schools; (2) no public grants or appropriation of money, property, or credit can be made to any institution not under the states' exclusive control; (3) no public appropriation may be made for any sectarian purpose, institution, or society; (4) no state aid may be granted to educational institutions controlled by a sectarian denomination; (5) no state aid may be extended to sectarian schools; (6) no state aid may be granted to private schools; (7) no public appropriation may be made for any school in which sectarian doctrines are taught.[24]

A similar policy has been formally adopted by Congress for the District of Columbia. This statute states:

> It is hereby declared to be the policy of the Government of the United States to make no appropriation of money or property for the purpose of founding, maintaining, or aiding by payment for services, expenses, or otherwise, any church or religious denomination, or any institution or society which is under sectarian or ecclesiastical control; and no money appropriated for charitable purposes in the District of Columbia, shall be paid to any church or religious denomination, or to any institution or society which is under sectarian or ecclesiastical control.[25]

New Hampshire has a rather unique constitutional provision which might be noted. Part I, Section 6 of its constitution permits public support of Protestant teachers of religion, piety, and morality and at the same time is tempered by a provision guaranteeing the freedom of conscience. It explains:

As morality and piety, rightly grounded on evangelical principles will give the best and greatest security to government, and will lay, in the hearts of men, the strongest obligations to due subjection; and as the knowledge of these is most likely to be propagated through a society by the institution of the public worship of the Deity, and of public instruction in morality and religion; therefore, to promote those important purposes, the people of this state, have a right to empower and do empower, the legislature to authorize, from time to time, the several towns, parishes, bodies corporate, or religious societies within this state to make adequate provisions, at their own expense for the support of and maintenance of public teachers of piety, religion, and morality. *Providing notwithstanding* that the various towns shall have the exclusive right of electing their own public teachers. And no person of any one particular sect or denomination shall ever be compelled to pay towards the support of the teacher or teachers of another persuasion, sect, or denomination.

This provision was adopted in 1784, and the litigation in which it played a part does little to aid us in ascertaining its intent. However, it might be noted that a New Hampshire Statute of 1819 took all power to build meeting halls and to support religious teachers from the towns where it had been placed by a statute of 1791, and conferred it upon religious societies. Any religious sect as well as any denomination of Christians was authorized to form such a society.[26] This constitutional provision has further been held to protect the rights of conscience of Roman Catholics as well as Protestants,[27] and to permit tax exemptions to a Catholic girls' school.[28] There is, however, no litigation involving Bible-reading exercises or related programs in New Hampshire.

The Model State Constitution and Religious Freedom

It might be interesting at this point to note how the Model State Constitution prepared by the Committee on

State Government of the National Municipal League handles this subject. Two sections deal specifically with it:

> Section 110. *Freedom of Religion.* No law shall be passed respecting the establishment of religion, or prohibiting the free exercise thereof.
>
> Section 111. *Appropriations for Private Purposes.* No tax shall be levied or appropriation of public money or property be made, either directly or indirectly, except for a public purpose, and no public money or property shall ever be appropriated, applied, donated, or used directly or indirectly, for any sect, church, denomination, or sectarian institution. No public money or property shall be appropriated for a charitable, industrial, educational or benevolent purpose except to a department, office, agency or civil division of the state.[29]

It is clear from the foregoing that the states' constitutions almost universally oppose sectarian instruction in the public schools and public aid to any type of sectarian establishment. What is not clear is what specific practices constitute sectarian teaching. Kansas, for example, has a provision in its constitution which states that no religious sect or sects shall ever control any part of the public or University funds.[30] But in *Billard* v. *Board of Education,* the Supreme Court of that state held that this provision did not prohibit Bible reading.[31]

STATUTES PROHIBITING SECTARIAN INSTRUCTION AND INFLUENCE

A host of state statutes prohibit sectarian instruction or influence in the public schools. These seemingly might prevent Bible reading in these schools, but in many cases they did not. Twenty-four states have enacted legislation prohibiting sectarian instruction in public schools in one form or another.[32]

The approach of the statutes varies. The very general type is illustrated by the Kansas statute, which states in part, "No sectarian doctrines shall be taught or inculcated in any public schools of the city . . ."[33] However, this particular law does not forbid Bible reading, since the next portion states, ". . . but the Holy Scriptures, without note or comment may be used therein." The other type of statute prohibiting sectarian instruction is much more specific, and deals particularly with books used in the school. Nevada's statute exemplifies this approach.

> No books, tracts, or papers of sectarian or denominational character shall be used or introduced in any school established under the provisions of this act; nor shall any sectarian or denominational doctrines be taught therein.[34]

From this it is apparent that the states want to keep the public school fund free from encroachment by parochial schools, and to prevent sectarian instruction of any sort that is aided by public funds. The National Education Association in its survey concluded that the least protected states regarding the use of public money for sectarian purposes were Maine, North Carolina, and New Jersey.[35] It might be noted that two of these states are segments of the old Puritan Commonwealth and one is part of the so-called "Bible Belt."

The states' constitutions are unclear as to what particular practices constitute sectarianism. And a most paradoxical issue confronting the states in the sectarian practices problem is the position of Bible reading. The problem has been summed up by one investigator in a series of questions that must be answered before a state policy can be inaugurated in this field: "Is Bible reading sectarian instruction? If so, is it prohibited by the principle of separation; (or) is Bible reading nonsectarian religious instruction? If it is, does it come under the ban of 'multiple establishment' of religion?"[36]

The majority of states, as we shall see, tended to regard Bible reading without comment, as nonsectarian religious or moral instruction. The states which permitted Bible reading seem not to have considered that this represents a form of "multiple establishment" of religion which was meant to be prohibited by the separation theory expounded by the framers of the First Amendment.[37]

STATUTES REGARDING BIBLE READING

Before the Supreme Court's ruling in 1963, a total of thirty-seven states permitted Bible reading in their public schools. At least thirteen of them arrived at this policy through the process of judicial interpretation. No state constitution prohibits Bible reading as such, and in all but one state the final decision as to the legality of the practice ultimately rested in the hands of the state judiciary. Only Mississippi's state constitution is explicit in regard to Bible reading. The section relating to religious liberty states, "The rights hereby secured shall not be construed to . . . exclude the Holy Bible from use in the public schools of the state."[38]

Though only Mississippi provides constitutionally for Bible reading, a number of states provide for Bible reading through statutes. Twelve states, as well as the District of Columbia, have statutes requiring that the Bible be read.[39] The Pennsylvania law, however, was declared unconstitutional in 1959 by a federal district court and this decision was upheld in a rehearing by the same court in 1962, even though the law had meanwhile been amended by the Pennsylvania legislature to make Bible reading in the public schools discretionary.⁴⁰ On appeal, the Pennsylvania law was declared unconstitutional in 1963 by the U.S. Supreme Court in the Schempp case.⁴¹

The state statutes authorizing Bible reading in the public schools take two principal forms. The first and more generalized form is exemplified by an Alabama statute which states: "All schools in this state which are supported in whole or in part by the public funds shall have once every school day reading from the Bible."⁴²

The more specific form which a number of states use is illustrated by an Arkansas statute:

> Every teacher or other person in charge shall provide for the reverent daily reading of a portion of the English Bible without comment in every public tax supported school up to and including every high school in the State, in the presence of the pupils; and prayer may be offered or the Lord's Prayer repeated; PROVIDED, any pupil shall be excused from the room on the written request of a parent or guardian.⁴³

The next section provides the punishment to be meted out for the violation of the above section. The first offense of omission on the part of an instructor is punishable by a twenty-five-dollar fine, the second results in the automatic termination of the teaching contract.

The specific type of statute such as the one cited above pays particular attention to two factors which are at the heart of most judicial battles over this question. These laws provide first, that the Bible must be read without note or comment, and second, those students who feel that their rights of conscience might be violated are allowed to absent themselves from the room in which the reading is taking place, upon presenting a written request from their parents or guardians. Nine of the states which permit Bible reading also stipulate that no note or comment may accompany such reading, and seven states include provisions which allow pupils who have conscientious objections to such reading to leave the room during this time.[44]

It might be noted that several courts holding Bible reading to be legal have added that they would not have so ruled had the reading been compulsory.[45]

Problems of Practice

A practical problem created by these laws has apparently been overlooked by the legislatures; that is, the question of which version of the Bible should be used. The laws are not specific on this. They merely speak of using "the Bible," "the Holy Bible," or the "English Bible," except for Maryland and Pennsylvania where the Douay Version is also permitted. Antagonism, however, usually results because Roman Catholics and Jews object to the use of the King James Version in fulfilling the Bible-reading requirement.

Choosing among Bibles is no minor problem. Notwithstanding the fact that some courts have taken the position that there is no difference between them,[46] the King James Version and the Douay Version of the Bible are not "essentially" the same, nor are they regarded as such by their partisans. Roman Catholics regard the King James Version, which excludes the so-called Apocryphal books upon which the theory of purgatory and other points of dogma important to Catholic theology is based, as incomplete and misleading. To Jewish children, any reading of the New Testament which deals with Jesus as the Messiah, gives the lie to their beliefs, and contradicts the teaching in their homes.[47] What version of the Bible to select has continually vexed educators and justices charged with the duty of determining and carrying out the intent of these legislative enactments.

The type of rationalization necessary to explain selections may be seen in a brief look at the rationale of a Pennsylvania case. This court felt that the "difference in emphasis or alleged mistreatment (resulting from a choice of either the King James or the Douay Version of the Bible) is an ecclesiastical matter, outside the scope of decision by civil government." It also pointed out that these are not matters for a judicial court to consider, for while the King James Version has been described as a nonsectarian book because it is used by many sects, the Douay Version has been held to be sufficiently similar to the King James Version to be used in the public schools.[48]

If the version to be used is, as the court has said, in the field of ecclesiastical affairs, and thus outside the realm of civil government, it might be asked where civil government gets the right to legislate on Bible reading in the first place? There is evidence to show that Madison and Jefferson would have denied any implied right such as this which allows civil government to legislate on religious matters,[49] and no one today has come up with an answer to how this may be done and still avoid sectarian disputes resulting from actions such as this.

Of the eleven states having laws requiring Bible reading (Alabama, Arkansas, Delaware, Florida, Georgia, Idaho, Kentucky, Maine, Massachusetts, New Jersey, Tennessee) and the District of Columbia, all but Idaho are on the eastern seaboard or in the South. In the eastern seaboard area, this possibly illustrates the pervasiveness of Colonial customs regarding religious instruction in the public schools; in the South, the importance of the Evangelist movement. Another point of interest is that seven of the twelve states also have laws prohibiting the teaching of sectarian religion in their public schools. With the exception of the Massachusetts statute, all of these laws are recent, having been passed since 1913.

Six states have statutes which permit but do not require

that the Bible be read in their schools: Indiana, Iowa, Kansas, North Dakota, Pennsylvania, and Oklahoma.[50] Prior to 1929, South Dakota was in this list, but in that year the provisions permitting Bible reading were declared unconstitutional by its courts.[51] The specific passage was deleted from the South Dakota Code.

Statutes *permitting* Bible reading have generalized and specific approaches as do the state statutes *requiring* Bible reading. The generalized approach is illustrated by the Indiana statue which says simply, "The Bible shall not be excluded from the public schools of the state."[52] A more comprehensive version sometimes used is illustrated by an Iowa provision:

> The Bible shall not be excluded from any public schools or institutions in the state, nor shall any child be required to read it contrary to the wishes of his parent or guardian.[53]

From conversations with several ex-public school students of these states, I have the impression that Bible reading is not always practiced in the states where it is permitted (but not required) by statutes.

Before being declared unconstitutional by the United States Supreme Court, Bible reading was permitted in nineteen states,[54] although no constitutional or statutory provision specifically providing for the practice existed. It was permitted either because the school boards and instructors believed it was not prohibited by state law and the taxpayers of the state condoned the practice, or because some citizen objected to it in court, and the state courts found it legal under the state's constitutional provisions.

In fourteen of these states it might be said that Bible reading was condoned, but in the five remaining states, Michigan, Colorado, Texas, Minnesota, and New York, the courts ruled that this practice was legal, even in the absence of specific permissory provisions. While court decisions which take a favorable view of Bible reading will be discussed in greater detail in the next chapter, it might be noted here that in states where statutory provisions existed which permitted or required Bible reading, and where litigation arose concerning the constitutionality of those provisions, the high courts of eight states, Kentucky, Kansas, Iowa, Massachusetts, Maine, New Jersey, Tennessee, and Georgia, found this to be a valid exercise of state power.

Summary

In summary, we find that, prior to the invalidation of such programs by the U.S. Supreme Court in 1963, thirty-seven states required, permitted, or condoned Bible reading in the public schools. Only one, Mississippi, had a specific provision in its constitution to this effect. Eleven states have statutes requiring Bible reading. Six states have statutes which permit, but do not require Bible reading. Six states, in the absence of statutory provisions, have court decisions which permitted Bible reading and which were equally binding. Fourteen states permitted Bible reading in the absence of any provisions whatsoever, and this practice was never challenged in the courts.

Obviously, then, despite the multitudinous state constitutional and statutory provisions forbidding sectarian instruction and public support of sectarian schools, the great majority of states did not feel that Bible reading came under these bans. In only eleven states was Bible reading felt to be sectarian instruction and, hence, illegal.[55] It will be remembered that *no state* has a constitutional or statutory provision forbidding Bible reading as such. Therefore, the conclusions regarding the illegality of Bible reading have resulted from judicial decisions in eight of the eleven states: Illinois, Louisiana, Nebraska, Ohio, South Dakota, Washington, Pennsylvania, and Wisconsin. In the remaining three states where the practice was held to be illegal, the people responsible for educational policy generally regarded Bible reading as being prohibited by either constitutional or statutory provisions.[56] An Arizona statute provides:

> Any teacher who shall use any sectarian or denominational books, or teach any sectarian doctrine, or conduct any religious exercises in his school, or who fails to comply with any provision of this chapter, shall be guilty of unprofessional conduct, and the proper authority shall revoke his certificate.[57]

While no court case has ever been brought to interpret this statute, the authorities in Arizona feel that this section appears to prohibit Bible reading since it specifically mentions "religious instruction."[58] It should be remembered, however, that many of the proponents of Bible reading argued that such programs were not religious or sectarian instruction, and the courts of a number of states have agreed with them.

California's position is indeterminate. The California Constitution has a section which provides:

> No public money shall ever be appropriated for the support of any sectarian or denominational school or any school not under the exclusive control of the officers of of the public schools; nor shall any sectarian or denominational doctrines be taught or any instruction thereon be permitted directly or indirectly in any of the public schools of the state.[59]

An additional statute to this effect in California's School Code says, "No publication of a sectarian, partisan, or denominational nature must be used or distributed in any school, or be made a part of any school library . . ."[60] The educational policy formulators in this state have felt for a long time that these provisions effectively prohibited Bible-reading exercises in the public schools.[61] The Supreme Court of California, however, in *Evans* v. *Selma High School,* concluded that these provisions did not prohibit the school board from purchasing Bibles to add to the school library, so long as these were not to be used for school-sanctioned Bible-reading exercises.[62]

But in the 1953 legislative session in California, twenty-one members of the California Assembly introduced Assembly Bill No. 682, which would authorize Bible-reading exercises in the public schools.[63] Several sections of the proposed legislation are noteworthy:

8301. As an aid to moral instruction in the public schools of California it shall be the policy of the Education Department to permit the reading of selected portions of the Bible.

8302. In each class or grade in the public schools selections from the Bible, from both the Old and New Testaments, from any recognized translation thereof, may be read aloud daily, or at other intervals, without sectarian application.

8303. The Department of Education shall authorize and publish a Syllabus of Graded Bible Readings which shall be made available to all public schools . . .

8305. Any exemption of pupils from such readings shall be arranged by the local school board.[64]

Following a series of unfavorable reports issued by several educator organizations, final action on the bill was delayed pending further study. (See Chapter 7 for a full discussion of this problem.)

The Nevada constitution, while it forbids sectarian control and instruction in a general manner,[65] is not as specific on these matters as the California constitution. Nevada's educators relied upon a statute that forbids the use of "sectarian or denominational books, tracts, etc.,"[66] for their belief that Bible reading was illegal. This question was never litigated, but authorities felt that the constitution and statutes of Nevada prevented the practice of Bible reading in that state.[67]

Montana is an enigma in regard to Bible reading in the public schools. It has not been included in any of the foregoing groups, although there is no evidence that Bible reading is practiced in Montana public schools. There is no evidence of any statutory provisions touching upon the subject of Bible reading, and no litigation exists specifically covering this topic. The National Education Association in its survey further reports that the State Superintendent of Education for Montana did not reply to its questionnaire inquiring whether the Bible was read in the schools.[68] The constitution of Montana contains rather specific prohibitions against public support of sectarian schools or instruction.

> No appropriations shall be made for charitable, industrial, educational, or benevolent purposes to any person, corporation, or community not under the absolute control of the state, nor to any denominational or sectarian institution or association.[69]

Peripheral Problems

A number of peripheral examples of state practices favoring Bible reading should be noticed. While Bible reading has been primarily a Protestant-sponsored phenomenon, it has been noted that in Louisiana, Roman Catholic instruction is sometimes conducted in the public schools by church officials.[70] It would seem a reasonable assumption that the reading of the Douay Bible is part of such instruction. In Alabama and Texas, high school credit is given for a course in Bible study. In Texas, however, the course must be taught from the point of view of literature rather than religion.[71] This practice has been attempted in other states, but in Washington, for example, the state's supreme court held that this violated the provision of the state constitution forbidding sectarian control and instruction in the public schools.[72]

The use of specific portions of the Bible is permitted by the statutes of some states. The Lord's Prayer is permitted by statute in Delaware, Maine, and New Jersey public schools.[73] Mississippi and North Dakota have statutes which permit the teaching of the Ten Commandments.[74] The North Dakota law, as a matter of fact, requires that the Ten Commandments be displayed in every classroom.

The practical difficulties facing an educational system allowing such things as instruction in the Ten Commandments and repetition of the Lord's Prayer have been summed up by Moehlman. He points out that the motive behind such plans may be laudable, but the practice may result in educational chaos, since there are several versions of the Lord's Prayer and the Ten Commandments, depending upon which Bible is used and to which religious denomination one belongs.[75] The primary purpose behind contemporary educational theory is to aid democracy by stressing the homogeneous nature of all Americans, regardless of religion or color.[76] Forcing someone else's version of the Lord's Prayer, the Ten Commandments, or the Bible upon a child is hardly calculated to achieve this end.

3

The Legality of Bible Reading

THE HIGH WATERMARK of the principle of separation of church and state seems to have occurred in the waning days of the nineteenth century and the early years of the twentieth. Since that time, Bible reading in the public schools has increased noticeably, especially since World War I. In 1952 and 1960 the United States Supreme Court refused to rule on the question because of jurisdictional reasons. In 1963, however, the Supreme Court declared that Bible-reading exercises in the public schools were unconstitutional. Prior to this, the high courts of twenty-one states, plus a federal district court in Pennsylvania (the Schempp case) ruled on the question. And their litigation has given rise to some lengthy and sometimes learned opinions.

Two generalizations may be made regarding these lower court opinions. The first relates to the almost completely divergent views held by the different judges on the central and essential issues running through all of the cases. The second is that while the fact situation in all the cases is not exactly the same, all of the cases discussed in this chapter and the next have the issue of Bible reading as their core. Other cases in which the question of Bible reading plays an incidental part will be discussed later.

The highest courts of fourteen states took an expressly favorable view of Bible reading in their public schools. These states are: Iowa, Kentucky, Kansas, Michigan, Minnesota, Massachusetts, Maine, New York, New Jersey, Texas, Tennessee, Colorado, Georgia, and Maryland.[1] The fact situations in these cases, as in all cases dealing with this question, ran the gamut from the Pfeiffer case to the Stanley case. In the former an action to restrain the Board of Education from using a textbook entitled *Readings From the Bible* as a supplementary textbook failed. The book was composed of selections taken mostly from the Old Testament and it contained no comment on the biblical passages. Nor did the teachers make oral comment on these passages. In addition to this, the pupils were not compelled to take part in the exercise if they presented a note from their parents asking that they be excused.[2]

In *People* ex rel. *Vollmar* v. *Stanley*,[3] the school board in a Colorado community had decreed that selections from the King James Version of the Bible be read aloud each day in the public schools. When the Roman Catholic pupils in these schools walked out of the room during this reading, the board proceeded to make attendance compulsory. A mandamus suit was then brought by the Catholic parents against the school board. The parents sought to prevent compulsory attendance at the time the Bible was being read. They also sought to prohibit this practice entirely in the public schools.

The Supreme Court of Colorado decided that although compulsory attendance violated the pupil's religious liberty granted by the State and Federal constitutions, nothing was inherently wrong with the practice of Bible reading, and the school board was entitled to continue the practice so long as it did not require compulsory attendance. The facts in other cases may differ slightly, but the essential ingredients of the litigation arising over Bible reading in the public schools are contained in the foregoing examples.

Basic Issues

The courts were confronted with three fundamental questions in connection with Bible reading. The first and most important question is: Is the Bible a sectarian book? The second question need be discussed in detail only if the first question is answered in the negative. It is: May the Bible without note or comment be used as a textbook in public schools? The third question is: May the boards of education and teachers require compulsory attendance during the period set aside for Bible reading?

While the remainder of this chapter, as well as the next chapter, will go into a detailed examination of representative opinions by various courts on these questions, a few general observations are in order at this point. In regard to the first question, the fourteen state courts which have held Bible reading to be legal believe that Bible reading in the public schools without note or comment is not sectarian instruction. Seven of these states have provisions in their constitutions prohibiting the use of tax revenue for sectarian purposes. [4] Five other states have statutes which prohibit sectarian instruction in their public schools.[5] It is interesting to note, however, that Kentucky, Maine, New Jersey, and Georgia which have statutes forbidding sectarian instruction in the schools, also have statutes which require

Bible reading.[6] In a similar vein, Kansas, which has a statute prohibiting sectarian instruction, also has a statute which permits Bible reading.[7]

In three states where the courts have held Bible reading to be legal, statutes exist which specifically refer to Bible reading in the public schools. Massachusetts and Tennessee have statutes[8] which require Bible reading, and Iowa has a statute[9] which permits this practice.

The attitude of the fourteen state courts which have held that the Bible is not a sectarian book seems to be based upon the conception that the constitutions and statutes of most states recognize the broad principles of Christianity, at least so far as its general moral teachings are concerned. This explains the ability of some courts to countenance Bible reading in public schools while at the same time believing in the importance and necessity of the provisions forbidding sectarian instruction in state constitutions and statutes. These courts which have viewed Bible reading favorably appear to think that,

> While Bible reading and exercises which merely tend to inculcate fundamental morality in pupils, and to quiet them in their studies are not prohibited, such exercises may be carried so far as to emphasize the teachings of a particular sect and this comes within a constitutional provision.[10]

The term "sectarian" is apparently viewed by most of these courts in a purely Christian context. It would seem likely that groups such as the Jews, Mohammedans, and Buddhists, would regard at least parts of the Bible as sectarian.

While the state courts are split in their views regarding the legality of using the Bible as a textbook, all of them recognize that it has great historical and literary value which would be an asset for pupils to acquire. They also generally acknowledge that it is rich in moral instruction, which all students should acquire in some way, but on how this is to be accomplished there is no agreement. It should also be mentioned that even courts opposed to Bible reading in the public schools felt that textbooks founded upon the Bible and emphasizing its fundamental teachings may be legally used in the public schools.[11]

The question whether compulsory attendance for Bible-reading exercises in the schools is legal has been most difficult for the state courts taking a favorable view of Bible reading to rationalize. Their problem was this: if the Bible is a sectarian book, reading it in school will restrict the religious liberties of some pupils. If it is not sectarian, it will not irritate the religious convictions of any sect, and since pupils are not excused from the other nonsectarian studies, such as arithmetic and chemistry, there is no reason why they should be excused from Bible reading. The facts seemed to indicate, however, that large sects, such as Roman Catholics and Jews, were opposed to reading the King James Version because it appeared to them to be inconsistent with their religious beliefs.

THE BIBLE IS NONSECTARIAN

From this somewhat perfunctory overview let us look more closely at basic issues faced by the courts in litigation arising over Bible-reading exercises in the public schools. The court that holds Bible reading to be legal obviously concludes it is not sectarian, or at least not of the type as was envisioned to be prohibited by the framers of the state constitutions and statutes.

A stumbling-block in the courts has been the semantic confusion surrounding the word "sect." It means many things to many people, but a working definition was offered by the Texas court which said a sect is, "A body of persons distinguished by peculiarities of faith and practice from other bodies and adhering to the same general system."[12] The court felt from this that a school in which Bible reading was practiced could not be a sect or religious society. It admitted, however, that:

> The right to instruct the young in the morality of the Bible might be carried to such an extent in the public schools as would make it obnoxious to the constitutional inhibition, not because God is worshipped, but because by the character of the services the place would be made a place of worship.[13]

The Colorado court in the Stanley case used a somewhat different approach to deny the intrinsic sectarian quality of the Bible. To the claim of the plaintiff that the King James Version was sectarian, the court replied, "The Bible is a compilation of many books. Even an atheist could find nothing sectarian in the book of Esther." It also explained that:

> Some of it [the Bible] is sectarian in the sense that it is relied upon by this or that sect to prove its particular doctrines, but that does not make its reading the teaching of a sectarian tenet or doctrine. If all *religious* instruction were prohibited, no history could be taught. Hume was an unbeliever and writes as such; Macauley is accused of partiality to dissenters; Motley of injustice to Roman Catholics. Nearly all histories of New England and indirectly of the United States are bound up with religion, religious inferences, implications, and often prejudices . . . . Even religious toleration cannot be taught without teaching religion.[14]

The Colorado court apparently takes a wider view of the term "sect" than does the Texas court, for the former speaks of an atheist's relation to the Bible, while the latter's view of a sect appears to be that it is merely a faction within an accepted religion. Perhaps what the Texas court meant by "the same general system," however, was any one of the monotheistic religions or even any belief in a primordial being. It would appear that some of the courts which have held Bible reading legal conceive the term sectarian as applying only to the Christian religion; this might have a tendency to curtail the religious freedom of non-Christian and eclectic groups. The logical gymnastics which are engaged in by some courts to get around this point are illustrated by the New York Supreme Court's rejecting the claim that Bible reading in the public schools is sectarian or that it violates the religious liberties of anyone. It said:

> A sect or tenet which is intolerant of those of a different sect or tenet is precisely the antithesis of religious liberty. Freedom is negated if it does not comprehend freedom for those who believe as well as those who disbelieve.[15]

It might be suggested that the freedom for those who believe has generally received a priority from the courts which have held Bible reading legal over the freedom of those who do not believe, or those who hold minority beliefs. Swancara has pointed out another important fact to be considered in a discussion of the sectarian nature of the Bible. He explains that even a nonsectarian book is capable of being used for sectarian purposes, and if we concede the Bible is nonsectarian we are forced to grant that it is generally used for sectarian purposes.[16]

HISTORICAL INVESTIGATIONS

Other courts, in discussing the potential sectarianism of the Bible, have looked to history for answers to the questions of what the founding fathers of the federal and state constitutions meant by religious freedom and sectarianism, and what they believed about the United States' being a Christian country. The Georgia court, after tracing the history of the separation principle in history, concluded that the founding fathers did not want or "have in mind a complete separation of Church and state." It was shocked to think anyone might think the Bible sectarian and thus incapable of use in the public schools of Georgia. It stressed:

> And so every denomination may object for conscience sake, and war upon the Bible and its use in common schools. Those who drafted and adopted our Constitution could never have intended it to meet such narrow and sectarian views. That section of the Constitution was clearly intended for higher and nobler purposes.[17]

These "higher and nobler purposes," the court believed, were to protect all religions, the Buddhists, pagans, Brahmans, etc., in the enjoyment of unrestricted liberty in their religion and to be assured that they would not be taxed or fined to support another religion. It is difficult to see how the court felt that reading the King James Version of the Christian Bible in public schools would aid the unrestricted religious liberty of non-Christian groups in the community.

The Texas court found from its historical investigations that the state constitutional provision forbidding sectarian instruction and an establishment of religion were calculated to prevent a condition such as existed in Texas when Mexico controlled that area. At that time, the Roman Catholic church was state-sponsored there, and received a portion of the tax revenue for its maintenance.[18] To assume that Bible reading came within the scope of these prohibitions was absurd, the court felt. "In fact," it went on to say:

> Christianity is so interwoven with the web and woof of the state government that to sustain the contention that the Constitution prohibits reading the Bible, offering of prayers, or singing songs of a religious character in any public building of the government would produce a condition bordering on moral anarchy.[19]

It pointed to examples of cooperation between church and state — chapels at the state's universities, chaplains in the state's prisons, and chaplains in the state's institutions for the blind — to fortify its position that Bible reading was a mild form of cooperation between church and state, and thus was not prohibited by the constitutional provision against sectarian instruction in the public schools.

The United States as a Christian Nation

Another element that the lower courts felt called upon to discuss involved the often-heard statement that the United States is a Christian country. If this is true, the Bible would then appear to be an essential part of our cultural background, and its place in the public school system apparently could not be ignored. The Minnesota court's rather condescending discussion of this question is characteristic of the courts which view Bible reading favorably. It said:

> We shall not stop to discuss whether or not this is a Christian nation; it is enough to refer to such discussions here-

inafter cited. However, we think it can not be successfully controverted that this government was founded on
the principles of Christianity by men either dominated
by or reared amidst its influence.[20]

It goes on to discount the importance of the Treaty with
Tripoli which states that the United States is not founded
upon the theories of Christianity[21] and concludes that the
contention that the short extract from the Bible read in
public schools constitutes sectarian instruction is in reality
"a trivial argument."[22] Perhaps if the Justices found themselves placed by religious upbringing on the opposing side
of the question the triviality of the argument would be
more difficult to discern.

A more legalistic approach to the historic analysis of
sectarianism, and Bible reading's place in the public schools,
is made by the Michigan court and is representative of the
approach used by some midwestern courts.[23] The Michigan
court explained that the state constitution of 1835 incorporated the Federal Ordinance of 1787. The Ordinance
said in part,

> Religion, morality and knowledge are essential to good
> Government and the happiness of mankind, and for these
> purposes, schools and the means to education shall ever
> be encouraged.

The court also pointed out that while the Ordinance did
not make the teaching of religion imperative, it precludes
the idea that the founders of the state's constitution meant
to exclude the Bible from the public schools.[24]

Justice Moore of the Michigan Supreme Court, in his
dissenting opinion, makes a frontal attack upon this theory
by pointing out its logical consequences. In objecting to the
argument concerning the incorporation theory of the Ordinance of 1787, he said:

> If his [Justice Montgomery's] position is sound, not only should the Bible be taught, but all forms of Christian religious instruction should be given in the schools. If this reasoning is sound, the constitution left it open to the school authorities to determine what variety of Christian religion they should teach, and the school board of the City of Detroit has the power today to have taught in the public schools . . . the theological tenets of any Christian church.[25]

He concludes with the ringing words used frequently by the courts which have held Bible reading to be illegal.

> A form of religion that cannot live under equal and impartial laws ought to die, and sooner or later must die. Legal Christianity is a solecism — a contradiction of terms.[26]

Public Funds and Sectarian Instruction

The next point that arises in litigation discussing the sectarian nature of Bible reading involves the expenditure of public funds for religious and sectarian purposes. As pointed out earlier this is generally forbidden by the constitutions and statutes of a number of these states. The courts which have viewed Bible reading favorably say that it does not constitute a public expenditure for sectarian purposes. The reasoning of the several courts, while not identical, follows a similar vein.

The Iowa court's summary is representative of the general attitude expressed by these courts. This court agreed that the possibility existed that Bible-reading exercises might be adopted with a potential view to worship; and in some sense the school might be considered a place of worship. It continued:

> But it seems to us that if we should hold that it [a school where Bible reading is practiced] is a place of worship, within the meaning of the constitution, we should put

a very strained construction upon it. The object of the provision, we think, is not to prevent the casual use of a public building as a place of offering prayer or of doing other acts of religious worship, but to prevent an enactment of a law whereby any persons can be compelled to pay taxes for building or repairing any place designed to be used distinctively as a place of worship. The object, we think, was to prevent an improper burden.[27]

The court went on to investigate the plaintiff's motives in bringing the suit and concluded that his real objection did not grow out of the question of taxation, but was to Bible reading as such. It tartly concluded:

> Possibly the plaintiff is a propagandist, and regards himself charged with a mission to destroy the influence of the Bible. Whether this is so or not, it is sufficient to say the the courts are charged with no such mission.[28]

The New York Supreme Court analyzed the motive involved in a suit questioning the practice of Bible reading in the same way. It felt that the plaintiff's attack was on the belief and trust in God, not on the expenditure of tax revenue for religious purposes. It continued by stating that these "beliefs and trusts, regardless of our own belief have received recognition in state and judicial documents from the earliest days of our republic."[29] After summing up the stock examples of cooperation between church and state, e.g., chaplains in the two houses of Congress and in the armed forces, and the inscription of the slogan "In God We Trust" on United States coins, the court rather paradoxically stated:

> These quotations are not intended to convey the thought that state and church should be brought into closer harmony. . . . The principle that religion has no place in public temporal education is so inexorable that a reaffirmation of it would be supererogatory.[30]

Bible Reading and Liberty of Conscience

While these fourteen state courts have held Bible reading to be legal, they were equally insistent that religious freedom and the liberty of conscience must be protected. They have, however, a tendency to speak in generalities, and some people might feel that the courts' actions belie their words. An example of the vociferous devotion to the principles of religious liberty may be found in the opinion of the Massachusetts court, which is illustrative of the views of the other courts which have held Bible reading to be legal. It feels that the school board has a right to require Bible reading in the schools, but it goes on to explain:

> We do not mean to say that it would be competent for a school committee to pass an order or regulation requiring pupils to conform to any religious forms or ceremonies which are inconsistent with or contrary to their religious convictions or conscientious scruples.[31]

Even though these courts pay homage to the principles of religious equality and the freedom of conscience they seem to suggest that these are ideals which cannot always be achieved in practical situations. Some have developed a theory which makes allowances for practices such as Bible reading, which have a tendency to ruffle the rights of free conscience for some people. The Maine court expressed this in one of the first cases on Bible reading. It pointed out that the legislature passes general laws for the guidance of the citizen:

> It is not necessarily true that they are unconstitutional because they conflict with his conscientious beliefs, nor is the citizen allowed to ignore them for that reason.[32]

To be sure, there is something to be said for this view, but in recent years some justices of the United States Supreme Court have pointed out that First Amendment rights,

including the right to freedom of conscience, have a somewhat preferred position when they come into conflict with
certain legislative enactments. In the Barnette case,[33] for example, the United States Supreme Court held that a religious aversion to saluting the United States flag with an
affirmation of a certain political belief had precedence over
an ordinance requiring that all students go through a flag
salute exercise in the public schools.

Another charge leveled against the practice of Bible
reading in the public schools is the allegation that the practice constitutes a legislative preference of one religion over
others. The Maine court, when called upon to answer this
charge, explained:

> If this were to be regarded as a legislative preference,
> much more must those laws by which the Sabbath is es-
> tablished as a day of rest, in which labor, except for neces-
> sity, is prohibited being done, be regarded as a subordi-
> nation of the religious views of all other sects to those
> holding that day as sacred.[34]

(This court apparently felt that the legality of Blue Laws
was above question.) This is a view concurred in by the
United States Supreme Court in 1961, when, in a series of
cases, it upheld the constitutionality of such laws.[35]

THE KING JAMES VERSION IS NONSECTARIAN

The King James Bible is the version almost invariably
chosen to be read in the schools. Nearly all of the litigation
resulting from the practice of Bible reading was brought
by Roman Catholics and Jews who objected to the selection
of this version as being sectarian. The courts which have
viewed Bible reading favorably have held these objections
to be invalid.

In this connection the general attitude taken by the
courts that have upheld the legality of Bible-reading exer-

cises is exemplified by the views expressed by the Kentucky court. It felt that a book is not sectarian simply because it is so comprehensive as to include the partial interpretation of the adherents of certain sects or because it is edited or compiled by persons of a particular sect. "It is not the authorship nor mechanical composition of the book, nor the use of it, but its contents that give it its character."[36]

The Kentucky court also had to determine the legality of a general prayer which was given at the beginning of the school day. The court concluded that neither the prayer nor Bible reading constituted sectarian instruction, since the children were not compelled to attend the exercises.

The Maine court saw the difference between the Protestant and Catholic version of the Bible as a mere translation problem, which should pose no serious difficulty. It explained that while the King James Version might be chosen by the school board of one area the Douay Version might be the choice of the board in another area. "The adoption of one is no authoritative sanction of purity of text or accuracy of translation."[37] The choice, it felt, was the result of the popular will, and could not be termed a preference of religion by law.

In regard to the Jewish taxpayers' objection that the reading of the New Testament constituted an expenditure of tax revenue for sectarian purposes, the Georgia court said:

> The Jew may complain to the court as a taxpayer just exactly when, and only when, a Christian may complain to a court as a taxpayer i. e., when the Legislature authorizes such reading of the Bible or such instruction in the Christian religion in the public schools as gives one Christian sect a preference over others.[38]

VERNON REGIONAL
JUNIOR COLLEGE LIBRARY

It went on to explain that it did not believe an ordinance which required the reading of the King James Version injured Roman Catholics or Jews, since they were not required to attend this exercise, and also because the Bible was read without note or comment. This, it felt, made it a study of a moral treatise on the same order as a study of the Koran might be.

Dissenting Views

The opinion of those who feel that Bible reading represents sectarian instruction is well summed up in Justice Wilson's dissenting opinion in the Kaplan case, heard by the Minnesota Supreme Court.[39] He said he did not feel it was proper to have Jewish children read the New Testament, for it has a tendency to show that their teaching at home is in error. This also holds true in regard to Roman Catholic pupils reading the King James Version of the Bible, or to Protestants' reading the theory of purgatory as explained in the Book of Maccabees of the Douay Bible, if the Board of Education happens to require the Douay Version be used in Bible reading exercise. "No man must feel that his religion is tolerated. His Constitutional rights of conscience should be indefeasible and beyond the control and interference of men. The Constitution says so."[40]

A somewhat unusual view is taken by Swancara[41] in objecting to the Colorado court's decision[42] which held that reading the King James Version was not sectarian. He states in connection with the court's rejection of the Roman Catholics' protest that their constitutional right to be free from sectarian instruction in the public school was being violated; "It reminds one of a Christian Science 'cure'; the disease is deemed imaginable only, and there is no occasion for seeking a cure."[43]

He also suggests that there is a correlation in this case between the Ku Klux Klan and the movement to have the King James Version read in the schools. He shows that the judge who dissented in this case because he felt that the reading should be compulsory, had been a speaker at a Klan meeting which was billed as the "Cosmopolitan Club" in the *Rocky Mountain News* on January 14, 1925. While at the meeting the judge was "lauded by other orators as a great judge and a man of the highest integrity." When the Roman Catholics lost the battle to stop Bible reading in the Colorado schools, Swancara states:

> Probably some Klanized Protestants thereupon rejoiced, not because any version of the Bible was read in the public schools [they insisted on the use of the King James Version only] but because of the ensuing vexation to some of the Catholic patrons, notwithstanding the fact that such rejoicing parties professed reverence for the Christian principle: 'Love thy neighbor as thyself.'

While this may be an extreme view, its uniqueness is noteworthy for a possible insight into the political forces at work behind a policy to institute Bible reading in the public schools.

One additional point is made by Swancara: when secular books which contain religious matters are read in class they do not give the pupils the impression that they are being influenced to favor one religion or another. The Koran, when used in school, is not read with a reverent tone. "This," he states, "is not true with the King James Version, it is meant to propagate the Protestant faith." If, as most of the courts suggest, the purpose of Bible reading

is to impart moral instruction, the Koran should receive
the same treatment as the Bible, for he concludes both are
rich in moral and ethical lessons.

THE BIBLE AND MORAL INSTRUCTION

The courts which viewed Bible reading favorably were
either not impressed by this argument or ignored it. They
generally maintained that the inculcation of the moral precepts of the Bible cannot be considered sectarian instruction. The Massachusetts court said:

> No more appropriate method could be adopted of keep-
> ing in the minds of both teachers and scholars that one
> of the chief objects of education, as declared by statutes of
> this commonwealth, and which teachers are especially en-
> joined to carry into effect is 'to impress on the minds of
> children and youths committed to their care and instruc-
> tion the principles of piety and justice and a sacred re-
> gard for truth.'[44]

The Kansas court stressed that moral instruction is a
public duty. It states that the public has a right to expect
that pupils coming out of the public schools have a more
acute sense of right and wrong, as well as higher ideals of
life. "The system ought to be so maintained as to make this
certain. The noblest ideals of moral character are found
in the Bible."[45]

The Minnesota court pointed out that the State Legislature provided for moral instruction in Section 2906, General Statutes, 1923, which read:

> The teachers in all public schools shall give instruction in
> morals; in physiology and hygiene and in the effects of
> narcotics and stimulants.

It then concludes: "What is more natural than turning
to that Book for moral precepts which for ages has been

regarded by the majority of the peoples of the civilized nations as the fountain of moral teachings."[46]

Some boards of education have gone to extraordinary
lengths to avoid the charge that they are using sectarian
texts in the Bible-reading exercises carried on in the public
schools. The New York Board, in an attempt to live up to
the constitutional and statutory provisions forbidding sectarian instruction in the schools, and yet to maintain a system of Bible reading, bought the Douay Version of the
Bible, the King James Version, a book entitled *Bible Readings,* the International Bible (authorized version) and portions of the Hebrew Bible in translation by Izaack Lessar.
These were to be read to the students at regular intervals.
The record is not clear as to which version was chosen to
be read to any given group of pupils, or how the selection
was arrived at. Nevertheless, the practice was challenged in
the Lewis case, and the Supreme Court of New York held
it to be legal.[47]

In addition to being rich in moral lessons, the Bible is
regarded by the courts of some states as being an excellent
disciplinarian. There are a number of cases where the stated
purpose of Bible reading was to quiet the pupils at the beginning of the school day, and to place them in a receptive
mood for the day's work. The Kansas court found nothing
objectionable when a teacher, for the purpose of quieting
the pupils, read the Lord's Prayer and biblical selections
without note or comment. The court could see "not the
slightest effort on the part of the teacher to inculcate any
religious dogmas."[48]

The Massachusetts court, in dismissing the charge
that Bible-reading exercises violated religious freedom by
being sectarian instruction, said:

But we are unable to see that the regulation with which the plaintiff was required to comply can be justly said to fall within this category. In the first place, it did not prescribe an act, which was necessarily one of devotion or religious ceremony.

It went on to say that the only thing required was the observance of quiet and decorum during the religious exercise with which the school is opened. The pupils were not compelled to join in the prayers and Bible-reading exercises, but "only to assume an attitude which was calculated to prevent interruption by avoiding communication with others . . ."[49]

THE BIBLE AS A TEXTBOOK

After the fourteen courts which looked favorably upon Bible reading had decided that the Bible was not a sectarian book, they investigated the legality of its use as a textbook in the schools. While they pointed out that since it was not sectarian, there could be no objection on that score, they went further and gave additional reasons for allowing the Bible to be used as a text. The consensus among the courts was that the choice of teaching materials rested with the state legislatures and their local educational counterparts, the school boards. The courts felt that judges had no right to set themselves above these agencies in matters of educational policy.

In *Nessle* v. *Hum*,[50] an early Ohio case which has not been previously cited since the question of Bible reading played only an incidental part in the litigation, the court addressed itself to the role legislatures play in the selection of educational material for the public schools. It explained that the legislature placed the management of the public schools under the exclusive direction of the Directors or the Boards of Education. It went on to point out that the courts have no authority to interfere with the boards by determining what instructions should or should not be given or what books should be chosen and what others should be cast aside.

The Maine court took a more extreme attitude. It repeated that the power of curriculum planning must rest somewhere, and it believed it rested with the legislature. However, it went on to explain that this power is general and unlimited. Even if the selection of text material was unwise or immoral, the court felt it had no power to interfere with it. There is only one recourse open to those who object to the educational material selected by school committees, and this is voting against the members of the school committee at the next election. An additional factor in this case was a damage claim made by the plaintiff which resulted from the expulsion of his son from school for a refusal to take part in the Bible-reading exercises. The court in dismissing this claim emphasized the immunity from liability of educational officials. It pointed out that even if the officials had been in error (which it did not concede) they could not be sued for making a mistake while in the good faith performance of their official duty.[51]

Judicial Reaction to Minority Group Views

In addition to stressing the power of the legislature and school boards in the choice of subject matter, the courts have also stressed the danger of allowing minorities to dictate or frustrate school policies. On this point also, the Maine court formulated the logical pattern to be used by later judges. It felt that if the objection to the Bible-reading exercise was allowed to stand, the choice of texts might be-come subordinate to an individual's will. It pointed out:

> The right of negation is, in its operation equivalent to that of proposing and establishing. The right of one sect to interdict or expurgate would place all schools in subordination to the sect interdicting or expurgating.[52]

This court, in rejecting the plaintiff's objections to Bible reading, concluded, "The right as claimed undermines the power of the state. It is that the will of the majority shall bow to the conscience of the minority or of one."

The Texas court discussed the danger of minority control of educational matters on a moral and ethical level. It said:

> But it does not follow that one or more individuals have the right to have the courts deny the people the privilege of having their children instructed in the moral truths of the Bible because such objectors do not desire that their own children shall be participants therein. This would be to starve the moral and spiritual natures of the many out of deference to the few.[53]

A lower Pennsylvania court once extended this view to a point which might shock our contemporary educators. It stated:

> The principle on which the common schools of this commonwealth were established was not a regard for children as individuals, but as part of an organized community for the working out of a higher civilization and freedom . . . They are the outgrowth of the state policy for the encouragement of virtue and the prevention of vice and immorality and are based upon the public conviction of what is necessary for the public safety.[54]

This court seemed to feel that the right of conscience is subordinate to the community need for uniformity.

The Bible as History and Literature

Another point which the courts investigate when looking into the merits of using the Bible as a text concerns its historical and literary aspects. It has been mentioned previously that even the courts which have ruled Bible reading to be illegal concede that it may make valuable historical and literary contributions to the pupil's education.

The New York court, speaking specifically about the Bible's literary value, said:

> Even those who do not accept the Bible as an accurate historical chronicle, enthusiastically regard it as possessing rare and sublime literary qualities. Suppose it were read in an English Class as an example of pure English. . . . It would be treading upon explosive ground for the courts to essay a regime for the public schools.[55]

When speaking of the historical importance of the Bible, the Kentucky court pointed out that if its contents were in another book not called by the same name, no one would object to its use in the schools. It then suggests the consequences inherent in the projection of the view that the Bible is a sectarian textbook.

> May it not be said then with equal force that to teach the Constitution, which itself teaches the right to perfect freedom in the worship of God, is sectarian, because some sect may deny that it was right to teach the children to worship God in any way except according to the teachings of that particular sect?[56]

Almost all of these courts felt that if they sustained the objection that the Bible was a sectarian textbook, they would be forced to banish from the schools any books even remotely touching upon religion. The Maine court explained that the Bible was used merely as a book from which reading exercises were given. If this was sectarian instruction, then the reading of Greek mythology would be instruction in paganism, it believed. The court then approached the question from a different angle by pointing out that:

> Because Galileo, Copernicus and Newton may chance to be found in some prohibitory index, is that a reason why the youth of the country should be educated in ignorance of the scientific teachings of those great philosophers?[57]

The Colorado court was appalled by the results which might stem from a doctrinaire view holding that any religious discussion in a textbook constituted sectarianism. It asserted that "if all religious instructions were prohibited, no history could be taught." It went on to predict that the "Star Spangled Banner" and "America" could not be sung in the school because they both mention God. Shakespeare or Milton could not be taught because of their frequent reference to God and to religion, nor could the student study the works of Webster, Clay, or Lincoln. From this and other similar analyses, it concluded that religious instruction was not always synonymous with sectarian instruction, and the Bible might advantageously be used as a text on some occasions.[58]

In *Evans* v. *Selma High School*,[59] where an unsuccessful attempt was made to enjoin the school authorities from purchasing a number of Bibles to be included in the high school library, the California court also drew a line between sectarian books which are prohibited and general books touching upon religion which may have a place in a high school library. After stating that the constitution and statutes of California do not exclude religious books from the schools, but prohibit the use of sectarian and denominational literature, the court declared:

> In a word, a book on any subject may be strongly partisan
> in tone and treatment. A religious book treating its sub-
> ject in this manner would be sectarian. But not all books
> of religion would be thus excluded. The fact that it is
> not approved by all sects of a particular religion nor by
> the followers of all religions would not class it as sectarian
> for library purposes.[60]

It concluded that the King James Bible was not a sectarian
book forbidden by any of the states constitutional or statutory provisions. "The mere act of purchasing it carries no
implication of adoption of the dogmas therein."

The dissenting justices in these cases have frequently
objected specifically to the use of the Bible as a textbook in
the public schools. The objections have a tendency to follow the same vein as expressed by the dissenting opinion
of the Michigan court. Here it was pointed out that there
is a great deal of difference between using the Bible as a
text or merely including occasional quotations from it in
other textbooks. In the latter case the quotations are not
placed there to give them authority as religious doctrine.
Then speaking of the Bible specifically, Justice Moore inquired:

> Does not the fact that the teacher reads the book without
> note or comment warrant the pupil in believing that
> what is read is recommended to him as true?[61]

Finally he dealt with the need for a moral and ethical
training in the schools, by explaining that as the efficiency
of the schools and other means of education increased, religion and morality and knowledge will prosper.[62]

BIBLE READING AND COMPULSORY ATTENDANCE

While the courts of fourteen states have agreed that
the Bible is not a sectarian book, and thus may be used in
the public schools, there is no unanimity among them as

to the question of compulsory attendance by students. There is agreement among most of the courts that pupils cannot be forced to attend Bible-reading exercises, but at least one — the Texas court — felt that since students are not excused from other nonsectarian instruction, such as geometry, there is no reason why they should be excused from Bible reading. This difference of opinion does not result from any essential difference in constitutional or statutory provisions affecting the subject. In *Church* v. *Bulloch*[63] and *People* ex rel. *Vollmar* v. *Stanley*[64] the constitutional and statutory provisions were similar, but the conclusions the courts of Texas and Colorado reached concerning the legality of compulsory attendance at Bible-reading exercises were quite different. The Texas court felt that the pupils must be present but need not pray, while the Colorado court stated that while the exercises were not contrary to the constitution of that state, pupils could not be forced to attend them.

The Colorado court reasoned that the "Right to liberty included the parents' right to determine what their children shall be taught, and refuse to have them taught what they think harmful." The one exception to this proposition, the court ruled, is that no one has a right to object to the teaching of good citizenship. The court did not believe, however, that Bible-reading exercises were essential to good citizenship, and therefore, the parents had a legitimate right to object to their children's being compelled to take part in such exercises. Compulsory attendance of this type would violate the individual's freedom guaranteed under the Fourteenth Amendment to the United States Constitution, this court concluded.[65]

In both the Colorado case and the Kaplan case in Minnesota, there was at least one judge who believed that compulsory attendance would be legal. In the former, this was expressed in one of the dissenting opinions, while in the latter Justice Stone concurred. He said, however, that while he was in agreement with the majority opinion, he did not think that the pupils would have to be released to make Bible reading legal in the public schools. He felt that it is merely, "considerate and tactful rather than legally necessary to permit certain children to absent themselves during the scripture reading."[66] This somewhat restrained view is not shared by one justice of the Colorado court who felt that Bible-reading exercises should be compulsory. He believed essentially that if the court felt the practice was legal and if the school authorities saw merit in the practice, all students should be compelled to attend.[67]

A problem facing courts that have ruled attendance at Bible-reading exercises could not be compulsory has been concerned with the effects upon pupils with conscientious objections who leave the room when the exercises begin. Counsels have argued that a youth is extremely gregarious and desires to be part of the group. Any forced separation from his school fellows, such as occurs when a child's conscience forbids him to attend Bible reading in which the majority of the class takes part, places a religious stigma upon the departing pupil which may result in social ostracism for him. In this way the pupil is denied his democratic right of equality. The courts have taken completely divergent views of this question, depending upon whether they have viewed Bible reading favorably or unfavorably.

The Colorado court's attitude on this question is representative of those courts which have looked favorably upon Bible reading. It rejected the above contention as an "idle argument," saying:

> We cannot agree to that. The shoe is on the other foot.
> We have known many boys to be ridiculed for complying
> with religious regulations, but never one for neglecting
> them or absenting himself from them.[68]

Possibly this represents a somewhat cloistered view.

DISSENTS AND DIVERGENCES

Chief Justice Wilson of the Minnesota Supreme Court,
in his dissenting opinion in the Kaplan case, objected to a
statement by the majority which was similar to the above-
mentioned view of the Colorado court. He pointed out that
excluding pupils from Bible-reading exercises because of
their conscientious objections constituted discrimination
against those pupils who leave the room. He explained that
a pupil's constitutionally guaranteed right to freedom of
conscience must mean that:

> He may not only worship as his conscience dictates, but,
> surely, he also has a right not to be annoyed by those
> things which directly interfere with what he genuinely be-
> lieves is wrong, even though they act only upon an inci-
> dental, but, to his mind, an important, angle of his way
> of worship.[69]

It might be noted further that not all of the fourteen
courts which upheld Bible-reading exercises were unanimous
in their respective opinions. Nor was there complete agreement among the majority opinions on points of philosophic
and historic interpretation. In the fourteen cases to come
before state courts where Bible reading was declared legal,
nine of the decisions were unanimous. Furthermore, the two
judges who dissented in the Colorado (Stanley) case did not
object to Bible-reading programs as such. Their objection
was directed at the court's decision to make such exercises

noncompulsory. One of the two dissenting votes in the Georgia court[70] was cast for exactly this same reason.

Thus in only four of the fourteen courts which upheld Bible reading was there any real difference of opinion regarding the actual practice. These were the courts of Michigan, Minnesota, Maryland, and Georgia.

Statistically then, we see that a total of eighty-five judges heard these cases in the fourteen state courts which upheld Bible reading. Of the eighty-five judges, only six dissented because of objections to Bible reading. This reveals a remarkable degree of agreement considering the explosive nature of the subject involved.

THE DOREMUS CASE

The Doremus case[71] has been reserved for separate consideration for several reasons. First, it was one of the more recent cases concerning Bible reading to be litigated. Secondly, it was the first case in which the United States Supreme Court gave us even the slightest insight as to how it stood on the question. It was not, however, the first case involving Bible-reading exercises to come before the Supreme Court of the United States. The first case was *State* ex rel. *Clithero* v. *Showalter*.[72] Here the court in a *per curiam* opinion dismissed for want of a substantial federal question, a mandamus suit seeking to force the school board to institute Bible reading in the public schools of Washington.

It should be noted that the Supreme Court in the Doremus case also refused to rule on the issues, and dismissed the appeal for lack of jurisdiction. Nonetheless, its reasoning is of particular interest since it not only reiterates some of the points already noted, but introduces some new approaches to the problem.

The facts in this case are similar to many cases previously discussed with several exceptions. The litigation involved a New Jersey statute[73] providing for the reading without comment of five verses of the Old Testament at the opening of each school day. No issue was raised under the state constitution, but the act was claimed to violate that clause of the First Amendment to the federal Constitution prohibiting the establishment of religion.

Doremus, who had no interest in the case other than being a "citizen and taxpayer," and Mrs. Anna Klein, whose seventeen-year-old daughter was a pupil in the school, brought the suit. There was no assertion that the Klein girl was offended, injured, or compelled to accept, approve, or listen to any dogma or creed when the Bible was read. Actually there was a pre-trial stipulation that any student at his own or his parent's request could be excused during Bible reading, and in this case no such excuse was asked. A point to be noted, however, is that the Klein girl had graduated from the high school before the appeal reached the Supreme Court of the United States.

In this case there was no trial held in the lower state court. The trial court denied relief on the merits on the basis of the pleading and a pre-trial conference. The Supreme Court of New Jersey, on appeal, held that the act did not violate the federal Constitution in spite of its jurisdictional doubts.[74] These doubts referred to Doremus' right as a citizen and taxpayer, for while the New Jersey court did not question this status, it did not concede, nor did it accept the proof that "the brief interruption in the day's schooling caused by compliance with the Statute adds cost to the school expenses or varies by more than an incomputable scintilla the economy of the day's work."[75]

The Supreme Court of New Jersey observed at the out-

set that no one in this case asserted that his religious practices had been interfered with or that his right of conscience
had been suppressed. The only purpose and function of the
plaintiffs, the court noted, is "that they assume the role of
actors so there may be a suit which will invoke a court ruling upon the constitutionality of the Statute." It went on
to deny that the intent of the First Amendment to the
United States Constitution was to negate the existence of a
Supreme Being or to suppress governmental recognition of
God. To prove this it cited the usual examples of state cooperation with religion and quoted a stanza from our national anthem which announces, "And this be our motto —
In God is Our Trust!"

Speaking more specifically of the Bible and of Bible-
reading exercises, the court said: "We consider that the Old
Testament because of its antiquity, its content, and its wide
acceptance, is not a sectarian book, when read without comment." It believed that the Bible is accepted by three great
religions — Jewish, Roman Catholic, and Protestant — and
in part, at least, by others. While the court conceded that
there were other religions in the United States beside the
ones mentioned it noted that they were numerically small
and "negligible" in point of impact on our national life.
This caused it to conclude that, "these minor groups had no
vital part in the formation of our national character."

This did not mean, the court hastened to point out, that
a small group thereby loses its constitutional rights. Since
"theism is in the warp and woof of the social and governmental fabric," the court concluded, there can be no constitutional objection to Bible-reading exercises on the grounds
that one religion is preferred above another. Furthermore,
it went on to explain, the statute in question has been in

operation forty-seven years, and courts have no right to invalidate a statute which has never been challenged for so many years unless its unconstitutionality is obvious.

The United States Supreme Court and the Doremus Case

Justice Jackson, speaking for the majority of the United States Supreme Court, delved into the fact situation before analyzing the merits of the case. He noted that since no trial was held in the state court, the United States Supreme Court had no findings of fact. Furthermore, the record contained "meager notes" of the pre-trial conference in the lower court. He then explained that though the highest state court believed that the plaintiffs had sufficient standing to maintain a suit to have a statute declared unconstitutional, and while this opinion was entitled to respect, it could not be binding upon the Supreme Court of the United States. He went on to state that the Supreme Court could make an independent examination of the record and upon so doing "we find nothing more substantial in support of jurisdiction than did the court below."[76]

He next discussed the significance to the case of the fact that the Klein girl had graduated from high school by the time the appeal was taken and pointed to the mootness of the question involved in the case as a result of this graduation. He explained:

> Obviously no decision we could render now would protect any rights she may have had, and this court does not sit to decide arguments after events have put them to rest.[77]

Justice Jackson pointed up the weakness of the argument advanced by Mrs. Klein when he stressed that there was no assertion that the child was injured or offended by this practice, since she was not even required to attend the Bible-reading exercise.

The controlling factor in cases such as this, the majority felt, was the requirement of substantial financial interests. They agreed that the motivation in this case was primarily of a religious nature, but they went on to say:

> It is not a question of motivation but of possession of the requisite financial interest that is, or is threatened to be injured by the unconstitutional conduct. We find no such direct and particular financial interest here.[78]

The court attempted to spell out what type of taxpayer action involving the question of Bible reading would present a "case or controversy" within the jurisdiction of the United States Supreme Court. It explained that this occurs only when it is a "good-faith pocket book" action seeking to litigate a direct and particular financial injury. When this is the case, it concluded, it does not matter that the taxpayer's dominant inducement is more religious than mercenary.[79]

Dissenting Views

Justice Douglas wrote a dissenting opinion in which Justices Reed and Burton concurred. He felt that the case deserved a decision on the merits, for no group is more interested in the operation of the public schools than taxpayers who support them and parents whose children attend them. He doubted if any taxpayers could show more interest than is present in this case, by showing that, "the Bible adds to the taxes they pay." He denied that the issues are "feigned" in this case, or that the suit is collusive. "The mismanagement of the school system that is alleged is clear and plain." He admitted that the rule of *Massachusetts* v. *Mellon*[80] would prevent a case such as this from being maintained if it were a suit to enjoin a federal law. But, he stressed, "New Jersey can fashion her own rules governing the institution of suits in her courts." Thus, if she gives these taxpayers status to sue, Justice Douglas could see nothing in the Constitution to prohibit it. He concluded:

> And where the clash of interests is as real and as strong as it is here, it is odd indeed to hold there is no case or controversy within the meaning of Art. III, sec. 2 of the Constitution.[81]

The Supreme Court is ever sensitive to public opinion as expressed by newspapers and legal journals. The tremendous furore which arose as a result of the McCollum case undoubtedly had a profound effect upon the sensibilities of the Justices in an area in which they have consistently expressed a deep solicitude, that of individual and religious liberty. Religious controversies such as those in the Doremus case have a habit of creating headlines and stirring up debates inevitably characterized by heat as well as light.

The action of the Supreme Court in the Doremus and more particularly in the Zorach case, (See Chapter 5) which was decided in the same year, perhaps indicated a retrenchment policy on the part of the Court calculated to smooth the ruffled feathers of highly vocal religious groups incensed by the McCollum decision.

THE TUDOR CASE

It is impossible to conclude a discussion of the Doremus case without calling attention to the remarkable change in attitude of the New Jersey Supreme Court one year afterward as revealed in the Tudor case.[82] This case also helps explain the attitudes of the New Jersey Supreme Court concerning matters of over-all religious education and related subjects. The Tudor case did not specifically deal with the problem of Bible reading in the public schools, but involved an action by parents of pupils in the public schools to determine the validity of a program involving the distribution of Gideon Bibles in the schools and to obtain an injunction against such distribution.

A temporary injunction was granted, but the Superior Court, law division, found in favor of the defendant Board of Education and vacated the restraining order, whereupon the plaintiff appealed. When the case reached the New Jersey Supreme Court, Chief Justice Vanderbilt, speaking for a unanimous court, held that permitting the distribution of King James Versions of the New Testament, or the so-called Gideon Bible, violated the constitutional provision prohibiting the making of any law respecting an establishment of religion as provided for in the First Amendment of the United States Constitution. Moreover, the court held that the practice also violated the New Jersey constitutional provision prohibiting an establishment of one religious sect in preference to another.

The court felt that although the school board's method of distributing the Gideon Bible was voluntary and no one was forced to take one and that no religious exercises or instruments were brought to the classrooms, there still existed, nonetheless, the preference of one religion over another and the distribution could not be sustained on the basis of mere assistance to religion as permitted in the Zorach case. The practice of distributing Bibles had been objected to by members of the Jewish and the Roman Catholics faiths.

In an intriguing exercise in logic, the New Jersey Supreme Court affirmed the Doremus case in the Tudor case but in so doing accepted the opposite set of arguments. In fact, the arguments accepted were those which had been advanced against the practice of Bible reading which was permitted in the Doremus case.[83]

There is little doubt that the New Jersey Supreme Court accepted a different notion of sectarianism in the Tudor case in contrast to the concept of sectarianism adopted in the Doremus case. The key difference between the two appears to be that in the Tudor case, the court felt that there truly were present examples of bona fide allegations of religious disapproval coming from Roman Catholic and Jewish groups. In the Doremus case, on the other hand, no one actually alleged injury. In other words, the court in Tudor clearly suggested that those things which religious groups consider unacceptable and which each group determines to be of doctrinal significance will be of controlling importance to the Supreme Court's interpretation of the concept of sectarianism. It would seem, therefore, that the New Jersey court had abandoned the technique of decision which is necessary to uphold programs of Bible reading in the public schools.

After hearing the testimony from Jewish biblical scholars who noted that, "the New Testament is in profound conflict with basic principles of Judaism," the New Jersey court held that the King James Version and the Gideon Bible were unacceptable to those of the Jewish faith. Moreover, after reviewing the Protestant version of the Bible and the Roman Catholic version of the Bible, the New Jersey court observed that:

. . . the King James version of the Bible is as unacceptable to Catholics as the Douay version is to the Protestants. According to the testimony in this case the Canon
Law of the Catholic Church provides that 'editions of the
original text of the Sacred Scriptures published by non-
Catholics are forbidden *ipso jure.*'

From these findings, the New Jersey Court concluded:

. . . to permit the distribution of the King James version
of the Bible in the public schools of this State would be to
cast aside all the progress made in the United States and
throughout New Jersey in the field of religious toleration
and freedom. We would be renewing the ancient struggles among the various religious faiths to the detriment
of all. This we must decline to do.

THE CARDEN CASE

Another case in which a state supreme court upheld the
validity of Bible-reading exercises in the public school occurred in Tennesse in the case of *Carden* v. *Bland.*[84] This
case requires a separate discussion not only because of its
contemporary quality but because of certain side issues which
would seem to have some long-range significance. It also has
more than its fair share of paradoxes.

The litigation involved proceedings brought by a citizen and taxpayer against the City of Nashville Board of
Education to enjoin the board members and others from engaging in certain practices pertaining to religion. Plaintiff
also sought to obtain a declaratory judgment declaring unconstitutional the state statute imposing upon the teachers the
duty to read at the opening of each school day a selection
from the Bible. The state statute is somewhat unique in
that it prohibits the same selection from being read more
than twice a month. The chancery court of Davidson county
sustained the demurrers and complainant appealed.

There were two major issues in the case, although the court in its opinion devoted the greatest share of its time to the second. Carden, first, sought a declaratory judgment prohibiting the public school teachers from requiring the students to attend Sunday school and to make a report of their attendance to the public school authorities. It was alleged that those students who failed to attend Sunday school were required as a penalty to copy many verses of the Bible; that on each Monday morning the teacher regularly followed a practice of requesting those pupils who had attended Sunday school the day before to stand; and those who remained seated were given special assignments, i.e. to copy some portion of the Bible. It was also charged that some of the teachers at Ross Public School kept on display in the classroom a record of the attendance of their pupils in Sunday school and that during school hours they conducted a devotional period consisting of reading from the Bible and saying the Lord's Prayer as it appeared in the King James Version.[85]

Secondly, Carden complained that it was a customary practice of his son's teachers to use school time to read or have some student read from the Bible and to ask questions of the pupils, including his son, concerning the contents of such passages; to repeat prayers, especially the Lord's Prayer; to sing hymns and other religious songs and to inquire of the pupils as to their attendance or nonattendance at Sunday school. The complainant stated that the practice of inquiring into a student's Sunday school attendance and the practice of Bible reading in the public school offended and embarrassed his son.

The court dealt very quickly with the question of requiring pupils to attend Sunday school. It noted that counsel had conceded that these practices and the penalties imposed for nonattendance had been discontinued by school authorities. The court therefore held that it was not necessary to consider and determine the legality of such practices. In no uncertain terms, however, it went on to say: "It is beyond the scope and authority of school boards and teachers in the public schools to conduct a program of education in the Bible and undertake to explain the meaning of any chapter or verse in either the Old or the New Testament."

The court thereupon stated that the sole question at issue was whether or not the state statute previously referred to violated the constitution of Tennessee and that of the United States.[86] In the court's opinion, the First Amendment of the United States Constitution and Article I, Section 3 of the Tennessee Constitution are practically synonymous. It felt that, if anything, the Tennessee Organic Law was broader and more comprehensive in its guarantee of freedom of worship and freedom of conscience.

Historical Analysis

The court first reviewed the bloody history of religious wars and the fight to establish religious freedom in the United States out of which emerged the First Amendment to the United States Constitution and Article I, Section 3 of the Tennessee Constitution. From this historical analysis, the court concluded that Bible-reading exercises are not a violation of the Constitutional mandate which guarantees to all men a "natural and indefeasible right to worship almighty God according to the dictates of their own conscience." Nor did the court feel it was reasonable to suppose such practices constituted, "the support of any place or form of worship" or an effort to "control or interfere with the rights of conscience."

The court attempted to answer those who argue the need for separation of church and state and for one's personal right to worship as he sees fit. It pointed out that they confused a short period of reverence or a simple act of spiritual devotion as being a form of worship sponsored and approved by an agency of the state "to the prejudice of other religious groups." It went on to explain: "We find it more or less difficult to conceive that these simple ceremonies amount to 'establishment of a religion,' or any attempt to do so, nor is it interference with any student's secular beliefs contrary to law."

The court next reviewed a number of state court decisions which it felt tended toward the consensus that the Bible is not a sectarian or denominational book. The court at this point, however, carefully refrained from mentioning any state supreme court decision which declared Bible reading in public schools to be unconstitutional. It did make reference to the Tudor case. But since that case was concerned with the distribution of Gideon Bibles to children in public schools, the court distinguished it from the present case on the basis of its facts.

Counsel for the complainant was given a brief but sharp lecture from the court because of the court's opinion that "they have taken a rather narrow and dogmatic view of these constitutional inhibitions." The court was of the opinion that in their concern for liberty of conscience and religious worship "they have overlooked the broader concept that religion per se is something which transcends all man-made creeds." If the complainants' views were sustained, the court believed that this would strike from the schoolroom and school libraries the great story of the Bible and prohibit the singing of great and "inspiring songs" such as "Faith of Our Fathers," and "America the Beautiful."

Judicial Reaction to Precedents

In acknowledging the brief filed by the American Civil Liberties Union as an amicus curiae the court took judicial note of the extent to which both state and federal courts have been engaged in reviewing state statutes involving Bible reading and religious instruction in the public schools. It agreed that such cases were numerous. It then went on to say in a highly misleading and indeed inaccurate statement: ". . . but these statutes have been stricken down only when instruction in the Bible is made compulsory."[87] To substantiate this statement, the court cited *People* ex rel. *Ring* v. *Board of Education*[88] where there was, in fact, a degree of compulsion in such Bible-reading exercises. It ignored those state supreme court decisions, however, involving exercises of this sort in which no compulsion was alleged, and where the supreme courts of several states nonetheless struck down the practice as violating the constitution.

The Tennessee court agreed that the separation of church and state is important but was of the opinion that the conception could not be tortured into meaning that the public school systems of the several states are compelled to be made Godless institutions as a matter of law. On the other hand, it emphasized, "We do not wish, however, to be understood as holding that any form of sectarian worship or secular instruction of the Bible is permissible under our statute and the constitution of this state."

The court concluded its decision by stating: "...the highest duty of those who are charged with the responsibility of training the young people of this state in the public schools is in teaching both by precept and example that in the conflicts of life they should not forget God . . . For this court to hold that the statute herein assailed contemplates the establishment of a religion, and that it is a subtle method of breaking down Mr. Jefferson's 'wall of separation' between church and state would be a spectacular exhibition of judicial sophistry."

In this decision the Tennessee Supreme Court clearly accepted the notion that the Bible per se is not a sectarian book. While the court was not willing to open the door to any form of sectarian instruction it was clearly of the opinion that voluntary Bible-reading exercises in the public school were not a violation of the United States Constitution or the constitution of Tennessee.

THE MURRAY CASE

On April 6, 1962, the Maryland Supreme Court, although badly divided, tended to follow the Tennessee court's general approach in upholding a program of Bible reading in the public schools.[89] By a vote of four to three the Maryland court concluded that programs involving Bible reading and recitation of the Lord's Prayer did not violate the religious clauses of the First Amendment in view of the fact that the use of school time and the expenditure of public funds for such programs was negligible. Furthermore, the court majority felt that the provision in the statute permitting a child to be excused from participating in such programs at the request of his parents further emphasized the validity of these programs.

Unlike many early cases, this one did not involve a challenge directed at a state law. The attack here was aimed at an administrative rule adopted by the Board of School Commissioners of Baltimore City pursuant to general authority conferred upon it by the state. The rule compelled each school in the district to be opened by reading without comment from the "Holy Bible" and/or the use of the Lord's Prayer. The Douay Version of the Bible might be used by the pupils who preferred it. In 1960, as a result of an opinion rendered by Attorney General C. F. Sybert who had become a member of the Maryland Supreme Court by the time this case was heard by that body, the rule was amended to permit any pupil whose parents requested it to be excused from these exercises. Judge Sybert did not participate in the decision of this case.

Along with the contention that the rule contravened their freedom of religion under the First and Fourteenth Amendments, the petitioners who claimed to be atheists argued that the rule "subjects their freedom of conscience to the rule of the majority." Moreover, they urged that the rule, by equating moral and spiritual values with religious values, had thereby rendered their beliefs and ideals "sinister, alien and suspect" thus tending to promote "doubt and questions of their morality, good citizenship and good faith."[90] This is a relatively new argument in a debate that has raged for a century, and is heard also in the Engel case (See Chapter 5).

When the case was tried in the lower court, the Board demurred on the grounds that the case did not state a cause of action for which relief could be granted properly by a writ of mandamus. The court sustained the demurrer and dismissed the petition without leave to amend. The trial court gave two reasons for this action. One, that the Board, in ordering such a program, was acting in the exercise of its discretionary power and thus its action could not be stayed by a writ of mandamus. Secondly, the trial court found that the facts in the petition for the writ of mandamus did not "spell out any violation of constitutional rights."

The case was argued twice on these grounds before the Maryland Supreme Court. The first time it was heard by five of the seven judges and the reargument was heard by seven judges, one of whom substituted for Judge Sybert. Judge Horney spoke for the majority, including Judge Prescott, Marbury, and L. L. Barrett, who was specially assigned to the case.

In dealing first with the jurisdictional arguments over the propriety of the use of a writ of mandamus in this case, the court concluded that "where the performance of a duty prescribed by law depends on whether the statute or regulation is constitutional or invalid, there is no reason why the question may not be determined on a petition for a writ of mandamus . . ." To bolster its position the court cited a substantial body of case law.[91]

The only other jurisdictional question — whether the petitioner had standing to sue — the court assumed in the affirmative, since they found the rule and practice constitutional. Some might regard this as an interesting, albeit somewhat unusual, device for getting to the jugular of constitutional issues without the nice-nelly inhibitions of judicial self-restraint.

Getting to the substantive issue, the court denied that the "Establishment Clause" or the "Free Exercise of Religion Clause" (of the First Amendment), or the "Equal Protection Clause" (of the Fourteenth Amendment) were violated by the practices under consideration. "Neither the First nor Fourteenth Amendment," the court insisted, "was intended to stifle all rapport between religion and government."[92]

It goes on to quote Justice Douglas' majority opinion in the Zorach case, to the effect that "We are a religious people." The Maryland court is of the opinion that the United States Supreme Court in both the Everson case and the Zorach case made it clear that programs of this type "where the time and money spent on it is inconsequential" do not violate the religious clauses of the First Amendment. Exercises such as these, the court felt, are in the same category as opening prayer ceremonies in the legislatures and courts of the states and the national government.

The fact that a student is not compelled to attend these programs, the Maryland court finds especially controlling. It regards as significant the fact that the United States Supreme Court remanded the Schempp case (See Chapter 4) back to the federal district court after the Pennsylvania legislature had amended the state law to provide for voluntary attendance on the part of the pupils, even though the programs themselves were mandatory in the schools. "It seems to us that the remand of this case [Schempp] at least indicated that the use of coercion or the lack of it may be the controlling factor in deciding whether or not a constitutional right has been denied," the Maryland court explained.[93]

While reading substantive judgments into the United States Supreme Court's remand of the Schempp case — a questionable practice at best — the Maryland court rejected the federal district court of Pennsylvania's subsequent ruling that the Bible-reading program in Pennsylvania violated the First and Fourteenth Amendments. The Maryland court argued that the case before it was not governed by the McCollum rule since the students were not compelled to attend the programs. It should be stressed that under the Pennsylvania program, struck down by the federal district court in 1962, the students were not required to participate in programs of this type.

Since there is no compulsion under the Maryland order, the court here refused to believe that the United States Supreme Court's 1961 ruling in *Torcaso* v. *Watkins*[94] that "neither a state nor federal government can constitutionally force a person 'to profess a belief or disbelief in any religion'" applied here. The distinction, as the court saw it, in the Torcaso case was concerned with the compulsion which required a nonbeliever to profess a belief in God in order to qualify for public office. Moreover, the Maryland court appears to accept the Tennessee court's erroneous notion that in other states when Bible-reading programs permitted optional attendance, the state courts invariably upheld such exercises.

Finally, the majority opinion deals with the allegations that the pupil has been denied the equal protection of the laws guaranteed him by the Fourteenth Amendment. The student relied on *Brown* v. *Board of Education*[95] — declaring segregation on the basis of color in the public schools to be unconstitutional — to support his contention that his self-exile from the opening exercises had a deleterious effect on his relationship with other students. The court had a quick answer to this argument. It felt that the equality of treatment guaranteed by the Fourteenth Amendment does not provide protection from the "embarrassment, the divisiveness or the psychological discontent arising out of nonconformance with the mores of the majority."[96]

Dissenting Views

In a vigorous dissent, concurred in by Judges Henderson and Prescott, Judge Brune pinpointed an element in the case ignored in the majority opinion. It was that the school board order made mandatory the reading of the Holy Bible in the public schools. Since there seems to be no substantial room for dispute that the reading of passages from the Bible and recital of the Lord's Prayer are Christian religious exercises, the dissenters felt that programs in the public schools involving Bible reading and reciting the Lord's Prayer, plainly favor "one religion and do so against other religions and against nonbelievers in any religion."[97] As such they violated the First Amendment's provision prohibiting any law *respecting an establishment* of religion.

Judge Brune observed that Chief Justice Warren of the United States Supreme Court, commented in this connection in the McGowan case:[98] "But the First Amendment, in its final form did not simply bar a congressional enactment *establishing a church;* it forbade all laws *respecting an establishment of religion.*"

The dissenters rejected the notion that such programs resist the taint of unconstitutionality simply because the pupils are not compelled to attend. "The coercive or compulsive power of the state is exercised at least to the extent of requiring pupils to attend school and it requires affirmative action to exempt them from participation in these religious exercises," Judge Brune explained. Moreover, the majority opinion tended to place too much specific weight on the general statement of Justice Douglas in the Zorach case, "We are a religious people whose institutions presuppose a Supreme Being," the minority believed.

Finally, Judge Brune noted that the United States Supreme Court recognized in the Brown case (when applying the Fourteenth Amendment to segregation by race in the public schools) that the psychological effects upon children may be of vital importance. He implied that if such reasons have significance to the Supreme Court they should be given equal weight by the Maryland court.

The dissenters also pointed out that since attendance at these religious exercises is compulsory unless a written parental excuse is presented to school authorities, this amounts to a formal profession of disbelief of the religion of the school which is required by the school authorities. This puts the child and the parents in peril of being subject to pressures from the majority. Thus Judge Brune feels that this case is the converse of the Torcaso decision where the United States Supreme Court held that no state or the national government may require a profession of belief in the existence of God as a condition for holding public office. "Neither a profession of belief or disbelief may be required," the minority felt. Judge Brune concluded by explaining:

> Hesitancy to expose a child to the suspicion of his fellows and to losing caste with them will tend to cause the surrender of his and his parents' religious or nonreligious convictions and will thus tend to put the hand of the state into the scales on the side of a particular religion which is supported by the prescribed exercises.

The Murray case was unique in several ways. First, there was the altered emphasis by plaintiff and the dissenters on the concept of compulsion, also revealed by the Supreme Court of the United States in the Schempp case (see Chapter 4) and the Engel case (see Chapter 5). In prior cases, there was a tendency for the courts to concern themselves solely with the question of whether student attendance at such exercises was mandatory or voluntary.

Secondly, the plaintiffs in this case called into question not only the due process clause of the First Amendment's provisions concerning religion, but they also raised the question of whether these practices violated the equal protection clause of the Fourteenth Amendment. The latter provision proved a mainstay in the Supreme Court's arsenal in handling civil rights cases in the decade from 1950 to 1960, particularly in the race relations field. It had the advantage of permitting a court to study psychological and other peripheral consequences of programs such as these and it made use of the sociological aspects of contemporary law in a fashion that the more philosophically based due process clause had difficulty achieving.

THE UNITED STATES SUPREME COURT AND THE MURRAY CASE

On appeal from the Court of Appeals of Maryland, the Murray case was heard jointly with the Schempp case as noted in Chapter 4, pages 144 ff. Since the United States Supreme Court majority and dissenting opinions are quoted in some detail in Chapter 4, it will be necessary here only to note that the Supreme Court rejected the rationale of the Maryland high court and declared that the state-sponsored program of Bible reading was unconstitutional on the grounds that it violated the Establishment Clause of the First Amendment.

It may or may not be significant that the Supreme Court chose to focus its primary attention on the Schempp case rather than the Murray case in 1963. The former involved a protest brought by Unitarians, a group which constitutes something of an organized sect. The Murray case, of course, concerned an action brought by self-avowed atheists. The potential for public misunderstanding of the court's position relating to religion would probably have been greater if the latter case had formed the nub of the court's opinion.

4

The Illegality of Bible Reading

WE NOW TURN OUR ATTENTION to the states in which the courts have looked with disfavor upon the practice of Bible reading in the public schools. The high courts of seven states (Illinois, Louisiana, Nebraska, Ohio, South Dakota, Washington, and Wisconsin) and a federal district court in Pennsylvania have studied the problem and concluded that it violates either constitutional or statutory provisions.[1]

The fact situations in these cases are roughly analogous to those mentioned in the last chapter. This involved the proposed or actual reading of the Bible by an instructor to his students during regularly constituted class time. It was generally the King James Version which was read, and such reading was without note or comment. The litigation which subsequently occurred was generally brought about by Catholic or Jewish parents who objected not only to the practice itself but to the choice of the King James Version as well. The one possible exception to the foregoing is the South Dakota case of *State* ex rel. *Finger* v. *Weedman*.[2]

Here the King James Version was read without note or

comment, but attendance was compulsory. When fifteen Catholic students refused to attend class during this reading they were expelled from school, and were notified that they would not be readmitted without a written apology for their actions. When the litigation came before the high court of South Dakota, it was asked to decide two questions. Are the pupils to be readmitted without a written apology, and might they legally be allowed to absent themselves during subsequent reading? The court held affirmatively in both cases, and thus did not rule as such upon the legality of Bible reading in the public schools. However, its written opinion contained a clearly enunciated *dictum* specifically pointing out the court's feeling that Bible reading in the public schools is inconsistent with the South Dakota constitution. Following this decision a South Dakota statute permitting Bible reading was deleted from the South Dakota Code.[3]

The same basic issues arise to plague the judges in these cases as those which confronted the judges who ruled Bible reading in the public schools legal. Is the Bible a sectarian book? May the Bible be used as a textbook? May school authorities make attendance compulsory in classes where the Bible is read?

There are, however, several significant differences between the approach of the courts that viewed Bible reading with favor and those that did not. Since the courts that held Bible reading to be illegal did so because they regarded it clearly as a sectarian book, they devoted less time to a discussion of its potential use as a textbook, and dealt summarily with the problem of compulsory attendance; for if Bible reading was illegal, it was obviously illegal to attempt to compel attendance.

Another noteworthy difference is that the opinions in these cases are characterized by a careful historical and philosophical study of the general problem of church-state relations in the United States, as well as the position of the practice of Bible reading in this relationship. This approach results in some eloquent and scholarly opinions dealing with as delicate a subject as a judge may rule upon. Probably the best example of this is the Wisconsin case, *State* ex rel. *Weiss* v. *District Board of Edgerton*,[4] for most of the later opinions, in which other state courts declare Bible reading to be illegal, borrow heavily from the rational and literary elements of the majority and concurring opinions in this case.

HISTORICAL BACKGROUNDS

Several of the courts begin their investigation as to the legitimacy of Bible reading by checking back into history to discover what the founding fathers of the United States Constitution regarded as the proper relationship between church and state. Their consensus is that most of the men responsible for the First Amendment to the United States Constitution, especially Madison and Jefferson, felt that it was necessary to keep the spheres assigned to the church and the spheres assigned to the state carefully separated. The Illinois Supreme Court in the Ring case may be taken as an example. After a thorough discussion of the role played by Madison and Jefferson, both in the State of Virginia and in the United States, to achieve religious freedom and keep church and state separate, the court concluded, "In the very nature of things, therefore, religion, or the duty we owe to the creator, is not within the cognizance of civil government, as was declared by James Madison in 1784 . . ."[5]

The authors of the national and state constitutions were apparently faced by the same charge that is levied today against anyone who favors maintaining the wall of separation between church and state. This is the claim that anyone who believes in this separation must be at least irreligious, but is more probably anti-religious. In answer to this type of reasoning, the Washington Supreme Court said:

> It is not that the men who framed and the people who adopted these constitutional enactments were wanting in reverence for the Bible, and respect and veneration for the sublime and pure morality taught therein, but because they were unwilling that any avenue should be left open for the invasion of the right of absolute freedom of conscience in religous affairs . . .[6]

The Ohio court in the Minor case developed a rather novel view of the separation principle as handed down by the founding fathers. In attempting to answer the question "how shall religious freedom be secured?" the court said:

> . . . it can best be secured by adopting the doctrine of the Seventh Section of our own Bill of Rights, and which I summarize in two words by calling it the doctrine of 'Hands Off!' Let the state not only keep its own hands off, but let it also see to it that religious sects keep their hands off each other.[7]

These courts generally feel that statutes and administrative decrees which permit Bible reading are ventures by the civil government into fields which it has no theoretic or historic right to enter. To bear this out they advanced some weighty arguments. The Illinois court explained that the law neither does nor should attempt to enforce Christianity. It said:

> Christianity had its beginnings and grew under oppression. Where it has depended upon the sword of civil authority for its authority it has been weakest. . . . It asks from civil government only impartial protection and concedes to every other sect and religion the same impartial civil right.[8]

In this same vein, the Ohio court reiterated the point that Christianity needs no help from the state. It echoed the Wisconsin court by pointing out that legal Christianity is a solecism. For Chrisianity to depend upon civil authority for the enforcement of its dogmas is to show its own weakness. "True Christianity never shields itself behind majorities . . . its laws are divine not human."[9]

Problems Involving Separation of Church and State

The courts which held Bible reading to be illegal are all deeply concerned with the possibility that the conflict over the separation of church and state might be fought out in the public schools. While the public schools provide a favorite whipping boy for some, to many thoughtful Americans they are believed to be the cornerstone of our democratic system. This fear is reflected in the concurring opinion of Justice Orton of the Wisconsin Supreme Court. He warned:

> There is no such source and cause of strife, quarrel, fights, malignant opposition, persecution and war, and all evil in the state, as religion. Let it once enter into our civil affairs, our government would soon be destroyed. . . . The common school is one of the most indispensable, useful, and valuable civil institutions this state has. It is democratic, and free to all alike, in perfect equality, where all the children of our people stand on a common platform, and may enjoy the benefits of an equal and common education.[10]

The Wisconsin Supreme Court was fully aware that by ruling Bible reading illegal in the public schools it was exposing itself to the charge that this action was derogatory to the Bible and its ideals. The Justices hastened to defend themselves from this charge, and by so doing established the line of reasoning which is frequently used by other state courts.

Justice Lyons pointed out in the majority opinion that:

> Religion teaches obedience to law and flourishes best where good government prevails. The constitutional prohibition was adopted in the interest of good government; and it argues but little faith in the vitality and power of religion to predict disaster to its progress because a constitutional provision enacted for such a purpose, is faithfully executed.[11]

In his concurring opinion, Justice Orton countered a charge which might have been taken from today's newspapers. He pointed out that there was a tendency to call the secular public schools Godless. "They are called so by those who wish to have not only religion, but their own religion taught therein." He continued, "They are Godless and the educational department of the government is Godless, in the same sense that the executive, legislative, and administrative departments are Godless."[12]

Another historical argument advanced by those who wanted to see Bible reading become a part of the public school curriculum was based on the Northwest Ordinance of 1787, and its present-day applicability to states which had once come under its provisions. The Illinois and Ohio courts in particular were called upon to answer this question.

In Ohio it was claimed that Bible reading should be legal under Article 7, Section 1, of the Ohio constitution.

This section was taken verbatim from the Ordinance of 1787 and reads:

> Religion, morality, and knowledge, however, being essential to good Government, it shall be the duty of the General Assembly to pass suitable laws to protect every religious denomination in the peaceful enjoyment of its own mode of public worship, and to encourage schools and the means of education.[13]

The court, however, interpreted these words quite differently, and refused to agree that Bible reading or any active state participation in the church's sphere is sanctioned by this section. It explained:

> . . . Religion, morality and knowledge are essential to government in the sense that they have the instrumentalities for producing and perfecting a good form of government. On the other hand, no government is at all adapted for producing and perfecting or propagating a good religion. . . . Religion is the parent and not the offspring of good government.[14]

The problem facing the Illinois court was slightly different. It was argued that even though the above-mentioned section of the Ordinance of 1787 was not in the Illinois constitution, it might be considered a part of the spirit upon which the constitution rests. The court denied this allegation, pointing out that the Ordinance of 1787 was superseded by the state constitution and by the admission of the state into the Union. It went on to explain that during the state's constitutional convention attempts were made to add a section to the constitution which would prohibit the exclusion of the Bible from the public schools. Because this move failed, the court felt justified in denying that the constitution carried an implication that Bible reading was legal.[15]

DISSENTS AND DIVERGENCES

It should be noted that not all of the seven state courts which held Bible reading to be illegal were unanimous in their decision, nor did all of the majority opinions agree on some of these points of historic and philosophic interpretation. It might be interesting at this point to note the number of judges who dissented from court decisions holding Bible reading to be illegal. In the nine cases to come before the high courts of the seven states and a Pennsylvania federal district court, six decisions were unanimous. Furthermore, Justice Holcomb of the Washington Supreme Court, in his lone dissent in *Dearle* v. *Frazier*,[16] agreed that Bible reading was illegal. He felt, however, that since the Washington constitution so clearly prohibits Bible reading, there was no need for the long and involved decision of his colleagues. He dissented because he felt the case should have been dismissed summarily.

In effect, therefore, only two of the courts were divided on the issue of Bible reading. In the Illinois case,[17] two of the seven supreme court justices were dissenters, while in the South Dakota case,[18] two justices out of five felt Bible reading was legal. Among the courts which ruled against Bible reading we have a total of 51 judges hearing nine cases before the high courts of seven different states plus one federal district court decision. Forty-seven of these judges felt that Bible reading in the public schools was illegal, while only four would allow this practice. There is a remarkable degree of agreement here considering the controversial nature of the issue involved.

The dissents in the South Dakota case were illustrative of the opposition's line of reasoning. Justice Brown in his dissent pointed out what he considered to be the complete impossibility of divorcing religion from the state. In addition, he did not believe that the founding fathers of the nation and the state had any intention of so doing. He used the stock examples to back up his argument; i.e., chaplains in the legislature and the armed services, the use of the slogan "In God We Trust" on United States coins, and the Presidential announcement of some religious holidays.[19]

There was also some disagreement in the majority opinions regarding the church-state relationship and the role of religion in American history and thought. This is indicated by the Louisiana court's opinion, which, while it held that Bible reading violated the right to religious freedom of the Jewish children, went on to say:

> There have been differences in expressions of opinion as to whether this is a Christian land or not . . . there has not been a question as to its being a Godly land, or that we are a religious people.

To demonstrate this fact, the court quoted from the "Declaration of Independence" and the "Articles of Confederation," both of which mention God.[20]

From this general attempt to analyze the historic forces active in determining the relationship between church and state in the United States, and the role of Bible reading in this process, the courts next looked more specifically at the possible sectarian quality of the Bible to determine whether or not this would justify a prohibition of the practice of Bible reading in the public schools.

THE BIBLE IS SECTARIAN

In their development of some working definition of the word "sect," a noticeable difference is seen between the fourteen state courts which held Bible reading to be legal, the seven state courts and the Pennsylvania federal district court which felt that it was illegal. It was the Wisconsin court which enunciated the most thorough definition of what (to it) constituted a sect, and this definition is characteristic of the state courts which held Bible reading to be illegal.

Justice Lyons, speaking for the majority of the court, spelled out its understanding of the meaning of the word "sect."

> It should here be said that the term 'religious sect' is understood as applying to people believing in the same religious doctrines, who are more or less closely associated or organized to advance such doctrines, and increase the number of believers therein. The doctrines of one of these sects which are not common to all the others are sectarian; and the term 'sectarian' is, we think, used in that sense in the constitution.[21]

To forestall any erroneous conclusions which might result from this definition, he quickly pointed out:

> It is scarcely necessary to add that we have no concern with the truth or error of the doctrines of any sect. We are only concerned to know whether instruction in 'sectarian doctrines' has been, or is liable to be, given in the public schools of Edgerton.[22]

These eight courts generally felt that the Bible was a sectarian book, and that portions of it were used by the different sects to prove various points of sectarian dogma. At least one court — the Louisiana Supreme Court — felt that it was impossible to read the Bible without conjuring up religious and sectarian overtones. In regard to reading the Bible in the public school, it announced:

> To read the Bible for the purpose stated requires that it be read reverently and worshipfully. As God is the author of the Book, He is necessarily worshipped in the reading of it. And the reading of it forms part of all religious services in the Christian and Jewish churches, which use the Word. It is as much a part of the religious worship of the churches of the land as is the offering of prayer to God.[23]

There seems to be general agreement among these courts that not all parts of the Bible are sectarian. The difficulty they foresaw is that it is impossible to determine with any certainty what portion of this book some sect might regard as sectarian. The Illinois court pointed out, "The only means of preventing sectarian instruction in the school is to exclude altogether religious instruction by means of reading the Bible or otherwise." This, it believed, was the only solution to the problem of determining exactly what parts of the Bible are sectarian. The Bible, in the last analysis, "cannot be separated from its character as an inspired book of religion."[24]

The Wisconsin court's view of the sectarian nature of the Bible was indicative of prevailing attitudes on this point in the eight states where Bible reading was held to be illegal. This court ruled that the sectarian instruction prohibited in the common schools (by Article 10, Section 3 of the Wisconsin constitution) was instruction in the doctrines held by one or another of the various religious sects and not by the rest. Bible reading in these schools came within this prohibition since each sect, with a few exceptions, based its peculiar doctrines upon some portion of the Bible, the reading of which tended to inculcate its beliefs.[25]

A minor variation on the theme of the sectarian nature of the Bible should be noted in the earlier Washington case, *Dearle* v. *Frazier*.[26] Here, the plaintiff hotly denied that the Bible was a sectarian book. The supreme court of Washington felt, however, that it was not necessary to prove the Bible sectarian, since the constitution of Washington states:

> No public money or property shall be appropriated for or applied to any religious worship, exercise, or instruction, or the support of any religious establishment.[27]

The court stressed the uniqueness of the Washington constitution, in that it speaks of "religious" and not "sectarian" instruction. It felt there could be no doubt that Bible reading in the public schools was religious instruction, or at least a religious exercise.[28] It went on to explain, "We have then, not only 'religious exercise' and 'instruction' which are prohibited, but their natural consequences — religious discussion and controversy."

The litigation in this case arose over the attempts by the plaintiff to compel the school authorities to give credit toward graduation for a course in Bible study. This was in keeping with a provision adopted by the State Board of Education several years earlier that proposed to give one-half of one high school credit for the study of the Old and New Testaments. All instruction was either to be given in the pupil's home or by a religious organization to which the pupil belonged. There was to be no high school supervision of the program other than preparing the syllabus of Bible readings, the setting up of the examination for the course, and the grading of the papers.

The court felt that the use of public money for the preparation of the syllabus and the final examination, as well as payment of teachers to grade the papers constituted an expenditure of public funds for religious purposes, which was forbidden by the state constitution.[29]

Use of Public Funds in Bible Reading

The questions of whether or not the taxpayers of an area may object to the use of public funds for various exercises such as Bible reading, and whether or not these exercises turn the school into a place of worship, have produced some varied opinions among the courts which held Bible reading to be illegal. The views of the Wisconsin court receive general acceptance by the other courts. This court believed that the reading of the Bible is an act of worship as the term is used in the Wisconsin constitution. Therefore, the taxpayers of any district who are compelled to contribute to the erection and support of common schools have the right to object to the reading of the Bible in these schools under the Wisconsin constitution, Art. I, Sec. 18, Clause 12, which states, "No man shall be compelled to support any place of worship."[30]

In this same vein, the Illinois court pointed out that Bible reading in the public schools violated Article 8, Section 3, of the Illinois constitution, which prohibits the appropriation of any public fund to aid any sectarian purpose.[31] The majority opinion of the Nebraska Supreme Court stated essentially the same view.[32] Justice Holcomb of the Nebraska court, in a separate concurring opinion, took issue with his colleagues on this point. He agreed that Bible reading may be regarded as sectarian instruction, but went on to say:

> As to the views apparently entertained and held to in the opinion to the effect that the exercises complained of constitute thereby the school house a place of worship within the meaning and contrary to the constitution. . . I do not agree.[33]

He explained this objection by saying he feared the majority view, if accepted, would prevent religious exercises in any penal or charitable institutions of the state.

A somewhat different view was presented by the Louisiana court, which seemed to suggest that the schoolhouse may be different things at different times.

> The school houses of the parish belong to the people of that parish, and they are under the control of the school

authorities of the parish. If, at any time when the school houses are not being occupied or used for school purposes, the school board were to permit the school houses to be used for religious or other purposes, the rights of the plaintiffs would not be infringed in any way, and they might not be heard to complain of such action by the school authorities.[34]

THE KING JAMES VERSION IS SECTARIAN

The courts holding Bible reading to be illegal show a deep concern for the rights of minority groups, and their decisions reflect an earnest attempt to work out some solution whereby no one's religious freedom is trampled under the foot of majority might.

When discussing the differences between the King James and the Douay Versions of the Bible, the Illinois court pointed out some practical political problems that might arise from using one or the other of them in Bible-reading exercises. The court suggested that struggles for control of the school board might occur between Roman Catholics and Protestants, for with control of the school board would go the power to choose which version of the Bible might be used. It concluded, "Our constitution has wisely provided against such a contest by excluding sectarian instruction altogether from the school."[35]

The Nebraska court likewise did not feel that the difference between the two versions of the Bible was negligible. This, it pointed out, was the major inadequacy of Section 7659 of Nebraska's Revised Code of 1919, which allowed Bible reading. It did not say which version of the Bible might be used in the schools, but it did forbid the teaching of sectarian dogmas in them. The court believed that the debate over Bible reading resulted from disagreements over the version of the Bible selected to be read, which in turn resulted in sectarian debates.[36]

While these courts in general agree that reading the
King James Version of the Bible violates the religious freedom of Catholic and Jewish children, and is sectarian instruction, the Louisiana court is a partial exception to this
rule. This court noted the difference between the Rabbinical Bible and the Christian Bible and concluded that
the Jews have a just complaint against the practice of Bible
reading. It did not feel that this is true in the case of Catholics. Since this court believed that the King James and the
Douay Versions of the Bible are essentially similar, the
Catholics could not validly complain of an injury. It concluded that while Bible reading violated the religious freedom of the Jewish children, it did not infringe on the religious liberty of the Catholics.[37] Finally, when speaking of
religious liberty for the Jewish child, the court said:

> Therefore, while we are grateful to God for religious free-
> dom, with other blessings, we may not interfere with any
> citizen's natural right to also worship the same God ac-
> cording to the dictates of his own conscience. The Jew
> will be permitted without interference to worship God
> according to his conscience, and so will others.

The court felt, therefore, that since Bible reading invaded
the rights of conscience of Jewish children it could not be
allowed in the public schools.

The Wisconsin Supreme Court took a broader view
of the effects of Bible reading on non-Protestant religious
groups. This is the more common interpretation among
the other state courts. It explained:

> . . . is it unreasonable to say that sectarian instruction
> was thus excluded [from the public schools] to the end
> that the child of the Jew or Catholic or Unitarian or Uni-
> versalist or Quaker should not be compelled to listen to
> the stated reading of passages of scripture which are ac-
> cepted by others as giving the lie to the religious faith and
> beliefs of their parents and themselves.[38]

Majority Rights

Generally inherent in the argument of those who favor Bible reading in the public schools, is a suggestion which presupposes the right of the majority to fix the type of educational policies they deem advisable. Several of the courts which held Bible reading to be illegal addressed themselves to this problem, and upheld the rights of minorities over majority might. Incident to this argument is the view sometimes advanced by those favoring Bible reading, which maintains that the religious freedom spoken of in state constitutions and statutes includes only the Christian religion.

The Ohio court was called upon to decide this latter question, and pointed out forcefully:

> When they [the founders of the state constitutions] speak of 'all men' having certain rights, they cannot merely mean 'all Christian men.' Some of the very men who helped to frame these constitutions were themselves not Christian men.[39]

It went on to stress, "If Christianity is a *law* of the state, like every other law it must have a sanction." In addition to this, there would have to be adequate penalties to enforce Christianity, and the court felt that this was obviously not the case.

Speaking more generally of minority rights in this country, the Illinois court said:

> It is precisely for the protection of the minority that constitutional limitations exist. Majorities need no such protection — they can take care of themselves.[40]

The Ohio court echoed this sentiment almost verbatim, saying, "the protection guaranteed by the section in question means protection to the minority. The majority can protect itself."[41]

As has been previously mentioned, these eight courts are concerned with keeping the public schools open to all children, regardless of religion. The only way that this could be accomplished, it appeared to them, was to prevent the teachings of the schools from injuring any child's religious sensibilities. The public schools were not the place to convert anyone to a given religious outlook, through programs of forcible attendance to what some children and their parents regard as sectarian instruction.

This view was especially well put by the Ohio court when it explained, "If you desire people to fall in love with your religion, make it lovely."[42] It went on to explain that one's attitude toward the advisability of government aid to religion depends upon who you are and where you are.

> No Protestant in Spain and no Catholic in this country will be found insisting that the government of his residence shall support and teach its own religion to the exclusion of all others and to tax all alike for its support.

The Nebraska court in a succinct passage might well speak for the other seven courts in voicing the desire to keep the public schools truly public. It stated, "It will be an evil day when anything happens to lower the public schools in popular esteem or to discourage attendance upon them by children of any class."[43]

THE BIBLE AND MORAL INSTRUCTION

One of the reasons given for favoring Bible reading is that it will aid in the general moral instruction of the pupils, quite apart from any sectarian connotations surrounding the book itself. They feel that the secular public schools have been lax in developing the moral awareness of the pupils, and all too frequently youngsters emerge from the public schools with a poor understanding of basic ethical principles. Those who subscribe to this belief seem to maintain that some common denominator of religious virtue might be inculcated through the practice of Bible reading. Very few agree, however, on what this common denominator is. What appears to be a common religious and moral tenet to one group frequently emerges as sectarian dogma to another.

The courts which held Bible reading illegal did not deny the possible benefit of added moral instruction in public schools. They were, however, deeply aware of the difficulty of arriving at major moral teachings which would be acceptable to all groups. At least one of these courts felt that determining what articles of religions constitute general morality was not within the scope of the judicial power. The Supreme Court of Washington pointed out:

> What guarantee has the citizen that the [school] board having a contrary faith will not inject those passages upon which their own sect rests its claim to be the true church under the guise of 'narrative or literary features,' and if they did so, where would the remedy be found? Surely the courts could not control their descretion, for judges are made of the same stuff as other men and what would appear to be heretical or doctrinal to one may stand out as a literary gem or as inoffensive narrative to another.[44]

Agreeing that it is nearly impossible to arrive at common moral and religious qualities which may be expounded through Bible reading exercises, the courts which looked upon Bible reading unfavorably felt that while it is important to teach these doctrines, the public school is not the place to do it. The Wisconsin court said:

> The priceless truths of the Bible are best taught to our youths in the church, the Sabbath and parochial schools, the social religious meetings, and above all, by parents in the home circle.[45]

Using essentially the same approach, the Nebraska court stated:

> . . . the state in its function as an educator must leave the teaching of religion to the church, because the church is the only body equipped to so teach, and on it rests the responsibility. . . . There need be no shock to the moral sense, nor to our religious and instincts, in barring religious subjects from our public schools and placing them where they belong, to be properly taught. Children of Catholics, Methodists, Presbyterians, Episcopalians, Baptists, or any other sect are not deprived of religious education, because it is not taught in the public school.[46]

The Illinois court also emphasized the necessity for keeping the spheres of church and state separate.

> The school like the government is simply a civil institution. It is secular, and not religious, in its purpose. The truths of the Bible are truths of religion, which do not come within the province of the public school.[47]

These courts then, feel that it is impossible to use the Bible as a textbook from which instructions in general morality may be garnered. Their views might be summed up by the Illinois court, which said:

> Any instruction on any one of the subjects [in the Bible] is necessarily sectarian, because, while it may be consistent with the doctrines of one or many of the sects, it will be inconsistent with the doctrine of one or more of them.[48]

THE BIBLE AS A TEXTBOOK

Since the courts which held Bible reading illegal did so because they believed it to be a sectarian book, they did not spend time looking into the potential virtues of using it as a text, as did the courts which looked with favor upon Bible reading. Several of the courts, however, made some interesting comments upon the Bible as a text.

The general tenor of these court opinions on the use of the Bible as a textbook is exemplified by that of the Louisiana court. It stressed the fact that the reading of the Bible was religious instruction, and when the New Testament was read it was Christian instruction. The character of the book, it felt, was religious, and it was not adaptable for use as a text without arousing religious overtones.[49]

Those who argued for the legality of Bible reading before these courts, stressed that if the practice were declared illegal, the public would derive the general impression that any textbooks founded upon the fundamental teachings of the Bible or using an occasional extract from it, would also be illegal for use in the public school. This argument was advanced by Justices Hand and Cartwright of the Illinois court in their dissenting opinion. They felt that freethinkers and atheists did not constitute organized sects, and that the constitutional prohibition against the teaching of sectarian religion in the public schools had no application to them or to their opposition to the teaching of general Christian morality. They concluded by announcing that if the majority opinion of the Illinois court was allowed to stand, it would result in the removal from the public schools of all literature which mentioned a Supreme Being.[50]

The majority opinion of the Illinois court, following the lead of the Wisconsin court in the Weiss case,[51] refused to believe that its decision presupposed the exclusion from the schools of books which use occasional extracts from the Bible or mentioned a Supreme Being. It relied heavily upon the argument advanced in the decision of the Wisconsin court. The Wisconsin court felt that while Bible reading itself was illegal under the Wisconsin constitution, this did not mean that textbooks founded upon the Bible and emphasizing its basic teachings of morality need be banished from the public schools.

This attitude is summed up by Justice Lyons of the Wisconsin court, when he stated:

> It should be observed, in this connection, that the above views do not, as counsel seemed to think they may, banish from the district schools such textbooks as are founded upon the fundamental teachings of the Bible, or which contain extracts therefrom. . . . [These extracts] pervade and ornament our secular literature and are important elements in its value and usefulness.[52]

The Courts and Educational Policy Formulation

One area of agreement exists between the courts looking favorably and the courts looking unfavorably upon the practice of Bible reading. They believed it was generally inadvisable for them to try to determine and dictate educational policies. They were reluctant to overrule the state legislature and the school boards in educational policies unless a clear-cut case could be made for the illegality of some educational program. In this connection it is necessary to point out a unique element in several of the cases where Bible reading was declared illegal.

In *Board of Education* v. *Minor*,[53] *State* ex rel. *Dearle* v. *Frazier*,[54] and *State* ex rel. *Clithero* v. *Showalter*[55] attempts were made to obtain court action which would have compelled the boards of education to institute a program of Bible reading in the schools, or to maintain such a program which had been discontinued because of a newly

adopted ordinance forbidding such exercises. In all three of
these cases the courts refused to interfere with the school
authorities' decisions.

The Ohio court in the Minor case[56] ruled that the constitution of the state did not enjoin or require religious instructions or the reading of religious books in the public
schools of the state. It explained that the legislature had
placed the management of the public schools under the
exclusive control of directors, trustees, and boards of education. The courts, therefore, had no rightful authority to
interfere by directing what instructions shall be given or
what books shall be read in the public schools of the state.
Justice Welch said, "There is no question before us of the
wisdom or unwisdom of having the Bible in the schools or
withdrawing it therefrom." He felt that the case presented
merely a question of the court's rightful authority to interfere in the management and control of the public schools.

The Washington court in the Frazier case[57] expressed
the same sentiments. The majority opinion pointed out that
a plan which would give high school credit for reading the
Old and New Testaments because of their "literary value"
(and which the superintendent of the school refused to follow) violated Article I, Section I, of the Washington constitution. It said:

> . . . the vice of the present plan is that public school
> credit is given for instruction at the hands of sectarian
> agents . . . . The Bible history, narrative and biography
> cannot be taught without leading to opinion and ofttimes
> partisan opinion is understood and anticipated by the
> school board.[58]

In addition to this, the Washington court concluded that
to compromise on this matter would be to make the courts

and not the school board the arbiters on matters of general educational policy.

In *State* ex rel. *Clithero* v. *Showalter*,[59] the Washington court disposed of the case on the basis of the rule laid down in the Frazier case.[60] The court felt there was no need to investigate the question anew, for it believed that if the people of the state seriously wanted the state's policy toward sectarian education in the public schools to change, the critics of the policy should strive to crystallize public opinion in favor of voting for a constitutional amendment. The court stressed that it is not the duty of the judiciary to revise the constitution because one group disapproves of certain provisions.[61]

Before concluding this section, one further point should be noted. While it is touched upon by only one of the courts holding Bible reading illegal, it presents a point of view which cannot be ignored by persons interested in the church-state relationship in the United States. The Ohio court not only felt that reading the King James Version of the Bible violated the rights of conscience of Roman Catholic and Jewish children, but it went on to express its concern for the rights of the Catholic or Jewish teacher who is required to read the Protestant Bible to children of all faiths.[62] The importance of this view should not be under-emphasized, for the teacher is caught between two equally distasteful alternatives. If for reasons of conscience he refuses to conduct the Bible-reading exercises, there is a good possibility that he may lose his position. On the other hand, if he performs the exercise as prescribed by law, his religious beliefs and principles will be violated. From an academic standpoint it may be interesting to speculate as to the outcome of a collision between economic interests and religious principles, but from the teacher's standpoint it is a decidedly uncomfortable decision to make. The Ohio court felt that the only way to keep such a situation from arising was to keep Bible-reading exercises out.

BIBLE READING AND COMPULSORY ATTENDANCE

The eight courts which held Bible reading to be illegal did not allow the question of compulsory attendance during such exercises to occupy much of their time, since they decided earlier that the Bible was sectarian and violated the religious sensibilities of certain groups. Several of the courts did touch lightly on this question, and the views of the Wisconsin court in particular are interesting as a direct antithesis of those presented by the Colorado court in the Stanley case. It has been previously mentioned that while the Colorado court held Bible reading legal, it stressed that at tendance at such reading could not be made compulsory. To the charge that such a system discriminated against the pupils who left the classroom during such exercises, the Colorado court replied:

> We cannot agree to that. The shoe is on the other foot. We have known many boys to be ridiculed for complying with religious regulations, but never one for neglecting them or absenting himself from them.[03]

The Wisconsin court took the opposite view. It explained that the practice of Bible reading in the public schools could receive no sanction from the fact that the pupils are not compelled to remain in the school while the Bible is being read. The withdrawal of a portion of them at such a time would tend to destroy the equality and uniformity of treatment sought to be established and protected by the constitution of Wisconsin.[64] Justice Lyons said: Even if the law allows pupils to leave during such reading, "the excluded pupil loses caste with his fellows, and is liable to be regarded with aversion, and subjected to reproach and insult," since he is leaving because of apparent hostility to the Bible that those who remain revere.

The Illinois court felt that compulsory attendance during Bible-reading exercises would certainly be a violation of the constitutional guarantee of the free exercise of religion. It pointed out that, "One does not enjoy the free exercise of religious worship who is compelled to join in any form of religious worship." It also felt that, "the free enjoyment of religious worship includes the freedom not to worship."[65] Like the Wisconsin court, the Supreme Court of Illinois held that even though attendance at Bible reading was optional, with the pupils being allowed to absent themselves from such exercises for reasons of conscience, the practice would still be unconstitutional. It said the very fact that the pupil left the room during such a program would serve to stigmatize him and put him at a disadvantage in school, which the law did not contemplate.[66]

The case which came before the South Dakota court was concerned only with compulsory attendance.[67] However, the *obiter dictum* in the decision against it was so critical of Bible reading in general, that the statute permitting it was deleted from the South Dakota Code.

THE SCHEMPP CASE

The Schempp case[68] is unique in the controversial area of Bible-reading exercises in the public schools for several reasons. First, it is a recent case involving questions of this nature to be litigated. Secondly, unlike all of the other major cases involving this question, this case was brought in a federal district court for the Eastern District of Pennsylvania rather than in the state courts, as is normally the case. It therefore gives us an opportunity to analyze the manner in which one federal court, at least, has applied the jurisdictional principles discussed by the Supreme Court of the United States in the Doremus case.

The suit was brought by Edward Schempp and Sidney Schempp as parents and guardians of their children who attended the public schools in Abington Township, Pennsylvania. Suit was brought under 28 U.S.C. Sections 1343 and 2281 and was heard by a three-judge federal district court under provisions of 28 U.S.C. Section 2284. The complainants attacked, as a violation of the First Amendment to the Constitution of the United States, the Pennsylvania state statute which provided for reading of ten verses of the "Holy Bible" by teachers or students.[69] Similar assertions were made in respect to reading ten verses of the Bible in conjunction with the pupils' practice of reciting the Lord's Prayer. The Schempps sought a permanent injunction enjoining these practices.

At the outset, the federal district court put its finger upon one of the knottiest problems arising in cases of this kind. It noted that the legislature of Pennsylvania did not define the term "Holy Bible." Nor, the court observed, did the legislature of Pennsylvania make any differentiation between the King James Version of the Bible frequently employed in the religious exercises of Protestants, and the Douay Version, the authorized Bible of the Roman Catholic church.

The court formally recognized that the complainants were Unitarians in Germantown, Philadelphia, Pennsylvania, and that they and their children regularly attended this church. The three children and the father testified, moreover, as to items of religious doctrine conveyed by a literal reading of the Bible, particularly the King James Version. Such tenets, they argued, were contrary to the religious beliefs they held. One complainant testified, for example, that he did not believe in the divinity of Christ, the Immaculate Conception, the concept of an anthropomorphic God, or the Trinity.

In addition, one child testified that during the reading of the Bible in the public schools a standard of physical deportment and attention of a higher caliber than usual was required of the students. While several of the children admitted that they had not objected to taking part in the practices complained of, one child clearly made known his objection. In November of 1956, Ellory Schempp's objection took the form of reading to himself a copy of the Koran while the Bible was being read. Moreover, he refused to stand during the recitation of the Lord's Prayer.

His homeroom teacher, thereupon, told him he should stand during the recitation of the Lord's Prayer, and he then asked to be excused from morning devotions. As a result, he was sent to discuss the matter with the vice-principal and the school guidance counselor. Following this discussion, he spent the period of "morning devotions" in the guidance counselor's office for the remainder of the year. At the beginning of the next academic year, however, when he asked his homeroom teacher to be excused from attending the ceremonies, she discussed the matter with the assistant principal. Thereupon, that official told him he should remain in the homeroom and attend the morning Bible-reading and prayer-recitation period as did the other students. The student obeyed these instructions for the remainder of the year.

School officials testified that no complaints had been received other than that of Ellory Schempp. The court found that this evidence was uncontradicted.[70]

Role of Biblical Scholars

After this careful exposition of the fact situation, the court next evaluated testimony presented by biblical scholars. Dr. Solomon Grayzel, editor of the Jewish Publications Society, emphasized that there were marked differences between the Jewish Holy Scriptures and the Christian Holy Bible. The most obvious, of course, was the absence of the New Testament in the Jewish Holy Scripture. Dr. Grayzel further noted that portions of the New Testament were offensive to Jewish tradition and, "from the standpoint of Jewish faith, the concept of Jesus Christ as the son of God was practically blasphemous." He noted instances in the New Testament which assertedly were not only sectarian in nature but tended to "bring the Jews into ridicule or scorn." Dr. Grayzel believed that such material from the New Testament could be explained to Jewish children in such a way as to do no harm to them. On the other hand, if portions of the New Testament were read to such children without explanation, they could be, he felt, psychologically harmful to the child. In addition, practices of the latter type caused a divisive force within the social media of the school, Dr. Grayzel believed.

Dr. Luther A. Weigle, Dean Emeritus of the Yale Divinity School, testified for the school board. Dr. Weigle believed that the Bible was nonsectarian. He later explained that the phrase "nonsectarian" meant to him nonsectarian within the Christian faiths. Although admitting that his definition of the Holy Bible would include the Jewish Holy

Scriptures, he also stated that the "Holy Bible" would not be complete without the New Testament. Reading of the Holy Scriptures to the exclusion of the New Testament, he believed, would be a sectarian practice. The Bible was of great moral, historical, and literary value, Dr. Weigle emphasized.

Counsel for the school board denied the charge that Bible-reading exercises in the public schools constituted a violation of the First Amendment. They contended that the reading of the "Holy Bible" at the opening of each school day did not affect, favor, or establish a religion or prohibit the free exercise thereof. They stressed that freedom of religion or of conscience does not include a right to practice one's beliefs or disbeliefs concerning the Bible by preventing others from hearing it read in the public schools. Reading the Bible without note or comment, they believed, was a substantial aid in developing the minds and morals of school children, and that the state had a constitutional right to employ such practices in its educational programs. Lastly, the school board argued, there was no compulsion upon the complainants in respect to religious observances, and they had not shown that they had been deprived of any constitutional rights.

Jurisdictional Considerations

In its decision, the federal district court had, at the outset, to come to grips with certain jurisdictional questions. First, it concluded that in light of the First Amendment liberties involved, the case contained a substantial federal question. Secondly, it rejected the notion that the doctrine of abstention was applicable in this case on the grounds that a United States District Court had the duty to adjudicate a controversy properly before it.[71] In reference to the doctrine of abstention, the court concluded, no interference with the administrative processes of the commonwealth of Pennsylvania was involved in this case, nor, by adjudicating the merits of the controversy, did the federal district court create "needless friction by unnecessarily enjoining state officials from executing domestic policies."

Third, the court confirmed the rights of the children of the parents in respect to their standing to maintain a suit at bar in this particular case. The court felt that the standing of the children was similar to that of the minor plaintiffs in *Brown* v. *Board of Education.*[72] The court believed that the parents had standing to bring suit in their own right in that they were the natural guardians of their children and had an immediate and direct interest in their spiritual and religious development.

Thereupon the court restricted itself in its decision to two major issues: One, the constitutional issues presented by the reading of ten verses of the Bible and two, the constitutional issues raised by reading of the Bible verses followed by the recital of the Lord's Prayer.

The Bible As Literature and History

At the outset of its evaluation into the merits of the case, the court said: "to characterize the Bible as a work of art, of literary or historic significance and to refuse to admit its essential character as a religious document would seem to us to be unrealistic." The court felt that the key question involved concerned whether or not to accept the Holy Bible as a religious document regardless of the version involved. The court agreed that Bible verses are of great literary merit but noted that these verses are embodied in books of worship regardless of the version. Furthermore, the Bible was devoted primarily to bringing man in touch with God. Moreover, the court felt that the manner in which the Bible was used as required by the state statute did not affect a clear division between religious dogmas and general moral truths. It noted that the daily reading of the Bible, buttressed by the authority of the state, backed with the authority of the teachers, could hardly do less than inculcate or promote the inculcation of various religious doctrines in childish minds. Thus, the practice required by the state amounted to religious instruction or a promotion of religious education.

It made no difference, the court felt, that religious "truths" may vary from one child to the other. Inasmuch as the Bible deals with man's relationship to God, the court believed that the Pennsylvania statute required a daily reminder of that relationship, that the statute aided all religions, and, "inasmuch as the 'Holy Bible' is a Christian document, the practice aids and prefers that Christian religion."[73]

The court also felt that by requiring public school teachers to read selections from the Bible that the commonwealth of Pennsylvania through statutory mandate was supporting the establishment of religion.

In answer to the defendant's argument that each listener might interpret what he heard in the fashion he desired, the court gave two reasons why this argument was invalid. First, the argument either ignored the essential religious nature of the Bible, or assumed that its religious quality could be disregarded by the listener. "This is too much to ignore and too much to assume," the court stressed. Secondly, the testimonies of the Schempps and Dr. Grayzel proved that, "interpretations of the Bible dependent upon the inclination of scholars and students, can result in a spectrum of meanings beginning at one end of the spectroscopic field with literal acceptance of the words of the Bible, objectionable to Unitarians such as the Schempps, and ending in the vague philosophical generalities condemned by fundamentalists."

The fact that during the morning exercises school children had to maintain a mien more in keeping with the devotional or religious rite than with order during classroom instruction also led to the conclusion that such exercises were sectarian in nature, the court believed. Indeed, these exercises were frequently referred to as "morning devotions" by the children and the school board, the court pointed out.

The school board had called to the court's attention the fact that several versions of the Bible plus the Jewish Holy Scriptures had been used in the exercises of the school. The court found, however, that this proved only "that the religion which is established is either sectless or is all-embracing, or that different religions are established equally. But none of these conditions, assuming them to exist, purges the use of the Bible as prescribed by the statutes of its constitutional infirmities."

Problems of Compulsion

The court also emphasized that a compulsory quality about the religious exercises required by Pennsylvania law could not be ignored. In the case of Ellory Schempp, the facts indicated he was compelled to attend the exercises by the assistant principal of his school acting under the authority of his office. On another occasion, Ellory Schempp was directed by his homeroom teacher to stand during the recitation of the Lord's Prayer. Moreover, the court believed that where a course of conduct is compelled for school teachers and school superintendents that the school officials will use every effort to cause the children committed to their guidance and care to form an audience for the reading of the Bible according to the terms of the statute. On this score, the court concluded that, "the arguments made by the defendants that there was no compulsion ignores reality in the face of social suasion."[74]

Nor did the court buy the argument that merely because the Schempps alone objected, the statute prescribed conduct which was not compulsory both as to teachers and pupils. "Indeed," the court pointed out, "the lack of protest may in fact attest to the success and subtlety of the compulsion." The court had little difficulty saying with finality that in schools conducted in accordance with the legislative fiat, the reading of the "Holy Bible" was compulsory as to teachers and pupils.

Finally, attention was called to the fact that the rights of parents were even more clearly interfered with by the Pennsylvania law. Parents have some interest in the development of their children's religious sensibilities, the court believed. Thus, if the faith of the child were developed, "inconsistently with the faith of the parent and contrary to the wishes of the parent, interference with the familial right of the parent to inculcate in the child the religion the parent desires is clear beyond doubt." The court forcefully concluded its evaluation of the case by emphasizing: "the right of the parent to teach his own faith to his child, or to teach him no religion at all is one of the foundations of our way of life and enjoys full constitutional protection."[75] On the basis of the points discussed, therefore, the federal district court flatly held the Pennsylvania statute to be unconstitutional. As suggested by my earlier analysis of the case it seems apparent that the district court's decision did not seem to turn merely on the fact that the state law made such exercises mandatory.

On the contrary, the decision seemed to rest upon a broader conception of First Amendment issues concerned with the Bible as a sectarian work and the ambiguity in the law which did not stipulate which version of the Bible was to be used for the programs in question. The district court pointed out that it was not merely the pressure of the statute, but the attitude of school officials resulting in "social suasion" which accounted for the compulsory features of the program. There was small reason to believe that the latter force would disappear merely because Bible-reading exercises were no longer demanded in the schools of Pennsylvania.

THE UNITED STATES SUPREME COURT
AND THE SCHEMPP CASE

Moving with especial rapidity, by federal court standards, the Schempp case came to the United States Supreme Court on appeal from the United States District Court for the Eastern District of Pennsylvania. The Supreme Court, on October 24, 1960, in a brief opinion *per curiam* vacated the judgment and remanded the case to the District Court for further proceedings appropriate in light of Act Number 700 of the Laws of the Pennsylvania General Assembly enacted on December 17, 1959.[76] This act amended by making discretionary the Pennsylvania law which made Bible reading in the public schools mandatory.

The United States Supreme Court apparently chose to believe that the federal district court's decision rested primarily on the feeling that the conclusive factor in the practices complained of rested in the fact that the Bible-reading exercises in the public schools were compulsory. Therefore, when the Pennsylvania law was amended making such programs discretionary, the Supreme Court seemed to feel that the original case became moot, and the court for jurisdictional reasons again refused to rule on the merits of Bible reading in the public schools.

While the Supreme Court's opinion in *Schempp* is brief to a point merging on inscrutability, it would seem that the court here, as in the Doremus case, hewed narrowly to the doctrine of avoiding a constitutional issue if a case can be decided on other grounds.

THE SCHEMPP CASE RETRIED

On February 1, 1962, the federal district court for the Eastern District of Pennsylvania reheard the Schempp case and once again unanimously held that the Pennsylvania statute, as amended, violated the Establishment Clause of the First Amendment as made applicable to the states by the Fourteenth Amendment.[77]

The court recognized that the schools' practices varied somewhat after the state statute was amended to provide that while Bible-reading exercises were mandatory in each public school of the state, students were not compelled to attend them. A few minutes after the children arrived at their "homerooms" at the start of the school day, the children sat "at attention" while ten verses of the Douay or Revised Standard Versions of the Bible, or Jewish Holy Scriptures, were broadcast without comment into each room through a loud-speaker. Immediately afterward, the students stood and repeated the Lord's Prayer and then gave the flag salute. General announcements were given next over the loud-speaker, after which the students went to their regular classes.

The children's father, Edward Schempp, testified that after careful consideration he had decided not to have his children excused from attending these exercises. He gave a variety of reasons for his position, among them his fear that his children might be regarded as "odd-balls" by teachers and students. Moreover, he recognized that it is common today to label all religious objections or differences "atheism," and furthermore, a tendency to equate atheism today with Communism or "un-Americanism." He felt too that by absenting themselves from the room during the Bible-reading exercises his children would probably miss the general announcements that followed immediately after the ceremony. And since those not attending these exercises were required to stand in the halls, this, in itself, carried with it the imputation of punishment for bad conduct.[78]

The court at the outset again rejected the contention that the doctrine of abstention applied, since the issue whether such programs violate the Establishment Clause of the United States Constitution contains a substantial enough federal question for a federal court to decide it before the Pennsylvania courts had an opportunity to rule on the matter. Judge Biggs, speaking for the court, next observed that the reading of the Bible, even without comment, "possesses a devotional and religious character and constitutes, in effect, a religious observance." This, the court believed, is made even more apparent by the fact that the Bible-reading exercise is followed immediately with the recital of the Lord's Prayer, by the students in unison.

The court went on to emphasize that even excusing students from the exercise does not mitigate the obligatory nature of the ceremony, even under the revised law, because the amended statute unequivocally requires that such exercises be held every school day. Moreover, they are held on school property, under the authority of the school officials, during school sessions. The law further requires that the "Holy Bible" be used, which, the court recognized, is a Christian document.

Thus it concluded that it was the intention of the Pennsylvania Legislature in Section 1516 of the School Code to introduce a religious ceremony into the public schools of that state in violation of the First and Fourteenth Amendments. The court felt that the decision of the Supreme Court in the McCollum case was controlling here, a point on which some may disagree even while agreeing with the court's holding.

The court finally perpetually enjoined and restrained the defendants from reading or permitting anyone subject to their control and direction to read to the students in Abington Senior High School, "any work or book known as the Holy Bible." The court went on to state, however, "that nothing herein shall be construed as interfering with or prohibiting the use of any book or works as educational source or reference material."[79]

THE UNITED STATES SUPREME COURT'S LAST WORD

The case was again appealed to the Supreme Court where it was joined with the Murray case. On June 17, 1963, the Supreme Court handed down its landmark decision and by a vote of eight to one held such laws and practices violated the Establishment Clause of the First Amendment.[80]

Justice Tom Clark, in the majority opinion, noted that "religion has been closely identified with our history and government." He went on to explain: "This is not to say, however, that religion has been so identified with our history and government that religious freedom is not likewise as strongly embedded in our public and private life." The court emphasized the importance of freedom of worship especially to a nation which is composed of citizens drawn from the four corners of the world and in which eighty-three separate religious bodies, each with over fifty thousand members, function. In addition there are, of course, innumerable smaller religious sects functioning in the United States.

Saying that the court had rejected "unequivocally" the contention that the Establishment Clause forbids "only government preference of one religion over another," and quoting Justice Rutledge in an earlier opinion, the court explained that:

> The [First] Amendment's purpose was not to strike merely at the official establishment of a single . . . religion. . . . It was to create a complete and permanent separation of the spheres of religious activity and civil authority by comprehensively forbidding every form of public aid or support for religion.

Justice Clark emphasized the First Amendment's requirement that the government remain neutral to religion, in the following words:

> The wholesome 'neutrality' . . . stems from a recognition of the teachings of history that powerful sects or groups might bring about a fusion of governmental and religious functions . . . to the end that official support of . . . Government would be placed behind the tenets of one or of all orthodoxies.

The court then fashioned a test to determine if a state law or practice violated the Establishment Clause. The test as the court saw it was: "What are the purposes and primary effect of the enactment?" The First Amendment is violated, the court announced, "if either [the purpose or primary effect of the law] is the advancement or inhibition of religion." To clarify this position the court emphasized again that there was a distinction between the Establishment Clause and the Free Exercise Clause, and a given action might violate one but not the other. "A violation of the Free Exercise Clause is predicated on coercion while the Establishment Clause need not be so attended," Justice Clark explained.

The programs attacked in these cases are prescribed as part of the curricular activities of students who are required by law to attend school. Moreover, the religious character of the exercise was admitted by the state, the court explained, since the alternate use of denominational versions of the Bible was permitted. This does not square, therefore, with the states' contention that the Bible was used either as an "instrument for nonreligious moral inspiration, or as a reference for the teaching of secular subjects," Justice Clark observed.

"It is no defense," the court noted, "to urge that the religious practices here may be relatively minor encroachments on the First Amendment. The breach of neutrality that is today a trickling stream may all too soon become a raging torrent." Quoting Madison, the court emphasized "it is proper to take alarm at the first experiment on our liberties."

Justice Clark denied that this decision would establish a "religion of secularism" in the schools. He went on to say that "one's education is not complete without a study of comparative religion or the history of religion." Moreover, the court saw the study of the literary and historic qualities of the Bible as worthy.

Finally the court rejected the argument that to prohibit a religious exercise approved by the majority would collide with the majority's right to free exercise of religion. The clause "has never meant that a majority could use the machinery of the state to practice its beliefs." The court felt that Justice Jackson in an earlier opinion effectively answered that contention. Jackson explained:

> The very purpose of a Bill of Rights was to withdraw certain subjects from the vicissitudes of political controversy, to place them beyond the reach of majorities. . . . One's right to . . . freedom of worship . . . and other fundamental rights may not be submitted to vote, they depend on the outcome of no elections.

In summary, the court's majority opinion makes it clear that religious exercises of this sort need not be compulsory for students in order for the practice to violate the Establishment Clause. Nor must they involve substantial expenditures of public funds to fail the test of constitutionality.

Concurring Views

In separate opinions, Justices Douglas, Goldberg and Harlan, and Brennan concurred with the majority decision. Justice Potter Stewart dissented.

In his concurring opinion, Justice Douglas noted that each of the cases under discussion violated the Establishment Clause in two different ways: first, the state is conducting a religious exercise and this cannot be done without violating the "neutrality" required of the state by the balance of power between individual, church, and state that has been

struck by the First Amendment, and, second, because public funds, though small in amount, are being used to promote a religious exercise — all the people being required
to finance a religious exercise that only some of the people
want and that violates the sensibilities of others.

Justice Brennan, in a résumé of the nation's historic
attempts to expound the meaning of the Constitution in
the intricate and demanding issue of the relationship between religion and the public schools, noted especially our
contemporary religious diversity:

> Today the Nation is far more heterogenous religiously,
> including as it does substantial minorities not only of
> Catholics and Jews but as well of those who worship ac-
> cording to no version of the Bible and those who worship
> no God at all. . . . In the face of such profound changes,
> practices which may have been objectionable to no one in
> the time of Jefferson and Madison may today be highly
> offensive to many persons, the deeply devout and the non-
> believers alike.

The highlights of his opinion relating to the nature of
public schools and to the McCollum and Zorach cases appear
in Chapter 5.

When turning specifically to the cases at issue, Brennan
felt that unless *Engel* v. *Vitale* was to be overruled, or the
court was to engage in wholly disingenuous distinction, it
could not sustain the nature of the exercises here challenged.
Daily recital of the Lord's Prayer and the reading of passages of scripture were quite as clearly breaches of the command of the Establishment Clause as was the daily use of
the rather bland Regents' Prayer in the New York public
schools. Indeed, Brennan went on, "I would suppose that
if anything the Lord's Prayer and the Holy Bible are more
clearly sectarian, and the present violations of the First

Amendment consequently more serious." Brennan noted that such a plainly religious means is necessarily forbidden by the Establishment Clause, in his opinion. Nor, said Brennan, is the justification valid that religious exercises may directly serve secular ends:

> . . . it would seem that less sensitive materials might equally well serve the same purpose. . . . without jeopardizing either the religious liberties of any members of the community or the proper degree of separation between the spheres of religion and government.

Justice Brennan cited the Pennsylvania district court's answer after the remand of the Schempp case as dispositive to the argument that excusing or exempting students absolved the practices involved insofar as these practices are claimed to violate the Establishment Clause; i.e., that the availability of excusal or exemption simply has no relevance to the establishment question, if it is once found that these practices are essentially religious exercises designed at least in part to achieve religious aims through the use of public school facilities during the school day. The question of the infringement of the Free Exercise Clause, under such circumstances, is more difficult, however, but in Brennan's opinion, "the excusal procedure itself necessarily operates in such a way as to infringe the rights of free exercise of those children who wish to be excused."

In a final important point, Justice Brennan refuted the contention by some that the invalidation of the exercises at bar permitted the court no alternative but to declare unconstitutional every vestige, however slight, of cooperation or accommodation between religion and government:

What the Framers [of the Constitution] meant to fore-close, and what our decisions under the Establishment Clause have forbidden, are those involvements of religious with secular institutions which (a) serve the essentially religious activities of religious institutions; (b) employ the organs of government for essentially religious purposes; or (c) use essentially religious means to serve governmental ends, where secular means would suffice. When the secular and religious institutions become involved in such a manner, there inhere in the relationship precisely those dangers — as much to church as to state — which the Framers feared would subvert religious liberty and the strength of a system of secular government.

But, Brennan explained, there may be many forms of involvements of government with religion which do not import such dangers and therefore should not in his judgment be deemed to violate the Establishment Clause.

Nothing in the Constitution compels the organs of government to be blind to what everyone else perceives — that religious differences among Americans have important and pervasive implications for our society. Likewise nothing in the Establishment Clause forbids the application of legislation having purely secular ends in such a way as to alleviate burdens upon the free exercise of an individual's religious beliefs. Surely the Framers would never have understood that such a construction sanctions that involvement which violates the Establishment Clause. Such a conclusion can be reached, I would suggest, only by using the words of the First Amendment to defeat its very purpose.

Finally, Justice Brennan dealt with six areas of involvement between government and religion in which there has existed both legal and lay confusion, but in which he denied there was conflict with the decision in the present cases under discussion. All these areas have been subjects of cases in lower federal and state courts: A. The Conflict Between Establishment and Free Exercise. B. Establishment and Exercises in Legislative Bodies. C. Nondevotional

Use of the Bible in the Public Schools. D. Uniform Tax Exemptions Incidentally Available to Religious Institutions. E. Religious Considerations in Public Welfare Programs. F. Activities Which, Though Religious in Origin, Have Ceased to Have Religious Meaning.

In their concurring opinion, Justices Goldberg and Harlan agreed that the attitude of the state toward religion must be one of neutrality. "But," Justice Goldberg noted,

> untutored devotion to the concept of neutrality can lead to invocation or approval of results which partake not simply of that noninterference and noninvolvement with the religious which the Constitution commands, but of a brooding and pervasive devotion to the secular and a passive, or even active, hostility to the religious. Such results are not only not compelled by the Constitution, but, it seems to me, are prohibited by it. Neither the state nor this Court can or should ignore the significance of the fact that a vast portion of our people believe in and worship God and that many of our legal, political and personal values derive historically from religious teachings. Government must inevitably take cognizance of the existence of religion and, indeed, under certain circumstances the First Amendment may require that it do so.

Finally, Justice Goldberg believed that opinions in the present and past cases made clear that the court would:

> . . . recognize the propriety of providing military chaplains and of the teaching *about* religion, as distinguished from the teachings *of* religion, in the public schools. The examples could readily be multiplied, for both the required and the permissible accommodations between state and church frame the relation as one free of hostility or favor and productive of religious and political harmony, but without undue involvement of one in the concerns or practices of the other. To be sure, the judgment in each case is a delicate one, but it must be made if we are to do loyal service as judges to the ultimate First Amendment objective of religious liberty.

Justice Goldberg concluded by noting:

> The First Amendment does not prohibit practices which
> by any realistic measure create none of the dangers which
> it is designed to prevent and which do not so directly or
> substantially involve the state in religious exercises or in
> the favoring of religion as to have meaningful and prac-
> tical impact. It is of course true that great consequences
> can grow from small beginnings, but the measure of
> constitutional adjudication is the ability and willingness
> to distinguish between real threat and mere shadow.

Justice Stewart's Dissent

In the sole dissenting opinion in the 1963 hearing of
the Schempp and Murray cases, Justice Potter Stewart (who
was also the sole dissenter in the 1962 Engel case, see page
197) said, "I think the records in the two cases before us are
so fundamentally deficient as to make impossible an informed
or responsible determination of the constitutional issues
presented. Specifically, I cannot agree that on these records
we can say that the Establishment Clause has necessarily
been violated." Stewart noted that neither complaint attacked the challenged practices as "establishments." "What
both allege as the basis for their causes of actions are, rather,
violations of religious liberty," he explained.

Taking issue again with the "conflict" between a "doctrinaire reading" of the Establishment Clause and the Free
Exercise Clause, Justice Stewart mentioned the using of
federal funds to employ chaplains for the armed forces, which
might be said to violate the Establishment Clause. "Yet a
lonely soldier stationed at some faraway outpost could surely
complain that a government which did *not* provide him the
opportunity for pastoral guidance was affirmatively prohibiting the free exercise of his religion. And such examples
could readily be multiplied."

Quoting opinions in the Everson and Zorach cases, and *Hamilton* v. *Regents,* and *Cantwell* v. *Connecticut,* Justice Stewart said,

> It is this concept of constitutional protection embodied in our decisions which makes the cases before us such difficult ones for me. For there is involved in these cases a substantial free exercise claim on the part of those who affirmatively desire to have their children's school day open with the reading of passages from the Bible. . . . What seems to me to be of paramount importance, then, is recognition of the fact that the claim advanced here in favor of Bible reading is sufficiently substantial to make simple reference to the constitutional phrase 'establishment of religion' as inadequate an analysis of the cases before us as the ritualistic invocation of the nonconstitutional phrase 'separation of church and state.' What these cases compel, rather, is an analysis of just what the 'neutrality' is which is required by the interplay of the Establishment and Free Exercise Clauses of the First Amendment, as imbedded in the Fourteenth.

Justice Stewart stated he thought religious exercises became constitutionally invalid only if their administration places the sanction of secular authority behind one or more particular religious or irreligious beliefs.

> There is no evidence in either case as to whether there would exist any coercion of any kind upon a student who did not want to participate. No evidence at all was adduced in the *Murray* case, because it was decided upon a demurrer [an objection that assumes the truth of the allegations but argues that no cause of action is shown]. All that we have in that case, therefore, is the conclusory language of a pleading. While such conclusory allegations are acceptable for procedural purposes, I think that the nature of the constitutional problem involved here clearly demands that no decision be made except upon evidence. In the *Schempp* case the record shows no more than a subjective prophecy by a parent of what he thought would happen if a request were made to be excused from participation in the exercises under the amended statute.

Justice Stewart concluded by observing that,

> What our Constitution indispensably protects is the freedom of each of us, be he Jew or Agnostic, Christian or Atheist, Buddhist or Freethinker, to believe or disbelieve, to worship or not worship, to pray or keep silent, according to his own conscience, uncoerced and unrestrained by government. . . . I think we must not assume that school boards so lack the qualities of inventiveness and good will as to make impossible the achievement of that goal.

One cannot conclude an investigation of the courts which have held Bible reading illegal without noting the great concern for the individual's right of freedom of conscience and religious beliefs uniformly expressed by these courts. Their decisions have generally upheld the rights of religious minorities in danger of having their religious sensibilities jolted by an impatient and occasionally unfeeling majority. These were difficult decisions to make and undoubtedly in many circles they were also unpopular decisions. It takes a courageous judge to rule against public opinion, particularly in a field as volatile as religion and its relation to the state. The courageousness of these judges is doubly apparent when one realizes that many state supreme court justices are elective, and thus lack the security of tenure of a federal judge.

5

Allied Problems in Religious Education

A NUMBER OF MISCELLANEOUS CASES were not included in the two previous chapters because, while Bible reading played a role of varying importance in each, it was not the controlling element or issue involved. In these cases the question of Bible reading was but one of the questions involving church-state relationships the judges were called upon to decide. It is interesting to note that while a number of the cases arose in states where the supreme courts had previously ruled on the question of Bible reading, the rationale and general rule of these peripheral cases were not always consistent with the conclusions reached by the state's high court in a Bible-reading case.

An example of this somewhat paradoxical situation may be seen in the state of Wisconsin. It has been noted that in 1890, the supreme court of that state ruled in *State ex rel. Weiss* v. *District Board* that Bible-reading exercises in the public schools were illegal under the Wisconsin constitution. Justice Lyons, speaking for the majority, pointed out that Bible reading, even without comment, was "religious instruction," for the "Bible contains numerous doctrinal passages upon some of which the peculiar creed of almost every religious sect is based, and that such passages may reasonably be understood to inculcate the doctrines predicated upon them." He felt that the practice was illegal even though the students were not compelled to attend. The departure of any student for reasons of conscience tended to destroy the equality of pupils and "puts a portion of them to serious disadvantages in many ways with respect to the others." Justice Orton's concurring opinion in this case also stressed that ". . . common schools are not common as being low in character or grade, but common to all alike, to everybody, and to all sects or denominations of religion, but without bringing religion into them." The inescapable impression from this is that the Wisconsin constitution as interpreted by the court, intends no right of the schools to engage in religious exercises or programs.[1]

BACCALAUREATE EXERCISES

In 1916, however, the Wisconsin supreme court in *State ex rel. Conway* v. *District Board*[2] took a somewhat different view. The litigation arose over the city of Elroy's practice of holding parts of the high school graduation exercises in different churches of that town. Various clergymen gave nonsectarian prayers and invocations. There was no compensation paid for the use of the church or for the clergymen's contributions to the program. A mandamus suit was brought seeking to restrain the board of education from continuing such a program, for it was charged that this violated Article X, Section 3, and Article I, Section 18 of the Wisconsin constitution. The former provision forbids sectarian education in the public schools of the state. The latter insures the rights of conscience and freedom from forcible support of a place of worship. The Supreme Court of Wisconsin ruled that the use of church buildings for high school graduation exercises and the practice of allowing clergymen of various faiths to offer nonsectarian prayers was permissible under the Wisconsin constitution.

When discussing the objection to the use of the church buildings for the graduation exercises, the court stated, "It is what is done, not the name of the place where it is done which is significant." The court in a rather curious manner dismissed the charge that the practices questioned here violated the individual's right of conscience. It explained:

> The individual cannot foreclose inquiry into the reasonableness of his request by his bare assertion (i.e., that his right of conscience has been violated). Some consciences are very tender and highly developed. . . they regard as wrong many things which the law sees as harmless.[3]

The court was concerned lest a misinterpretation of its action in this case might lead some to conclude that the door was now open to bring into the public schools sectarian instruction, prayers, and similar practices. It pointed out that this could not be condoned, and in a passage notable for some fuzzy logic explained why.

> We do not underrate the efficacy of prayer. Neither are we prepared to say that the average high school graduate may not need it. But whenever it is likely to do more harm than good it might well be dispensed with. It is not at all times wise or politic to do certain things although no legal rights would be invaded by doing them.[4]

In the present case the court apparently felt the exercises did more good than harm, and thus permitted their continuation. One cannot help but wonder if this view can be squared with the rule of the Weiss case, or, if the implications of this view are followed, to what degree the two previously mentioned constitutional provisions are a safeguard against sectarianism in the public schools.

RELIGIOUS INSTRUCTION AT STATE UNIVERSITIES

The Illinois Supreme Court is also an example of a court which held Bible reading in the public schools illegal.[5] But it took a more favorable view of religious instructions at the state university in an earlier case.[6] The judicial logic presented in this case is studiously ignored by the Illinois court in the Ring case, which deals specifically with Bible reading, and is as critical of this practice as is the Wisconsin court in the Weiss case. The earlier Illinois case centered around a rule of the University of Illinois which required that the students of this school must attend nonsectarian religious exercises in the university chapel. A student named North petitioned for a writ of mandamus to force the Board of Trustees to reinstate him in the university after he was expelled for refusing to attend these exercises without asking to be excused. The board had ruled it would not compel anyone to attend these services if he asked to be excused.

The Illinois Supreme Court held that the Board's directive did not conflict with the Illinois constitution, Article II, Section 3, which states: "No person shall be required to attend or support any ministry or place of worship against his consent." The court pointed out that the petitioner admitted it was not his right of conscience which was interfered with; that, in fact, he had attended these chapel services for five years previously, and that he did not claim:

. . . that the exercises at the chapel meetings were sectarian and, therefore, objectionable; but the only objection to those exercises was and is that they were in part religious worship.[7]

The major issue involved the right of the faculty to inaugurate such a policy.

The court felt that the faculty had this right so long as it stayed within constitutional limits. There could be no doubt that this program was legal, it explained, since anyone might be excused from it if he presented a reason for his wish to the board. It was this feature which prevented the program from forcing anyone to attend religious services against his will. The court pointed out that the faculty had certain rights over the plaintiff of which he was surely aware when he voluntarily entered the institution; and it concluded:

> We think the conclusion is irresistible that in his controversy with the faculty he was not attempting to protect himself in the exercise of a constitutional privilege, but was only using the clause of the Constitution as a shield for himself and endeavoring to furnish others an excuse for disobedience.[8]

This is another example of a case in which the court found the motives of an individual questioning religious exercises in public schools to be of greater importance than the issue of the constitutionality of the religious instruction as such.

Another case in the Illinois Supreme Court, while not involving the question of Bible reading specifically, does have as its core the use of public funds for sectarian purposes, and might be briefly noted at this time. The case involved the payment of public funds to Roman Catholic institutions for the education of delinquent children. Religious instruction was required of all students in these institutions. The Supreme Court of Illinois approved this program on the theory that since the sum paid to the Catholic institution was less than the actual cost of such a program, it was the state and not the church which benefited.[9]

The Maryland Supreme Court was faced in 1961 with a somewhat related problem concerning religion and the state university. In the case of *Hanauer* v. *Elkins*,[10] the Maryland court held that the University of Maryland which requires students to take basic military training as part of its curriculum was not imposing a religious test contrary to the charter of the University of Maryland and to the First Amendment of the United States Constitution.

CHURCH CONTROL OVER PUBLIC SCHOOLS

In a number of cases the fact situation was more complicated, and the question of Bible reading and religious instruction played a subsidiary role. These arose where the school was purportedly a public school, but where, in fact, a church exercised some control over the school. In some cases, classes were held in conjunction with a religious institution or teachers were basically church people who taught religion either directly or indirectly. The supreme courts of Iowa, Kentucky, Kansas, Michigan, Missouri, Nebraska, New Mexico, and Wisconsin held that a denominational school does not become a public school simply by calling it one, and the courts felt that these schools were not entitled to state financial aid.[11]

The case of *Knowlton* v. *Baumhover*[12] which went to the Iowa Supreme Court is representative of the cases which involve the mingling of a public school with a religious school. Here, in a predominantly Roman Catholic area, the board of education allowed the public school building to fall into disuse and instead leased a room in the Roman Catholic school to serve as the public school. A nun taught in the purportedly public school room, and this room was decorated with pictures and images of the Roman Catholic faith. Religious services directed by priests were conducted in both rooms of the school and daily instructions in the Roman Catholic catechism were given by the nuns who were the teachers. In the course of time, pupils from the public and the parochial school became intermixed, with action finally being taken to place all the younger students in one room and the older ones in the other. The school authorities pointed out that if any public school pupil objected to this arrangement he would be placed in the room which was nominally the public school. There was, however, no record of this ever having occurred. After the transfer from the public school building to the parochial school had taken place, the Sister's salary for teaching was raised from fifty to seventy dollars a month.

The court ruled that the maintenance of a sectarian school as a public school, even if sanctioned by the people of a district, did not justify the appropriation of public money for its support. It felt that before the law, every church or other organization upholding or permitting any form of religion or religious faith or practice is a sect, and as such is denied the use of public funds for the advancement of religious or sectarian teaching. Of particular importance to this study, however, is the fact that the court refused to enjoin the practice of reading the scriptures without comment and the recitation of the Lord's Prayer in any rejuvenated public school.[13] Iowa, it should be noted, does have a statute which permits Bible reading and recitation of the Lord's Prayer in the public schools.[14]

Speaking generally of the situation which prevailed in

this school district, the court did not feel that this condition was due to a mere irregularity, as the school board had contended. The judges felt that the board had given at least tacit support to the program by its inaction.[15] Nor did the court feel that it was enough that non-Catholic pupils were not required to attend services if they did not choose to, since the "gregarious instincts of children impel them to go with the crowd." Justice Weaver said:

> This principle of unfettered individual liberty of conscience necessarily implies what is too often forgotten, that such liberty must be so exercised by him to whom it has been given as not to infringe upon the equally sacred right of his neighbor to differ with him. . . . The right of a man to worship God or even refuse to worship God, and to entertain such religious views as appeal to his individual conscience without dictation or interference by any person or power, civil or ecclesiastical is as fundamental in a free government like ours as is the right to life, liberty and the pursuit of happiness.

The Iowa court felt that a program such as is questioned here:

> . . . [W]ould mean sectarianism in the public schools and to put sectarianism into the schools would, according to the opinion prevailing when the Constitution was ratified, be to put venom into the body politic.[16]

Finally, the court pointed out to those who argued for the continuation of this program, in similar cases which had come before this court,[17] it had been the Roman Catholics who had brought the action, claiming that the King James Version of the Bible was sectarian and pleading to be free from sectarian control. "They can not [now] complain if they are subject to the same rule," the court explained.[18]

Combining Public Schools and Religious Schools

In one of the most recent cases of this nature, the New Mexico court, after it decisively ruled that a public school combined with a religious school was illegal, skillfully sidestepped the issue of how much, if any, religious instruction might be given in the public school.[19] It hoped that the issue would be settled by the United States Supreme Court in the Doremus case (pending at this time).

> As the highest court of our land has held the provisions of the First Amendment to the United States Constitution were made applicable to the various states by the Fourteenth Amendment its decision will be binding upon this case and the State of New Mexico. We have another case pending before us which involves only one school[20] . . . which will serve as a vehicle for the adoption of the correct rule when it is announced by our highest court.[21]

One can almost hear the judges sigh with relief after dodging this explosive problem.

A year later, in *Miller* v. *Cooper*[22] (which the court was holding in abeyance while waiting for the United States Supreme Court's decision in the Doremus case), Judge McGhee announced the New Mexico court's unhappiness over the fact that the Doremus case was dismissed without a ruling on the merits.[23] Lacking the sense of direction which such a handling of the case would have given it, the New Mexico court finally ruled that baccalaureate services and commencement exercises of the public high school might legally be held in a church building.[24] However, on the other major issue facing it, the court ruled to enjoin public school teachers from placing religious pamphlets of a sectarian nature in the classrooms so that they might be readily available to the students. The school, the court felt, cannot be used as a medium for the dissemination of religious pamphlets.

The Missouri court in a similar case[25] also stressed that merely because parents acquiesced for a long period of time to the merging of the public school with a parochial school, did not mean they waived their right to protest. "The public interest cannot be waived." The constitutional provisions guaranteeing religious liberty are mandatory and must be obeyed, the court stated.[26] Justice Douglas of the Missouri court expostulated: "Certainly the school board may not employ its powers to enforce religious worship by children even in the faith of their parents."[27]

Faced by a similar series of facts, the Wisconsin court[28] felt that the religious exercises carried on in this hybrid-type school constituted a violation of the Wisconsin constitution's provision forbidding public support of places of worship[29] as well as its being sectarian instruction in the public schools.[30] It held, however, that a suit brought to recover from the school board the money spent to maintain such a school was not justified since the taxpayers were guilty of laches by tolerating the practice for such a long period of time.[31] The court also felt the Board might legitimately continue to rent part of the parochial school for use as a public school, so long as the religious exercises and programs common to the former were kept completely out of the public school. The school board had the right to select the site for the public school, the court pointed out.[32]

Rental of Church Property

In addition to the Wisconsin Supreme Court, the highest courts of Illinois, Indiana, Kentucky, and Connecticut approved the rental of space in buildings owned and operated by churches, so long as the board of education retained the essential element of control.[33]

The Illinois court was faced by a situation where the board of education had rented the basement of a Roman Catholic church to be used as the public school.[34] The board hired only Roman Catholics to teach in the school, and it was alleged that the children of Catholic parents and the teachers were "regularly to attend mass in the church at 8 A.M., and from 8:30 A.M. to 9 A.M. to listen to instruction in the Catholic catechism in the school room." It was also noted that the district had voted down a proposal to bond the district to erect a new schoolhouse.

The court believed that the school board had a right to obtain a building to serve as the public school from whomever it chose, especially since no public school existed. In regard to the board's hiring of all Catholic teachers, the court said: "The school authorities may select a teacher who belongs to any church, or no church, as they may think fit." In answer to the charge that Roman Catholic children were compelled to attend church to hear mass, the court felt that since no one had charged the board of education with compelling the pupils to do this, no relief could be sought from the board. The court answered the charge that such practices constituted religious and sectarian instruction by stating:

> Had the board of education required any religious doctrine to be taught in the public schools, or established any religious exercises sectarian in character, and complainant's children were required to receive such religious instruction in the school, and conform to the sectarian exercises established, he might have good ground for complaint, as our public schools are established for the purpose of education. The schools have not been established to aid any sectarian denomination, or assist in disseminating any sectarian doctrine.[35]

A critic of the court's decision might feel that the board of education's inaction (in regard to stopping such religious exercises) constituted some form of action.

In a 1945 case involving the school board's right to choose the site for a public school, the Connecticut Supreme Court felt that this right extended to renting part of a Catholic orphanage and allowing nuns to teach in the public school, so long as the exclusive control rested with the state and the school was free from sectarian instruction.[36] It held that even though all the children who attended the school were Roman Catholics this fact was not determinative, since any child residing in the area might attend if he wanted. To the charge that the nuns conducted religious exercises, the court replied that it did not feel these were sectarian since they occurred before the school sessions began.

The Indiana high court stated in the Johnson case that a parochial school building which was being rented for a public school and where Catholic pictures and the holy water font were displayed in the classroom could not be considered an example of sectarian control of public schools.[37] Nor did it believe that the children's attending mass prior to the beginning of school constituted an example of sectarian instruction.

This case arose in the late 1930's during the latter days of the depression. Religious authorities in charge of the parochial school had previously announced they would be forced to close the school because of lack of funds. This meant that parochial students would be shifted to the public school system, which was not equipped to absorb such an influx. The school board, by renting the parochial school, was attempting to forestall a situation of overcrowding. It is possible that the court took this extraordinary condition into consideration when confronted by this case.

WEARING OF DISTINCTIVE RELIGIOUS GARB

Another question faced by the Indiana court in the Johnson case[38] related to the right of public school teachers to wear distinctive religious garb. This practice has caused controversy in a number of areas in the United States. Critics of such practices maintain that religious attire, such as the raiment of a nun, has a tendency to inspire respect and sympathy for the religious denomination of which it is a symbol, and is thus a sectarian influence. Here, as in other cases dealing with potential sectarian influences, there is little agreement among the states' high courts.

Some courts upheld the teacher's right to wear religious garments, as in Indiana, North Dakota, and Connecticut.[39] The rationale of these courts suggests that mere style of dress is not sectarian instruction, for it is simply illustrative of a church affiliation that is well known anyway. The North Dakota court noted:

> We are all agreed that the wearing of the religious habit described in the evidence here does not convert the school into a sectarian school, or create sectarian control within the purview of the constitution. . . . The laws of the state do not prescribe the fashion of dress of the teachers in our schools. Whether it is wise or unwise to regulate the style of dress to be worn by teachers in our public schools, or to inhibit the wearing of dress or insignia indicating religious belief is not a matter for the courts to determine. The limit of our inquiry is to determine whether what has been done infringes upon and violates the provisions of the constitution.[40]

The Pennsyslvania court, which once upheld the right of teachers to wear distinctive garb,[41] later sustained a statute preventing the wearing of any dress indicating the teacher's membership in any religious order, sect, or denomination.[42] In the earlier case no statute covered the subject. While the court agreed that religious habit might impart to the pupils the idea of membership in a sect, it felt that the religious affiliations of the teachers were well known to the pupils even without such attire. The court noted that the legislature might prohibit the wearing of such garments, but it doubted that such action would curtail the knowledge that a teacher adhered to a specific creed.

One year later the Pennsylvania legislature enacted a statute preventing public school teachers from wearing raiments which denoted membership in any religious order or denomination.[43] This law was upheld by the Pennsylvania high court in *Commonwealth* v. *Herr*.[44] The court concluded that the prohibition was directed against the actions of a teacher while in performance of her duties, and not against her beliefs.

The courts of New York, Iowa, and New Mexico have also frowned upon public school teachers wearing religious garb.[45] These courts felt that such costumes inspired sympathy and respect for the religious denomination to which the instructor belonged. To this extent, the judges argued, this constituted sectarian influence. Oregon and Nebraska have statutes forbidding teachers to wear such attire, but they have not been tested in the courts.[46]

In 1951, Wisconsin State Superintendent of Public Instruction Watson cut off state financial aid to a number of schools in the western portion of that state. Superintendent Watson felt that reflections of religious influence in these schools, such as nun teachers, crucifixes and other symbols of the Catholic faith, violated the state constitution and statutory provisions against granting public support to sectarian instruction. As a result, a number of these schools became bona fide parochial schools.[47]

The right of a public school instructor to dress himself in a garb dictated by his religious belief is not absolute. The legislatures appear to enjoy a large range of discretion, if it may be reasonably assumed that sectarian inferences may be derived from an instructor's distinctive raiment.[48]

RELEASED AND DISMISSED TIME

The question of "released" and "dismissed time" religious instruction has received considerable attention in recent years because of the Supreme Court's action in the McCollum[49] and Zorach[50] cases. The issue of Bible reading is not necessarily of primary importance in these cases, since the religious instruction covers a much wider field than the mere reading of the Scriptures.

Certain semantic difficulties frequently cause confusion in this problem. For our purposes, "released time" will be applied to those programs in which public school pupils are released from their regular classes to attend religious exercises conducted by representatives of the different denominations *within* the school building. This instruction takes place during periods when classes would ordinarily be in session. Those who do not want to attend are placed in a separate room where they may use the time for study.

According to President Butler of Columbia University, the cooperative practices of the public schools to aid in religious instruction had their beginnings in France after the educational reforms of 1882.[51] A system of "released time" was adopted by Dr. William Wirt, Superintendent of

Schools in Gary, Indiana, in 1914.[52] The apparent success of this program convinced educators in other parts of the country that here was an answer to the often-complained-of lack of religious and moral instruction in the public schools.

The situation in Elgin, Illinois, is illustrative of the influence of the Gary plan. In 1937, the Elgin Council of Christian Education, after surveying the potential causes for increased juvenile delinquency and other youth problems, concluded that the schools' "approach to the problem of living was hopelessly inadequate." The council believed that the breakdown of character and the failure to develop character was due to the complexity of modern civilization, the breakdown of homes, a pervasive attitude of materialism, and a generally cynical attitude toward morality. The council attributed these horrors to a lack of religious training for youths. To remedy the situation it suggested weekday religious training, to be held in the public schools.[53] These conclusions were submitted to the board of education in the form of a report, which said in part:

> It is the opinion of the committee that religion supplies the motivating force and authority for all ethical actions. In order that character may be based upon this necessary foundation, the committee respectfully suggests that the public schools dismiss all children whose parents give consent for one hour per week for the purpose of religious instruction in their respective churches, to be taught by teachers who can meet the public school requirements. In order that the children, whose parents do not consent to their dismissal, be not deprived of all character education it is suggested that the Board of Education provide opportunity for ethical instruction during the time the children are dismissed for religious instruction.[54]

These proposals were accepted by the board of education in 1938. While the committee had not been entirely clear as to where this instruction was to take place, the board decided that it should be held in public school buildings with the possible exception of churches with parochial schools.[55] It should be noted that this program was inaugurated prior to the McCollum case and would now be illegal, since it is clearly within the scope of that case.

While many schools adopted the Gary plan, some made a significant alteration in the basic design: religious instruction was to be held outside the public school, with pupils dismissed from their regular classes to attend. Those who did not were required to remain in school and continue with their studies. This is the type of program generally called "dismissed time."

The educators who adopted it felt there would be fewer objections to this plan than to one of "released time," since no charge could be made that public property was being used for sectarian or religious purposes. In a number of states, however, high school credit is given for programs such as this, where responsible groups report that high school students have completed satisfactory courses of Bible study. In 1927, twenty-five of the forty-eight states, including New York and Illinois, granted credit for such programs.[56] (The Ring case, as has been noted, held Bible reading in the public schools of Illinois to be illegal.) Dr. Stokes points out that this number has increased in recent years, until interfered with by the McCollum case. The Zorach case, however, made it clear that religious instruction outside of public school buildings was not covered by the McCollum case decision, and is legal. It is important to remember that the McCollum case dealt with "released time" instruction, while the Zorach case involved "dismissed time."

The McCollum Case

The McCollum case, by outlawing "released time" programs, caused a great deal of debate and has become one of the most controversial decisions in years. Mrs. Vashti McCollum, the wife of a University of Illinois professor, who was a "rationalist," objected to the "released time" program in the Champaign, Illinois, public schools. The program, suggested by a voluntary association of Roman Catholics, Jews, and Protestants, provided that the classes were to be composed of students whose parents had signed printed cards requesting that their children be permitted to attend. Classes were to be held weekly and were to last thirty minutes for the lower grades and forty-five minutes for the higher grades. The instruction was given in the public school buildings, but the instructors were employed at no expense to the school board, although they were subject to the approval and supervision of the superintendent of schools. The classes were taught in three separate groups by Catholic priests, a Jewish Rabbi, and Protestant teachers. Those pupils who did not attend were required to go to some other part of the school building and continue their secular studies.[57]

Mrs. McCollum's son attended a Champaign public school. She brought a mandamus suit as a parent and taxpayer in the Circuit Court of Champaign County. She alleged that this "released time" program constituted a use of public funds for sectarian purposes contrary to the Constitution of Illinois and the state's school code. She contended that the plan denied the equal protection of the laws, and more important, by segregating public school pupils into sectarian groups for religious instruction, it violated federal and state guarantees of the freedom of religion. She was supported in her suit by the Chicago Civil Liberties Committee and other groups opposed to "released time."[58]

The circuit court denied the writ of mandamus and stated:

> . . . So far as federal constitutional provisions are concerned, and conceding that they are binding upon the State of Illinois, and upon the defendant school board, there is nothing in any expression of the Federal Supreme Court that remotely indicates that there is any constitutional objection to the Champaign plan of religious education.[59]

The Illinois Supreme Court unanimously affirmed the holding of the lower court.[60] It distinguished the Ring case, which outlawed Bible reading, by stating that released time was voluntary, that it was not part of the public school program, and that it caused no additional expense to the school board since the religious organizations bore all expenses. Any incidental expenses, the court believed, were *de minimis*. Finally, it maintained, the rule of the Latimer case[61] which upheld a "dismissed time" plan in Chicago, governed the Champaign plan also. Judge Thompson stated:

> Our government very wisely refuses to recognize a specific religion, but this cannot mean that the government does not recognize or subscribe to religious ideals. . . . To deny the existence of religious motivation is to deny the inspiration and authority of the Constitution itself.[62]

When this case came to the United States Supreme Court, Mrs. McCollum had picked up support from various church and public-service groups. Of special interest is the brief filed by the American Civil Liberties Union. It pointed out that while the church, sectarian schools, and the home are all proper places for religious instruction, this was not the case with the public school. It explained the confusion and dangers which would result if such programs were tolerated.

> [The schools] would be flooded with sectarian publications, crowded with religious teachers, many in clerical garbs. Pupils would be classified and segregated according to their diverse beliefs or lack of beliefs. There would not be enough room to hold all of the classes. The public school system for all practical purposes would cease to exist and its ideal of secular education would be a mockery . . . . [R]eligion is not a civil function or a public matter. An education which includes religious teaching is a private matter and function . . . . An approval of the Champaign plan would seriously interfere with the general welfare and the tranquility of the whole country . . . . [The] public ideal of the secular education and the inspired concept of separation of Church from State should not be tarnished by compromise. They invade the religious rights of no one. They assure freedom for all.[63]

The Supreme Court by an eight to one vote, Justice Reed dissenting, reversed the state court. The court, speaking through Justice Black, held that this program constituted the "use of tax-supported property for religious instruction and the close cooperation between the school authorities and the religious council in promoting religious instruction." Using the *dicta* of the Everson case, Justice Black rejected the argument that historically the First Amendment was intended to forbid only governmental preference of one religion over another and not impartial governmental assistance to all religions. He explained that all of the justices in the Everson case agreed that the "First Amendment has erected a wall between church and state which must be high and impregnable." He went on to say, "[T]he First Amendment rests upon the premise that both religion and government can best work to achieve their lofty aims if each is left free from the other within its respective sphere." Justice Black concluded:

> [Punctuation *sic*] Here not only are the state's tax supported public school buildings used for the dissemination of religious doctrines. The state also affords sectarian groups an invaluable aid in that it helps to provide pupils for the religious classes through use of the state's compulsory public school machinery. This is not separation of church and state.[64]

In a concurring opinion written by Justice Frankfurter, with whom Justices Rutledge, Jackson, and Burton agreed, Frankfurter sought to prove that the constitution forbids "the co-mingling of sectarian instruction with the secular instruction in the public schools."[65] He agreed that many of the earliest Colonial schools devoted considerable time to religious instruction. He went on to show that following the theories of men like Madison and Horace Mann, who felt it was necessary to keep sectarianism out of the public schools, state after state had disassociated religion from the public schools. He explained:

> The claims of religion were not minimized by refusing to make the public schools agencies for their assertion. The non-sectarian or secular public school was the means of reconciling freedom in general with religious freedom.[66]

This happened before the adoption of the Fourteenth Amendment, which in this respect, "merely reflected a principle then dominant in our national life."[67]

An important feature about this opinion is the unwillingness of these four justices to sweepingly declare illegal all forms and varieties of religious programs similar in any way to the Champaign plan. Frankfurter made it fairly clear that the court was dealing with one plan of "released time," and left the door open for a different decision regarding "dismissed time." He noted:

> We do not consider as indeed we could not, school programs not before us which, though colloquially characterized as 'released time,' present situations differing in aspects that may well be constitutionally crucial. Different forms which 'released time' has taken during more than thirty years of growth include programs which, like that before us, would not withstand the test of the constitution; others may be found unexceptional.[68]

Justice Jackson's concurring opinion expressed doubts whether the facts of the case authorized the court to take jurisdiction. He could not see that anyone's freedom was endangered by the Champaign plan, for he doubted that the constitution protected anyone, "from the embarrassment that always attends non-conformity, whether in religion, politics, behavior, or dress." Justice Jackson did not believe a claim to the deprivation of property could be sustained, since, "any cost of this plan to the taxpayers is incalculable and negligible." He also questioned the advisability and possibility of excluding all potential religious instruction from the public schools. He explained:

> Perhaps subjects such as mathematics, physics, and chemistry are, or can be, completely secularized. But it would not seem practical to teach either practice or appreciation of the arts if we are to forbid the exposure of youth to any religious influences.
>
> Music without sacred music, architecture minus the cathedral, or painting without the scriptural themes would be eccentric and incomplete even from a secular point of view.[69]

Finally, Justice Jackson felt that the order granting mandamus was too far-reaching in its terms. About the only thing upon which Jackson agreed with the majority seemed to be the final decision. By what logical method he arrived at this conclusion is an interesting matter for speculation.

Justice Reed dissented alone, and pointed out the many instances of cooperation between church and state in American society, such as the compulsory chapel services at West Point and Annapolis. Reed had difficulty determining from the opinions of Black, Frankfurter, and Jackson exactly what was unconstitutional about the Champaign plan. He found it difficult to believe that the constitution prohibited religious instruction in the public school during regular school hours. He commented:

> . . . The prohibition of enactments respecting the establishment of religion does not bar every friendly gesture between church and state. It is not an absolute prohibition against every conceivable situation where the two may work together any more than other provisions of the First Amendment — free speech, free press — are absolutes . . . . A state is entitled to great leeway in its legislation when dealing with important social problems of its population . . . . The constitution should not be stretched to forbid national customs in the way courts act to reach arrangements to avoid federal taxation. Devotion to the great principles of religious liberty should not lead us into a rigid interpretation of the constitutional guarantee that conflicts with accepted habits of our people.[70]

The McCollum decision was a great disappointment to some religious groups. The Roman Catholics were especially up in arms about it. The National Catholic Welfare Council bitterly denounced it as an "entirely novel" interpretation of the First Amendment, as well as being a victory for "doctrinaire secularism."[71] This approach was enlarged upon by James O'Neill, a Catholic layman, who modestly attacked the Supreme Court Justices' literary, logical, and legal abilities.[72] A somewhat more restrained view was taken by the Liberal Catholic weekly, *Common-weal*.[73] Stokes points out that while Protestant Evangelicals were disappointed by the results, it was praised by "most Jewish agencies, by the *Christian Century,* by Unitarians and more liberal Christian groups, and even by many Baptists who saw its importance from the standpoint of Church-State separation."[74] While he also feels that this decision of the court was expected by many constitutional lawyers, it should be pointed out that a number of well-known men in this field disagreed quite vehemently with the decision.[75]

Dismissed Time

The decision in the McCollum case leaves little doubt that "released time" programs are unconstitutional in the United States. The question of "dismissed time" was logically the next thing to be decided. Since programs of "dismissed time" are, if anything, more common than "released time," a Supreme Court ruling on this point would be more far-reaching than the McCollum decision.[76] Several things that might have had a bearing on the court's opinion of "dismissed time" should be kept in mind. One is the suggestion of Frankfurter in the McCollum case that the rule of that case applied only to the specific type of program common in that school system. The door was thus left open to reach a different conclusion on "dismissed time." Another is that a rash of criticism resulting from the McCollum case flooded legal journals, newspapers, and religious periodicals. The influence of these attacks, while unreckonable, cannot be ignored in attempting to analyze the decision in the Zorach case.

The courts of several states had been confronted with the specific problem of "dismissed time" in the years just preceding the Zorach case. The New York Court of Appeals in 1927 ruled that a "dismissed time" program in the White Plains school system did not violate the state Education Law or constitution.[77] The New York Supreme Court took the same view of a similar program in the New York City Schools in 1948.[78] The court emphasized that the McCollum decision applied only to a system of "released time" and had no bearing on "dismissed time" programs. The Illinois court in 1946 was unanimous in upholding a program of "dismissed time" which had existed for sixteen years in the Chicago school system.[79] In 1947, the California Court of Appeals for the Second District sustained a "dismissed time" program. It held that among other things religious education such as this would cut down juvenile delinquency by stressing moral integrity.[80]

The Zorach Case

On July 28, 1948, the New York City "dismissed time" program was again challenged in the Zorach-Gluck suit. Their petition, filed in the Supreme Court of New York, County of Kings, alleged:

(a) that the public school authorities cooperate closely with the Greater New York Coordinating Committee on the Released Time in the management of a program in promoting religious instruction;

(b) that the administration of the program necessarily entails the use of the tax-supported public school system (use of public property);

(c) that the state compulsory attendance laws are employed coercively to insure attendance at religious instruction;

(d) that the released time[81] program has resulted in the accentuation of differences in religious beliefs in both classrooms and community;

(e) that the limiting of participation to the "duly constituted religious bodies" effects an unlawful censorship and preference favoring certain religious groups.[82]

After a period of legal fencing,[83] the case came before the New York Court of Appeals. The court sustained Section 3210 of the New York Education Law permitting "dismissed time" over the contention that this violated the Fourteenth Amendment of the United States Constitution and Art. I, Sec. 3 of the New York constitution.[84] Judge Froessel, speaking for the majority, distinguished the rule of the McCollum case since it applied only to "released time," while the issue at stake in New York concerned "dismissed time" programs.

The New York Education Law permits its public schools to release students during school hours, on written requests of their parents, so that they may leave the school building and grounds and go to religious centers for devotional purposes or religious instruction. Students who do not attend these exercises stay in their classrooms and the church reports those pupils who leave the school, but do not attend the exercises.[85] The New York program, the court felt, did not involve religious instruction in the public schools or the use of public money. These were the major bones of contention in the McCollum case. There was no supervision or approval of religious teachers and no solicitation of pupils or distribution of cards by public school personnel. "All that the school does besides excuse the pupil is to keep a record — which is not available for any other purpose — in order to see that the excuses are not taken advantage of and the school deceived...."[86]

The New York Court cited Justice Frankfurter's concurring opinion in the McCollum case to support the view that the rule referred only to "released time" programs of the same type as that of Champaign, Illinois. It explained, "the constitution does not demand every friendly gesture between church and state shall be discountenanced."[87] The court pointed out that parents have the right to educate their children in places other than public schools so long as state requirements are met. Thus, if parents wish to have their children educated in the public schools, but to withdraw them from the schools once a week for religious instruction, "the school may constitutionally accede to this parental request."[88] It was suggested that some of the teachers may have used undue pressure upon the students to take part in this program. The court explained that if such were the case, disciplinary action might surely be brought against such offenders, but this would in no way invalidate the statute.

Judge Desmond, in a concurring opinion, agreed that the McCollum case was not controlling. It was, rather, the New York Court's rule in the Lewis case,[89] which must be followed. Furthermore, he did not see how the release of other parent's children impinged in any way on any "right" of the petitioners. Desmond pointed out that the statute in question was defended by the then-Governor Lehman, whose devotion to constitutional liberties needs no "encomium."[90] He denied that any total separation of church and state has ever existed in the United States.

> The true and real principle that calls for assertion here is that of the right of parents to control the education of their children, so long as they provide them with the state-mandated minimum of secular learning and the right of parents to raise and instruct their children in any religion chosen by the parents.[91]

He disagreed with Chief Justice Fred Vinson, when he said in the Dennis case,[92] "there are no absolutes" and "all concepts are relative." Desmond went out on a limb and stated "freedom of religion is a right which is absolute and not subject to any governmental interference whatever."[93]

Judge Fuld dissented alone. He followed Justice Black's opinion in the McCollum case. He concluded that the rule of the court stated, *"That any use of a pupil's school time, whether that use is on or off the school grounds, with the necessary school regulations to facilitate attendance, falls under the ban."*[94] He felt that the state offered sectarian groups an invaluable aid through the use of the state's compulsory public school machinery, thus violating the principle of church-state separation. The social pressures exerted within a school using a "dismissed time" program are enough to force otherwise reluctant students to take part in such a program. He explained that the major objections to the Champaign plan as well as the New York plan are the "utilization by state authority of the 'momentum of the whole school atmosphere and school planning' behind released time."[95] If this were not the case, the school authorities and religious groups might adopt the French system where one school day is shortened to allow all children to go where they please.

This case came on appeal to the Supreme Court of the United States.[96] On April 28, 1952, the court in a six to three decision (Black, Frankfurter, and Jackson dissenting) affirmed the decision of the highest New York court. Justice Douglas, speaking for the majority, ruled that New York's "dismissed time" program had neither prohibited the free exercise of religion nor made a law "respecting an establishment of religion within the meaning of the First Amendment, as applied to the states by the Fourteenth." The court felt, "It takes obtuse reasoning to inject any issue of 'free exercise' of religion into the present case."[97] It went on to explain the "First Amendment does not say that in every and all respects there shall be a separation of Church and State." If complete separation existed, churches could not be required to pay property taxes, nor could police and fire protection be given by the municipality to churches.[98] To show the dangerous extremes to which this logic might be extended, Justice Douglas noted: "A fastidious atheist or agnostic could even object to the supplication with which the court opens each session, 'God save the United States and this Honorable Court.' "[99]

Furthermore, Douglas believed, "we are a religious people whose institutions presuppose a Supreme Being." But we are also a people tolerant of the religion of others. The government may show no partiality to any sect. However, "when the state encourages religious instruction or cooperation with religious authorities by adjusting the schedule of public events to sectarian needs, it follows the best of our traditions."[100] (It is difficult to imagine that these sentiments emanate from essentially the same court which decided the McCollum case).

The court felt that while the First Amendment forbade government financing of religious groups and undertaking of religious instructions, the First Amendment did not require governmental hostility to religion. Finally, when dealing with the allegation that coercion was used to get public school students into religious classrooms, the court held that there was no evidence existing to support the contention. It noted, however, that if such evidence of coercion existed, a wholly different case would be presented.[101]

In his dissenting opinion, Justice Black could see no significant difference between the illegal system which existed in Champaign, Illinois, and the New York system, held legal by the court in this case. He thought the McCollum case made it clear that the decision would have been the same even if the religious classes were not held in the public school building.[102] He also took note of the attacks on the court which resulted from its decision in the McCollum case. This may have been directed at his more sensitive and thin-skinned colleagues who, he may have felt, back-tracked on their stated principles in the McCollum case. He agreed with Douglas that Americans are "a religious people," but pointed out that it was for the very reason that "Eighteenth Century Americans were a religious people divided into many fighting sects that we were given the constitutional mandate to keep Church and State completely separate." He pointed out the danger of government-coerced religious orthodoxy which seems inherent in the "dismissed time" program and concluded: "The First Amendment has lost much if the religious follower and the atheist are no longer to be judicially regarded as entitled to equal protection under the law."[103]

Justice Frankfurter in his dissent agreed with Justice Jackson, but deigned to "add a few words." These relate to the intrinsic coerciveness of any "dismissed time" program. He agreed with the majority that the school might close its doors when it wished to allow its pupils to attend religious instruction. The point he objected to was that the school did not close its doors or suspend operations.

> There is all the difference in the world between letting the children out of school and letting some out of school into religious classes. . . . The pith of the case is that formalized religious instruction is substituted for other school activities which those who do not participate in the released time program are compelled to attend.[104]

It appears to this writer that this is the controlling element in the Zorach case. It is one which the majority studiously side-stepped. Finally, Frankfurter was critical of the majority for its admission that if evidence of coercion existed, an entirely different case would be presented. He explained:

> The court disregards the fact that as the case comes to us, there could be no proof of coercion, for the appellants were not allowed (by the New York court) to make proof of it. . . . When constitutional issues turn on facts, it is a strange procedure indeed not to permit the facts to be established.[105]

Justice Jackson also reiterated the indirect but extremely important aid given to religious denominations under a program of "dismissed time." He pointed out that the greater effectiveness of this system over a strictly voluntary program of religious instruction which takes place after school hours "is due to the truant officer who, if the youngster fails to go to the church school, dogs him back to the public school room." Thus the school "serves as a temporary jail for a pupil who will not go to church." Jackson felt that indirect actions violating the First Amendment are just as unconstitutional as direct actions. As an individual who sent his children to a private church school, Jackson took issue with the majority opinion for suggesting that the only opposition to such programs comes from anti-religious or atheistic groups. He explained, "It is possible to hold a faith with enough confidence to believe that what should be rendered to God does not necessarily need to be decided and collected by Caesar." He concluded with a thought which might well be worth remembering. "The day that this country ceases to be free for irreligion, it will cease to be free for religion — except for the sect that can win political power."[106]

The fundamental question which arises from all of this relates to the legal status of "dismissed time" and "released time" programs. One would have to be recklessly rash or a superior soothsayer to answer this with complete certainty. The most that can be said is that the McCollum case appears to outlaw programs of "released time" while the Zorach rule upholds the rights of communities to have "dismissed time" programs of religious instruction for their public schools. Thus, the First and Fourteenth Amendments are violated if the public schools release students from classes to attend religious exercises in the public school buildings; but it is legal for the schools to dismiss their charges from classes to attend religious instruction outside of the public school physical plant.

CLASSROOM PRAYER

The Engel Case

On June 25, 1962, the Supreme Court of the United States handed down a decision of monumental importance concerning the role of religion in the public schools. In *Engel* v. *Vitale*[107] the court by a six-to-one vote struck down a state-sponsored optional program of a nondenominational prayer in the public schools of the state of New York.

The facts in the case can be briefly summarized. Acting upon a recommendation of the New York State Board of Regents, the Board of Education of New Hyde Park, New York, directed the School District's principal to cause the teachers to open each school day with the following prayer:

> Almighty God, we acknowledge our dependence upon Thee, and we beg Thy blessings upon us, our parents, our teachers and our country.

This prayer resulted from months of laborious discussion on the part of representatives of most of the religious denominations in New York, who, at the behest of the State

Board of Regents, sought to devise a nondenominational prayer acceptable to all groups.[108] While not all of the denominations originally involved with fashioning an acceptable nondenominational plan approved of the prayer under attack in this case, the New York Board of Regents recommended and published it as a part of their "Statement on Moral and Spiritual Training in the Schools." The Regents commented: "We believe that this statement will be subscribed to by all men and women of good will and we call upon all of them to aid in giving life to our program."

Soon after the practice of reciting the Regents' prayer was adopted by the New Hyde Park School District, the parents of ten pupils brought action in a New York court alleging that the use of this prayer in the public schools was contrary to the beliefs and religious practices of both themselves and their children.[109] They challenged the constitutionality of both the state law and the School District's regulation ordering the recitation of the prayer on the grounds that this official governmental action violated the First Amendment of the United States Constitution which provides that "Congress shall make no law respecting an establishment of religion."

This provision of the First Amendment was made applicable to the state of New York and all other states by the "incorporation doctrine" of the Fourteenth Amendment, first announced in 1925 in *Gitlow* v. *New York*[110] and applied to the "establishment of religion" clause of the First Amendment in the McCollum case in 1948. The "incorporation doctrine," as devised by the Supreme Court, provides that those rights of the Bill of Rights necessary for an ordered freedom are incorporated into the clause of the Fourteenth Amendment which stipulates that no state shall "deprive any person of life, liberty or property without due process of law." Thus the provision of the First Amendment applies to both the national and state governments.

The trial court rejected these allegations and upheld the constitutionality of the state-sponsored programs of prayer. The trial court made clear, however, that the Board of Education must set up procedures to protect those who objected to reciting the prayer. The New York court looked with favor upon that portion of the Regents' regulation making it clear that neither teachers nor any other school authority could comment on the participation or nonparticipation of pupils in the exercise. Nor could the school officials suggest or require that any posture or language be used, or dress be worn. The court held that provisions must be made for those not participating in such programs, and while suggesting several different approaches, left the final determination of the methods to be followed up to the Board of Regents.

The New York Court of Appeals, over the vigorous dissents of Judges Dye and Fuld, sustained an order of the trial court upholding the power of New York to use the Regents' prayer in the public schools so long as the schools did not compel any pupil to join in the prayer over his or his parents' objection.[111]

The case came to the Supreme Court of the United States and Justice Hugo L. Black spoke for the majority in overruling the decision of the New York State Court.

From the outset of his discussion in the case, Justice Black left no doubt that the court agreed the "State of New York has adopted a practice wholly inconsistent with the Establishment Clause," of the First Amendment. The program of prayer is a "religious activity" and a "solemn avowal of divine faith and supplication for the blessing of the

Almighty." By its very nature, such prayer is religious and this fact was not denied by any of the respondents, the court noted.

The court agreed with petitioner's contention that the law permitting the Regents' prayer is unconstitutional because the prayer itself was composed by governmental officials and was part of a governmental program to further religious beliefs. The constitutional prohibition against the establishment of religion, the court stated emphatically, must at least mean that in this country, "it is no part of the business of government to compose official prayers for any group of the American people to recite as a part of a religious program carried on by government."[112]

Justice Black then traced the long and bitter religious and political struggle in England associated with the adoption of the *Book of Common Prayer* in 1548 and 1549, and concluded that it was because of this controversy that many early colonists left England for America. He recognized, however, that once most of these groups arrived in the New World they enacted laws establishing their own religion as the religion of their colony. It was only after the Revolutionary War that successful attacks were made on the practice of state-established churches by such men as Thomas Jefferson and James Madison, the author of the First Amendment. At the time of the adoption of the Constitution, the court felt, there was a widespread awareness among Americans of the dangers of a union of church and state. Americans of that day "knew the anguish, hardship and bitter strife that could come when zealous religious groups struggled with one another to obtain the Government's stamp of approval."[113] The Constitution, the court pointed out, was adopted with the intention of averting part of this danger by placing the government in the hands of the people rather than in the hands of a monarch. But realizing that this was not a sufficient safeguard, the founding fathers added the First Amendment to insure that the content of their prayers and the privilege of praying whenever they wanted was not left to the whims of the ballot box. The First Amendment, the court explained, was designed to stand as a guarantee that, "the people's religions must not be subjected to the pressures of government for change each time a new political administration is elected to office."

The court had no doubt that the New York State prayer program establishes the religious beliefs embodied in the Regents' prayer. Moreover, it rejected the argument that the practice should be upheld on the grounds that all pupils were not required to recite the prayer, but those who wished were permitted to remain silent or to leave the room. Such an argument "ignores the essential nature of the program's constitutional defects."

In discussing the difference between the Establishment Clause and the Free Exercise Clause of the First Amendment, the court noted that while the two might overlap in certain instances, they forbid two quite different kinds of governmental encroachment upon religious freedom. Then, getting to the crux of the entire issue as the court majority saw it, Justice Black said: "The Establishment Clause, unlike the Free Exercise Clause, does not depend upon any showing of direct governmental compulsion and is violated by the enactment of laws which establish an official religion whether those laws operate directly to coerce nonobserving individuals or not."[114]

Clearly observing a practical problem arising from a program such as the one complained of, the court went on to explain that when the prestige, power, and financial support of government is placed behind a particular religious belief, "the *indirect* coercive pressure upon religious minorities to conform to the prevailing officially approved religion is plain."[115]

Discussing the purposes underlying the Establishment Clause, the court found the first and most immediate purpose rested on the belief, "that a union of government and religion tends to destroy government and to degrade religion." Thus, the court explained (quoting from James Madison), this clause lives as an expression of principle on the part of the Founders of the Constitution that "religion is too personal, too sacred, too holy, to permit its 'unhallowed perversion' by a civil magistrate."

Another purpose behind the Establishment Clause, as the court saw it, rested on the awareness of the facts of history which show that governmentally established religions and religious persecution go hand in hand.

The court flatly rejected the argument that if it applied the Constitution in such a way as to prohibit state laws respecting an establishment of religious services in public schools, such action would be commonly regarded as indicating a hostility toward religion or toward prayer. "Nothing . . . could be more wrong," the court insisted, for the "history of man is inseparable from the history of religion."[116] Nor were the men who drafted the Bill of Rights hostile to religion or prayer. The founders drafted the First Amendment, the court pointed out, "to quiet well-justified fears which nearly all of them felt arising out of an awareness that governments of the past had shackled men's tongues to make them speak only the religious thoughts that government wanted them to speak, and to pray only to the God that government wanted them to pray to."[117]

It is neither sacrilegious nor antireligious, the court commented, to say that all government should "stay out of the business of writing or sanctioning official prayers and leave that purely religious function to the people themselves or those the people choose to look to for religious guidance." In a footnote, however, the court made it clear that nothing in this decision should be construed as discouraging school children and others from reciting historical documents such as the Declaration of Independence, containing references to the Deity or singing "officially espoused anthems" which contain the composer's profession of faith in a Supreme Being. "Such patriotic or ceremonial occasions," the court insisted, "bear no true resemblance to the unquestioned religious exercise that the state of New York has sponsored in this instance."[118]

The majority opinion closed by refuting the argument of those who contend that since the Regents' official prayer is so brief and general there could be no danger to religious freedom in its governmental establishment. The court felt that James Madison, the author of the First Amendment, aptly came to grips with this viewpoint when he wrote:

> [I]t is proper to take alarm at the first experiment on our liberties. . . . Who does not see that the same authority which can establish Christianity, in exclusion of all other Religions, may establish with the same ease any particular sect of Christians, in exclusion of all other Sects? That the same authority which can force a citizen to contribute three pence only of his property for the support of any one establishment, may force him to conform to any other establishment in all cases whatsoever?[119]

Justices Frankfurter and White took no part in the decision of this case.

The majority opinion seemed to rest primarily on the general base that an official government enactment requiring or permitting a specific religious practice violates the Establishment Clause. It suggested that government on any level in the United States has no business legislating on matters of religion. It is immaterial whether or not such governmental programs require an expenditure of public funds even to a minute extent.

Justice Douglas Concurring

In a concurring opinion, however, Justice William O. Douglas, while of course agreeing with the final action of the majority, tended to center his objections on his disapproval of the program for utilizing public funds. At the outset he explained, "The point for decision is whether the government can constitutionally finance a religion." He went on to point out that our government on all levels is "honeycombed with such financing." Nonetheless, Justice Douglas insisted, "I think it is an unconstitutional undertaking whatever form it takes."[120]

He went on to point out certain things that the case does not involve, such as the coercing of anyone to utter the prayer on pain of penalty. This would clearly violate the Bill of Rights. The only person compelled to utter the prayer is the teacher, and Justice Douglas observed that no teacher was complaining in this case.

Moreover, Douglas insisted that the doctrine of the McCollum case[121] must be distinguished from the case under consideration. The former differed from the present case since in the latter, the teaching staff made no attempt to indoctrinate pupils and there was no attempt at exposition. The New York prayer, as Justice Douglas saw it, "does not involve any element of proselytizing as did the McCollum case."

Then he returned to his theme that the court here was confronted with the narrow issue of whether New York oversteps constitutionality when it finances a religious exercise. After all, Justice Douglas explained, "what New York does on the opening of its public schools is what we do when we open court." The Marshall of the United States Supreme Court traditionally announces the convening of the court by saying, "God save the United States and this honorable court." Since this may be regarded as a supplication or prayer, Douglas noted that the Justices are in the same position as the public school pupils of New York. They may join in or refrain from participating.

Furthermore, the New York program under attack is similar to the manner in which Congress opens each day's business, Justice Douglas believed, since the official chaplains of each house ask for divine guidance for the congressmen.

These situations have one thing in common, Justice Douglas felt. The New York teachers, the Marshall of the Supreme Court, and the Chaplains of the House and Senate are on the public payroll. And while the amounts of public money involved in such programs are minuscule, each situation involves a public official on a public payroll performing a religious exercise in a governmental institution. Moreover, Douglas saw a subtle element of coercion in all of the exercises since "Few adults, let alone children, would leave our courtroom or the Senate or the House while those prayers are being given. Every such audience is in a sense a 'captive' audience."

Having reached this juncture, Justice Douglas rather paradoxically observed: "At the same time I cannot say that to authorize this prayer is to establish a religion in the strictly historic meaning of the words." But, he went on, getting to what he appears to consider the crucial element in determining his decision, "once government finances a religious exercise it inserts a divisive influence into our communities."[122]

Quoting his words in the Zorach case[123] Justice Douglas again acknowledged that "We are a religious people whose institutions presuppose a Supreme Being." But he went on to point out that "if a religious leaven is to be worked into the affairs of our people, it is to be done by individuals and groups, not by the government."[124] There are those who may see some inconsistency between the attitudes expressed by Justice Douglas in the Zorach case when compared to those expressed in the situation here.

The First Amendment, Justice Douglas emphasized, leaves government in a position of neutrality and not of hostility to religion. It teaches that government neutrality toward religion better serves all religious interests.

Then in a highly interesting and significant passage Justice Douglas commented:

> My problem today would be uncomplicated but for *Everson* v. *Board of Education*[125] . . . which allowed taxpayers' money to be used to pay 'the bus fares of parochial school pupils'. . . . The Everson case seems in retrospect to be out of line with the First Amendment. Its result is appealing, as it allows aid to be given to needy children. Yet by the same token, public funds could be used to satisfy other needs of children in parochial schools — lunches, books, and tuition being obvious examples.

He concluded by quoting Justice Rutledge's dissent in the Everson case which calls attention to the fact that the underlying principle of religious liberty is that it be maintained free from sustenance, and other interferences by the state. Public money assisting religious activities causes a struggle of sect against sect which can result only in the destruction of cherished freedoms. The end product of such a struggle will be that the dominant group in a society will achieve the dominant benefits, in the opinion of the late Justice Rutledge and concurred in here by Justice Douglas.[126]

The Douglas concurrence raises some interesting avenues of speculation. On the one hand, in centering his objections to the constitutionality of programs of this type primarily upon the use of public monies for their support, his basis of decision appears much narrower than the decisional base of the majority. The latter appears convinced that any legislative action or administrative order or rule establishing an official religion, constitutes a violation of the Establishment Clause whether it operates directly to coerce nonobserving individuals or not. Moreover, the majority opinion suggests that the Establishment of Religion Clause is violated not only if the financial support of government is placed behind particular religious beliefs, but also if governmental *power* and *prestige* are used in such a fashion.

While moving from a narrower base, however, Justice Douglas steps out considerably further in some respects in his opinion than does the majority. Reversing his opinion in the Everson case in which he voted to uphold the constitutionality of state programs permitting the use of public funds for the payment of transportation of pupils to parochial schools, he now sees the Everson case "out of line with the First Amendment."

If Justice Black, who authored the majority opinion in both the Everson case and the present case agreed on this subject, he certainly did not deem it necessary to comment on his change of viewpoint. Indeed, this may be the primary reason behind Justice Douglas' separate concurring opinion, i.e., to spotlight this substantive disagreement over the extension of the Engel doctrine to areas other than state-sponsored programs of public prayer.

Furthermore, the Douglas opinion may serve as an inducement for further attempts to challenge programs of state support of bus transportation to parochial schools, since Justice Black is the only member of the court originally hearing the Everson appeal still on the bench who has not disavowed the Everson decision. In the original case, the decision was narrowly arrived at by a five-to-four vote with Justices Frankfurter, Rutledge, Jackson, and Minton dissenting. The composition of today's court has so changed that it would be idle to speculate on the outcome if it should be faced with a second Everson case.

Justice Stewart Dissenting

The sole dissenter in the Engel case was Justice Potter Stewart. He pointed out that the court did not hold here, nor could it, that the New York practice interfered with the free exercise of anyone's religion since this was not a compulsory program. He was of the opinion that the court had misapplied a great constitutional principle, for he could not understand how an "official religion" is established by "letting those who want to say a prayer say it."[127]

To deny the wishes of the pupils who want to pray is denying them the opportunity of "sharing in the spiritual heritage of our nation," Justice Stewart believed. Moreover, he insisted that what is dealt with here is not the establishment of a state church, but whether public school pupils who want to begin their day by joining in prayer are prohibited from doing so. There are those who might counter this point by noting that the majority opinion would not prevent the students from such a practice if they entered into it voluntarily. What the majority opinion attacks is a governmental regulation establishing such a program, albeit on a voluntary basis.

Justice Stewart was critical of the use of such "metaphors," as the "wall of separation," a phrase that does not appear in the Constitution. And he rejected the majority's heavy reliance upon the history of religious controversies in England under an established church. He would prefer to study instead the religious traditions of our people, "reflected in countless practices of the institutions and officials of our government."

He too observed that the Supreme Court is opened each day of the session with an invocation calling for the protection of God, and called attention to the opening prayers for the daily sessions of Congress. Moreover, he observed that every President from George Washington to the present has asked the help and protection of God upon assuming office.

Justice Stewart also pointed out that the third stanza of "The Star-Spangled Banner," which was officially adopted as our National Anthem by an Act of Congress in 1931, contains the statement, "And this be our motto 'In God is our Trust.' " Furthermore, he noted that in 1954, Congress added to the Pledge of Allegiance the phrase, "one nation *under God.*" And that in 1952, legislation enacted by Congress called upon the President to proclaim each year a National Day of Prayer.[128]

He challenged Justice Douglas' statement that the only question before the court was whether government "can constitutionally finance a religious exercise," by pointing out that the official chaplains of Congress and in the military are paid with public money. And prison chaplains in both federal and state prisons also receive their pay from the public treasury.[129]

He concluded by expressing doubt that any such practices or the prayer program in New York establishes an official religion. What they do, he explained, is to "recognize and to follow the deeply entrenched and highly cherished spiritual traditions of our nation — traditions which come down to us from those who almost two hundred years ago avowed in the Declaration of Independence their 'firm reliance on the protection of divine providence' when they proclaimed the freedom and independence of this brave new world.[130]

Whether one agrees or disagrees with the outcome of this case, it seems clear that the court in this decision did a commendable thing in taking a positive, significant step toward clarifying the meaning of the Establishment Clause of the First Amendment. The newspaper editorial comment that followed the decision tended to favor the court's position; the New York *Times* and the New York *Herald Tribune* among them.[131]

Some important churchmen were critical of the decision — including Cardinal Spellman of New York, Cardinal McIntyre of Los Angeles, and the Right Reverend James A. Pike, Bishop of the Episcopal Diocese of California.

On the other hand, the New York Board of Rabbis, and Dr. Dana McLean Greeley, president of the Unitarian Universalist Association, praised the ruling.[132] The New

York Board of Rabbis, representing the Orthodox, Conservative, and Reform rabbinate of Greater New York, said, in part, "The recitation of prayers in the public schools, which is tantamount to the teaching of prayer, is not in conformity with the spirit of the American concept of the separation of church and state. All the religious groups in this country will best advance their respective faiths by adherence to this principle."[133]

Bishop Pike was quoted by the New York *Times* as saying, "I am surprised that the Court has extended to an obviously nonsectarian prayer the prohibition against the 'establishment of religion' which was clearly intended by our forefathers to bar official status to any particular denomination or sect."[134]

In the 1962 session of Congress, some sentiment was discernible toward initiating a constitutional amendment to permit governmental agencies to authorize practices of this nature. It seems fair to predict that this issue will remain prominent on the American scene for years to come.

COMMENT BY JUSTICE BRENNAN
CONCERNING RELIGIOUS EDUCATION

It is interesting to note here the portion of Justice Brennan's concurring opinion in the Schempp and Murray cases in 1964 relative to the United States Supreme Court's past rulings in such cases as Everson, McCollum, and Zorach.[135]

Justice Brennan noted that the court in past decisions had consistently recognized that the Establishment Clause embodied the framers' conclusion that government and religion have discrete interests which are mutually best served when each avoids too close a proximity to the other.

It is not only the nonbeliever who fears the injection of sectarian doctrines and controversies into the civil polity, but in as high degree it is the devout believer who fears the secularization of a creed which becomes too deeply involved with and dependent upon the government.

Justice Brennan explained,

'. . . our tradition of civil liberty rests not only on the secularism of a Thomas Jefferson but also on the fervent sectarianism . . . of a Roger Williams. . . .' Our decisions on questions of religious education or exercises in the public schools have consistently reflected this dual aspect of the Establishment Clause. *Engel* v. *Vitale* unmistakably has its roots in three earlier cases which, on cognate issues, shaped the contours of the Establishment Clause. First, in *Everson* the Court held that reimbursement by the town of parents for the cost of transporting their children by public carrier to parochial (as well as public and private nonsectarian) schools did not offend the Establishment Clause. Such reimbursement, by easing the financial burden upon Catholic parents, may indirectly have fostered the operation of the Catholic schools, and may thereby indirectly have facilitated the teaching of Catholic principles, thus serving ultimately a religious goal. But this form of governmental assistance was difficult to distinguish from myriad other incidental if not insignificant government benefits enjoyed by religious institutions — fire and police protection, tax exemptions, and the pavement of streets and sidewalks, for example.

"But," Brennan was quick to explain,

even this form of assistance was thought by four Justices of the *Everson* Court to be barred by the Establishment Clause because [it was] too perilously close to that public support of religion forbidden by the First Amendment.

The McCollum case and the Zorach case, Brennan felt, must be considered together. So far as these two cases are concerned, Brennan stated,

I reject the suggestion that *Zorach* overruled *McCollum* in silence. The distinctions which the Court drew in *Zorach* between the two cases is in my view faithful to the function of the Establishment Clause. . . . However, . . . *McCollum* and *Zorach* do not seem to me distinguishable in terms of the free exercise claims advanced in both cases. The nonparticipant in the *McCollum* program was given secular instruction in a separate room during the times his classmates had religious lessons, the nonparticipant in any *Zorach* program also received secular instruction, while his classmates repaired to a place outside the school for religious instruction.

The crucial difference, in Brennan's opinion, was that the McCollum program offended the Establishment Clause while the Zorach program did not. This was not, he said, because of the difference in public expenditures involved. The McCollum program involved the regular use of school facilities while, under the Zorach program, the religious instruction was carried on entirely off the school premises, and the teacher's part was simply to facilitate the children's release to the churches. "The deeper difference," Brennan emphasized, "was that the *McCollum* program placed the religious instructor in the public school classroom in precisely the position of authority held by the regular teachers of secular subjects, while the *Zorach* program did not."

Brennan summed up the differences as follows,

The *McCollum* program, in lending to the support of sectarian instruction all the authority of the governmentally operated public school system, brought government and religion into that proximity which the Establishment Clause forbids. To be sure, a religious teacher presumably commands substantial respect and merits attention in his own right. But the Constitution does not permit that prestige and capacity for influence to be augmented by investiture of all the symbols of authority at the command of the lay teacher for the enhancement of secular instruction.

MISCELLANY

Finally, a number of miscellaneous cases not readily categorized, should be noted here.

A New York court held in 1926 that the provisions of a private school's contract which required students to attend Sunday services in Christian churches was a violation of a Jewish student's constitutional right to freedom of conscience.[136] The New York court relied heavily upon the Ohio Supreme Court's decision in the Minor case,[137] and went on to explain:[138]

> This republic was founded by our forefathers, not to escape the injustices of political aggression, but to seek freedom in a region where every man could worship God according to his own conscience. . . . It was for this that they braved the savage wilderness. . . .[139] It is plain to me that the strenuous effort of the plaintiff to compel the defendant's son, a boy of Jewish faith, to attend the church services of various Christian churches in the village of Germantown, against his will, and in opposition to his religious faith and convictions, is clearly a violation of his constitutional rights.

In a case dealing with the issue of public support of sectarian institutions, the Wisconsin Supreme Court held in 1920 that the Educational Bonus Act of 1919, under which Wisconsin veterans received $30 a month while attending school, was not invalid because they might attend nonpublic religious institutions.[140] The court pointed out that the schools are simply reimbursed for the actual increased cost to such schools resulting from the attendance of the beneficiaries of the act. "Mere reimbursement is not aid," the court concluded.[141]

Another case, while not truly related to the subject of this investigation, does give some insight into one court's opinion of religious books as such. In 1947, the California high court held that the assessment of an *ad valorem* tax on books and pamphlets belonging to an incorporated Bible and tract society, while in storage and awaiting distribution or use by members of a religious society, is not a violation of the guarantee of religious freedom.[142] The court pointed out that:

> The purpose . . . is to secure equality of taxation which results from subjecting all property to the same burden. . . . There is, therefore no discrimination in the instant tax and it is not even remotely aimed at any possible restriction on the exercise of religion . . .[143]

The court concluded by stating that while the power to tax may involve the power to destroy, it is certain no such result will stem from the tax in question.[144]

On December 23, 1960, the high court of Florida, in the Brown case, followed the example of the New Jersey Supreme Court in the Tudor case, and declared a program of distributing Gideon Bibles in the public schools of Orange County to be a violation of the freedom of religion clause of the First and Fourteenth Amendments.[145] The fact situation in the Florida case was similar to that involved in the Tudor case, and the Florida court relied heavily on that decision in its determination of the Brown case.

The Florida court pointed out that being a Gideon required membership in a Protestant church and that the Bible in question was the King James Version. Furthermore, it explained that under even the strictest interpretation, the First Amendment forbids preferential treatment by the government, either federal or state, of one sect or religion over others.

The court went on to observe that state power is no more

to be used to handicap religions than it is to be used to favor them. But it felt that distribution of Gideon Bibles in the public schools approximated an annual promotion and endorsement of certain religious sects or groups. Moreover, this impairs the rights of the plaintiffs and their children to be free from governmental action which discriminates in the free exercise of religious belief.

The court put the shoe on the other foot by explaining that if the Gideons distributed in a strongly Protestant area, the Douay Bible exclusively, or the Koran or the Talmud, "we surmise that the Protestant groups would feel a sectarian resentment against the actions of the school authorities."[146] Narrowing the question even further, the court was of the opinion that if the doctrinaire books of either the Methodists, Baptists, Presbyterians, or other of the numerous Protestant groups were distributed throughout the school system to the exclusion of the other groups, "considerable legal action would justifiably ensue."

The court concluded with the words of Thomas Jefferson, one of the architects of freedom of religion in the United States:

> Believing . . . that religion is a matter which lies solely between man and his God, that he owes account to none other for his faith or his worship, that the legislative powers of government reach actions only, and not opinions, I contemplate with sovereign reverence that act of the whole American people which declared that their legislature should 'make no law respecting an establishment of religion or prohibiting the free exercise thereof' thus building a wall of separation between church and state.[147]

On this basis, the Florida court revealed no hesitancy in declaring that a program of distributing Gideon Bibles in the public schools of Florida violated the First Amendment of the United States Constitution.

Pledge of Allegiance Problems

In 1957, a proceeding was brought in the Supreme Court of New York State to compel the Commissioner of Education to revoke a regulation recommending the use in the public schools of that section of the pledge of allegiance including the words "under God."[148] On June 14, 1954, Congress had amended Federal law[149] by inserting between the words "nation" and "indivisible," the words "under God." As amended, the pledge of allegiance to the flag reads:

> I pledge allegiance to the flag of the United States of America and to the Republic for which it stands, one nation under God, indivisible, with liberty and justice for all.

New York law makes it the duty of the Commissioner of Education to prepare for use in the public schools a program providing for a salute to the flag, a pledge of allegiance to the flag, for instruction in its correct use and display, and such other patriotic exercises as may be deemed by him to be expedient.[150] The Commissioner of Education for the state of New York promulgated a regulation providing:

> It is recommended that the schools use the following pledge to the flag: 'I pledge allegiance to the flag of the United States of America and to the Republic for which it stands, one nation indivisible, with liberty and justice for all.'

Following the action of Congress in 1954, the New York Commissioner of Education revised the regulation to provide for the inclusion of the words "under God" in the pledge of allegiance.

Petitioners did not object to the earlier pledge but contended that the Commissioner of Education had the duty to revoke the revised regulation deleting the words "under God" on the grounds that this violated the First Amendment to the United States Constitution and the Constitution of New York State.[151] Lewis argued that freethinkers, nonbelievers, atheists, and agnostics should not be compelled to recite the present pledge of allegiance because it included the words "under God" and that such compulsion violated their constitutional rights.

The court, however, rejected these contentions and dismissed the petition on several grounds. It felt it was clear that in amending Regulation 150 in accordance with the New York education law and with an act of Congress, the Commissioner of Education was performing his duties. It believed that to sustain the contention of petitioners would imply that the Commissioner of Education had not only the right but the duty to determine the constitutionality of an act of the state legislature or of Congress and to refuse to perform where in his judgment such an act was unconstitutional. Clearly, the court concluded, it was in the exclusive domain of the judiciary to determine the constitutionality of an act of Congress or of the state legislature.

In response to the queries concerning the First Amendment raised by the petitioner, the court noted that as it understood the intent, design, and purpose of the First Amendment, it was conceived to prevent and prohibit the establishment of a state religion; "it was not intended to prevent or prohibit the growth and development of a *religious state.*" If Lewis' contentions were sound, the court wondered whether the public school curriculum might properly include the Declaration of Independence and the Gettysburg

Address. Moreover, it felt that it would be questionable whether the song "America" might be sung in public schools without offending the First Amendment or whether the Presidential oath of office had a questionable constitutional status.

The court, however, was concerned about the social suasion which might operate to require, in fact, a child to recite the words "under God," even though it might violate his religious beliefs. It felt, however, that the child had a perfect right to simply omit the words "under God" in reciting the pledge. His "nonconformity," if such it be, will not in the circumstances of this particular case, set him apart from his fellow students or bring "pressure" to bear upon him in any real sense. The petitioner's right to disbelieve is guaranteed by the First Amendment, the court emphasized, and neither they nor their children can be compelled to recite the words "under God" in the pledge of allegiance. But at the same time the First Amendment afforded them no preference over those who believe in God and who, in pledging their allegiance, chose to express that belief, the court concluded. To grant Lewis' application would, in fact, be preferring those who believe in no religion over those who do believe, the court emphasized in closing.

Textbooks in Parochial Schools

In 1961, the Oregon Supreme Court outlawed the state program of providing school textbooks to parochial schools by declaring unconstitutional a state law which had existed for twenty years.

The law provided that local school districts in Oregon purchase textbooks out of state funds for use in church-sponsored and other private schools. The Oregon high court, in a six-to-one decision said, "[Roman] Catholic schools operate only because Catholic parents feel that the precepts of their faith should be integrated into the teaching of secular subjects. Those who do not share in this faith need not share in the cost of nurturing it."[152]

The court based its decision primarily on the Constitution of the State of Oregon, Article I, Section 5, which reads, "No money shall be drawn from the treasury [of the state or its subdivisions] for the benefit of any religious or theological institution . . ."

The court pointed out that the constitutional section in question was designed to keep separate the functions of state and church, thus preventing one from influencing the other. The court went on to explain that since the expenditure for such programs amounted to $4,000 a year, this constituted a substantial benefit to the parochial schools, and brought the program within the prohibition of the constitutional restriction.

The constitutional provision, the court concluded, required the state to be neutral in its relation with believers and unbelievers.

Summary

These cases, while covering a crazy quilt of subjects and issues, do seem to have one element in common: the complete lack of agreement on what constitutes sectarian instruction, and the justification of extending public funds to sectarian institutions. In Wisconsin, for example, the courts have held Bible reading illegal. But public high school baccalaureate exercises in which various clergymen gave nonsectarian prayers and invocations were upheld by the courts of that state. In Illinois, the courts have prohibited Bible reading in the public schools, but they have taken a favorable view of religious instruction at the state university.

In a number of instances where a church exercised some control over a school, the courts of eight states have ruled that a denominational school does not become a public school simply by calling it one. These courts, as has been seen, have decided that such schools are not entitled to state financial aid. It is interesting to note that a majority of these states either permit or require Bible-reading exercises in the public schools. There is little agreement among the courts of the various states regarding the legality of public school teachers wearing distinctive religious garments. Three states permit such practices, and five states prohibit them. There is no correlation between a state's stand on this question and its attitude toward Bible reading.

"Released time" programs of religious instruction which have been fairly common in various state-supported schools have been banned by the United States Supreme Court in the McCollum case. However, this court has added to the confused status of religious exercises in the schools by upholding (in the Zorach case) "dismissed time" programs in the public schools. But the court has made clear that state-sponsored prayers in the public schools are unconstitutional even though individual students are not compelled to participate in such programs.

It seems clear from this that the Supreme Court approaches matters in this area on a case-to-case basis rather than attempting to fashion a ringing absolute principle of law. Although those seeking the "final answer" may lament this approach, it has much to commend it, pertaining as it does to our highly dynamic and rapidly changing human society. Moreover, the probability of an infinite variety of such programs seems to preclude a single, all-encompassing rule of law.

6

Religious Group Attitudes and Pressure

THE CONTROVERSY CONCERNING Bible reading, and the larger issue of religious education in the public schools, has grown in importance as evidenced by its increased airing in newspapers and popular magazines. The magnitude of the issues has moved the debate outside the arena of religious and educational journals. But though an attempt to crystallize public opinion on one side or the other has been made, it is doubtful that the basic elements have been much clarified by the mass media's increased scrutiny.

In 1952, two Wisconsin newspapers commented editorially on the practice of Bible reading in the public schools. The Milwaukee *Journal* noted that the National Council of Churches of Christ (a Protestant organization) had publicly stated that it hoped to find a constitutional way to promulgate Bible reading in the public schools.[1] The paper felt that "The sincerity of purpose — to make pupils aware of the American 'heritage of faith' — is beyond question. But the thinking is fuzzy." It went on to stress the differences in the various versions of the Bible, and noted the impossibility of choosing one version agreeable to all sects. The editors felt such practices would result in sectarian controversies and law suits; these would result in pitting faith against faith and intensifying bigotry. The decision of the Wisconsin Supreme Court in the Weiss case was applauded for preventing such sectarian conflagrations by prohibiting Bible reading in the schools of Wisconsin.

Nor did the editors share the concern of the Council of Churches that "our culture is in danger of becoming pagan." They pointed out that American churches claimed to have grown to nearly 90,000,000 members in the prior year. This meant that they were gaining members faster than the population was growing, which raised the question:

> Aren't those thousands of churches and millions of homes and the religious schools the places to give children a knowledge of religion and an inclination toward its great moral concepts? Is religion wise to seek to lean upon the state as a crutch? What strange parent, himself neglecting the religious education of his children, would nevertheless expect the public school to attend to it?[2]

These sentiments were substantially reiterated by the Madison *Capital Times*[3] which shortly afterward commented upon the Milwaukee *Journal* editorial. As an example of the intensity of feeling generated by the difference in Bible versions, the Madison paper noted the case of a minister in North Carolina who presided over the burning of copies of the new revised version of the Bible which he considered to be heretical. It explained:

> The simple and lamentable fact is that there is far more prejudice and bigotry about religious matters than most of us want to admit. If sectarian doctrine is introduced into our schools we run the risk of transmitting the prejudices of adults to our children who fortunately, are comparatively free of it. The differences which divide adults might well become a part of the life of school children and do serious damage to public education.[4]

The conclusion here is that religion is a matter between man and his God. "The lesson of history is that whenever another individual or a state attempts to intervene, you had better watch out. There is going to be trouble."

The churches of the United States are, of course, greatly concerned with furthering the moral education of the young. There is little agreement, however, among the sects, or within the sects for that matter, on how this is to be accomplished. This debate centers mainly around the public schools, and their role in propagating ethical and religious ideals. Churchmen are definitely divided regarding the place of religion in the public schools.

Life magazine, in an editorial, gave a rather thorough sketch of the elements present in the contemporary debate.[5] It noted that the Catholic hierarchy's annual statement on religion in America paid special attention to the public schools, and expressed the belief that our materialism had produced a greater danger than materialism itself — secularism. The hierarchy felt the growth of secularism could be traced to the reluctance of the Supreme Court, liberals, and educators to permit religious instruction at public expense.

Life reported that the Catholic statement immediately drew a reproof from the Baptist Joint Committee on Public Affairs, which declared that any government aid to church institutions is unconstitutional. "They politely called the Catholics un-American." According to the editorial, two elements are at the core of this dispute. The first is that American Protestants are concerned over some of the extreme pronouncements of the Catholic church, which seems "unable to renounce the goal of a clerical monopoly of all worship and education, even where, as in the United States, most Catholic laymen have no such ambitions." Since the Protestants have adopted sectarian tolerance as an absolute principle, they are suspicious of any new Catholic proposal whether it is good or not. The second element is more fundamental. "It is the conflict between those who care whether God lives in American life and those who do not."

Life is convinced that our founding fathers aimed at a system of church-state cooperation. Then, clearly becoming partisan in the debate, it stated:

> This suggestion of a monopoly of truth is what gives non-Catholics ground for reasonable objection. But they register their objection at a different and unreasonable point. The Baptists actually defend secularism and accuse the Catholics (who explicitly deny it) of using the word as a smokescreen with which to kill the public schools! And they duck the much more serious issue that the religious 'neutrality' of the public school has become in fact a form of irreligion.

A great many educators and a number of religious leaders would object to this statement, as will be pointed out later in this chapter.

Finally, the editorial praised an article by Will Herberg,[6] "a religious Jew," for sorting out the issues in this controversy. Herberg felt that the authors of the Constitution did not intend to erect a wall of separation between church and state. He explained that the public schools, like most democratic institutions, are Protestant creations, but they were never intended by their founders to be completely devoid of religious influence. This has resulted from a shaky alliance between the followers of John Dewey (who wished to set up democracy itself as the main purpose of schooling), and Protestant groups who fear the growing power and influence of the Catholic church.

Life reported that Herberg thought Protestants surrendered intellectual leadership to nonreligious forces, with the result that they have been "maneuvered into an unreal, contradictory and panicky position." While the editorial noted some "honorable exceptions" to this charge,[7] it believed that if the present alliance continued, "it threatens to make democracy itself the established religion of the schools, and eventually, of the nation." The editorial concludes by explaining:

> The temptation of Protestantism is that when it succeeds in solving a social problem, as it did by creating American democracy and the public school, the solution attracts devotion that belongs to God who sponsored it. The glory of Protestantism is that its problems are the hardest, since they are addressed to innumerable free consciences.[8]

With this general preview of some contemporary attitudes, let us now turn to the views of the major sects. Several points should be noted at the outset: Though a denomination may feel that it is important for schools to impart religious and moral values, this does not necessarily mean that it favors Bible reading and religious exercises within the schools. Also, since many of the sects in the United States are established along congregational lines, the pronouncement of one individual or organization does not, of necessity, imply that this is the official stand for the entire denomination. Even in sects organized along hierarchial lines, it cannot always be taken for granted that a statement by a member of the hierarchy or by an important layman reflects official and doctrinaire pronouncements of the policy-formulating body. An attempt has been made here to present representative views of the major sects. In some cases they may be seen to form a consensus while in others a wide diversity exists which may reflect the congregational nature of the group, or a lack of an established policy.

THE ROMAN CATHOLIC POSITION
ON BIBLE READING

Before getting into a discussion of Roman Catholic views, some mention should be made of Catholic attitudes toward Bible reading in general. Considerable confusion surrounds this point since some Protestants believe Bible reading by Catholic laymen to be frowned upon by the church hierarchy. This is stoutly denied by the Catholics. Space does not permit a full investigation of this problem. But the contention will be presented and some of the more contemporary evidence bearing on it.

Stokes points out that the:

> Roman Catholic Church has been cautious about commending the reading of the Bible by laymen, without authoritative notes giving the Catholic point of view, except when it can be interpreted by a priest or other authorized representative.[9]

He admits, however, that there are many examples of Catholic pupils attending public schools where the King James Version of the Bible is read and where the local priests have raised no objections.

Paul Blanshard, after studying Canon 1399 of the Catholic Church, concludes that, "It is a grave sin for a Catholic under ordinary circumstances knowingly to own or use a Protestant Bible."[10] It might be stressed that this refers only to the Protestant Bible. He goes on to explain that Father Francis W. Connell, Associate Professor of Moral Theology at the Catholic University of America, has outlined a whole code for Catholic teachers in public schools in his book *Morals in Politics and Professions,* published in 1946. The Catholic teacher, he writes,

. . . should avoid the Protestant Bible if possible and bring her own Bible to class and read it to the pupils, when custom calls for the reading of the Bible in the public school. When the recitation of the Lord's Prayer is called for, neither the Catholic teacher nor the Catholic pupil should recite the phrase, 'For thine is the Kingdom, etc.' because, 'in practice these words have taken on a Protestant connotation, so their use would constitute an implicit approval of heresy.'[11]

The mere mention of Blanshard's name stimulates the Catholic's olefactory perception so that he detects burning crosses and the resurrection of the *Menace*. Therefore, it is not surprising that James O'Neill, a leading Catholic layman, who has taken up the cudgels against most of Blanshard's conclusions about the Catholic church, should object to the above statements regarding the Bible. O'Neill believes that when Blanshard states " 'Catholics are forbidden to read the Bible,' one should be understood to mean exactly that."[12] He then states:

> The truth is that Catholics are taught and urged to read the Bible. The only documentation that Mr. Blanshard offers for his untrue statement is Canon 1399. If anyone will take the trouble to read Canon 1399, he will find that Mr. Blanshard's [statement] will need a good many qualifications put in order to make it even partially true. Canon 1399 is a long and complicated treatment of books, of interest chiefly to the clergy (as is all canon law) and contains nothing to substantiate Mr. Blanshard's criticism. . . .[13]

In the interests of accuracy it should be pointed out that Blanshard referred only to a prohibition against Catholics reading the Protestant Bible. Mr. O'Neill has a tendency to confuse this with a categorical prohibition against reading any of the several versions extant.

The Bible's Role in Life

Other Catholics have followed a more positive approach in discussing the Bible's role in their life. Writing in *Commonweal* several years ago, Alban Baer stressed the importance to the lay Catholic of reading the Scriptures and the Holy Writers.[14] He thought a person should not always distrust his own judgment when he feels one of the pious books is dull. However, prudence and caution should be exercised in arriving at such conclusions. Next to the Holy Scriptures, Baer believed, the most valuable spiritual reading is found in the Fathers and Doctors of the Church, for they aid and guide Catholics in interpreting the scriptures.* He suggested following St. Augustine's advice, "Read not to contradict and confute; nor to believe and take for granted; nor to find talk or discourse; but to weigh and consider." He points out to the laity that they should not be so awestruck by the greatness of these writings that they never read them. For:

> To know anything is to love it: to know God's word spoken directly through His inspired writers and indirectly through all whom He, through His church has commissioned and encouraged to speak or write of Him — to know God's word is to love its author.[15]

A 1953 article in *America,* the Jesuit weekly magazine, made a frontal attack upon the contention that Catholics are discouraged by church officials from reading the Bible.[16] It commented on the celebrations marking the publication of the new version of the Catholic Bible in September, 1952. (This was, incidentally, the same month that the newly

---

*Fathers of the Church are those teachers of the first twelve, and especially of the first six, centuries whose teaching had great authority; Doctors of the Church are ecclesiastics noted for the greatness of their learning and the holiness of their lives; often declared Saints by the Church.

revised Protestant Bible issued from the presses.) The Catholic Bible resulted from the work of United States biblical scholars under sponsorship of the Episcopal Committee of the Confraternity of Christian Doctrine, with the approval of the American hierarchy. These celebrations took various forms.

> On the school level, the Bible, at least for a week, had a place of honor in both curricular and extra-curricular activities. Thousands of assemblies featured 'spelldowns,' pantomimes and playlets. The *Catholic Boy, Catholic School Journal,* the *Messengers,* and *Treasure Chest* supplied teachers with 'how to do' materials.

This activity was apparently restricted to Roman Catholic parochial schools. However, the article went on to point out:

> Typical of community participation was that of the Sisters of Charity of Leavenworth, who produced two original plays to be presented in 53 grade schools, 11 high schools, and 14 schools of nursing. . . . The Mission Helpers of the Sacred Heart, experts in the catechetics field, prepared 8 lessons on the Bible for the more than 3.5 million Catholic pupils in public elementary schools. Public high school students in Hartford and San Francisco had a four week course on the scriptures.

In addition to this, historic and ancient Bibles were displayed in the vestibules of several Catholic churches. All of these are examples of the Catholic Church's endeavors "to keep the Good Book *for,* not *from* the people," *America* explained. It felt that Catholic efforts in 1952 let the United States citizenry know that the Bible is a Catholic Book, and that the "Church which in the past preserved the Bible, gave it to the world and lost whole peoples rather than compromise on its teachings, still honors and cherishes it."

The article concluded: "Unquestionably, love of the Bible and a closer acquaintance with it would be a potent factor in the moral 'revision' our times need."

While these are not necessarily official pronouncements of the Roman Catholic hierarchy, *America* and *Commonweal* are two of the most widely read Catholic periodicals.

The Bible in the Public Schools

When examining the attitudes of Roman Catholics regarding Bible-reading practices in the public schools, one fact in particular stands out: Most of the litigation seeking to enjoin such exercises has been brought by Catholic and Jewish citizens. They have objected to the use of the King James Version of the Bible in these programs.[17] Professor Howard Beale of the University of Wisconsin has explained that Catholics objected to Bible reading and religious instruction in the public schools, because such programs were a direct reflection of Protestantism.[18] He pointed out that in their fight to exclude the Bible from the schools, the Catholics and Jews were joined in 1870 by a "so called liberal movement." This movement "fanatically attacked all vestiges of religion in American life and tried to exclude from public places not only the Bible, but all reference to deity." In addition to this group the Catholics and Jews picked up support from a group of ministers whose dogmatism had been shaken by the disproving of many tenets which the authoritarian religion of their youth told them must be accepted without question. They concluded that nothing could be gained by forcing religion upon pupils and teachers, for required exercises did not best serve the interests of religion itself.

The dilemma facing the Catholics in regard to their

stand on Bible reading has been expertly summarized by Beale. He explained:

> The Catholics were torn between a desire to keep their own children in parochial schools and a concern to free their children and their teachers in the public schools from using the Protestant Bible. They never would admit that they wished religion or the Bible excluded from the schools, for the whole argument in favor of parochial schools was that religion formed a major part of education.

The major objection was, of course, not to Bible reading itself, but the version read, and the person doing the reading. This is an important distinction to keep in mind when encountering some later, seemingly paradoxical, views relating to religious instruction and Bible reading.

The Church tends toward the opinion that the way to impart religious education is through recognized members of the clergy. Religious education by public school teachers would be at best inadequate. It is for this reason, plus its opposition to Protestant influence in the public schools, that the Catholic hierarchy, early in the history of the United States, sought to create parochial schools.

Some of the clearest enunciations of this view came from Bishop John B. Purcell, later archbishop of Cincinnati. In 1837 he objected to Protestant Bibles being placed in the hands of Roman Catholic pupils, and sought provisions that would prohibit teachers from injecting sectarian bias in their instruction. In addition to this, he advocated a program which would permit public school pupils to be instructed by their own pastor once or twice a week.[19]

This attitude of the Roman Catholics, which Purcell had aided in developing, was given expression in the pastoral letter of the Third Provincial Council of Cincinnati to the laity and clergy in 1861. The arguments against the public schools and reasons for public support of parochial schools are much the same as those heard today. The letter said in part:

> As this religious training is not possible in the public schools as at present organized and conducted, our children are necessarily excluded from them, as effectively as they would be by locks and bolts. . . . After paying our due proportion of common taxes for the support of schools which are thus virtually closed against us, we feel constrained to erect others, at enormous expense for the Christian education of our own children. . . . In a country so divided in sentiment as ours is on the subject of Religion, the only system which would be fair and equitable to all, would be that which would make education like religion, and all other important pursuits, *entirely free;* and if taxes are collected from all for its encouragement and support, to apportion the amount of these taxes fairly among the scholars taught, certain branches up to a certain standard, no matter under what religious or other auspices. This system would elicit educational industry and talent by stimulating competition; and we have not a doubt that it would lessen the cost of education, greatly extend its blessings, and render it both sounder and more widely diffused. It would satisfy all classes, and it would render the schools really public and common which they certainly are not at present except in name.[20]

Some Roman Catholic Attitudes Toward Public Schools

In recent years Catholics have been particularly sensitive to the charge (occasionally heard) that they are opposed to public schools. This has been vehemently denied by high Catholic sources.[21] Msgr. Frederick G. Hochwalt, Secretary General of the National Catholic Educational Association, undertook to answer the question of how Catholics stand on public education. He pointed out:

> (1) Catholics believe in the public schools! (2) Catholics believe that as citizens, like all other citizens, they have

an obligation to pay taxes for the adequate support of the public schools in their community. (3) Catholics have not nor will not interfere with the justifiable expansion of the public schools in their community. (4) Catholics have a civic duty to take an active interest in the welfare of the public school system.[22]

Stokes asserts that even if the Douay Version was substituted for the King James Version, the Catholics frankly conceded they would not discontinue their efforts to build up parochial schools. "Indeed the Douay version is permitted in some places without substantially altering the church's position."[23] These objections are based on the view that Bible reading alone, if considered from the standpoint of religious instruction, is entirely inadequate.

The magazine *America* summed up these contentions. Additionally, it objected to the weakness of Bible-reading programs because the Bible was read without note or comment. (This is an attempt to avoid the charge that such reading constitutes sectarian instruction.) It pointed out:

> No child is taught anything by listening to the reading of a book without note or comment. They [public school teachers] cannot teach religion in that manner with any greater success than they could teach grammar or arithmetic. In fact, the very custom of Bible reading may harm religion. If the Bible is God's work, it should be heard with reverence and a docile heart. If it is merely a human document, containing more or less well authenticated facts of history together with a tribal code of morals, it has no more claim to respect than the works of Herodotus or Confucius, and the attempt to enforce reverence is rank superstition.[24]

Cardinal Gibbon was one Catholic leader who favored Bible reading in the public schools. He believed such exercises had definite advantages, and should receive Catholic support when no other form of religious instruction could be provided. In a letter addressed to the president of the Chicago Women's Education Union, he explained:

> The men and women of our day who are educated in our public schools will, I am sure, be much better themselves, and will also be able to transmit to their children an inheritance of truth, virtue and deep morality, if at school they are brought to a knowledge of Biblical facts and teachings. A judicious selection of Scripture readings; appropriate presentation of the various Scripture incidents, born of reflection on the passages read and scenes presented, cannot but contribute, in my opinion, to the better education of the children in our public schools, and thus exercise a healthy influence on society at large, since the principles of morality and religion will be silently instilled while instruction is imparted in branches of human knowledge.[25]

Problems of Secularism

While many Catholics have been critical of Bible reading in public schools, they have been even more outspoken in their opposition to what they call "secularism" in these schools. There appears to be a consensus among Catholic writers and journals in recent years that the problems of youth could be solved in a great measure by having some type of general religious training in the public schools. What these basic and nonsectarian dogmas are is not made clear.

As early as 1926 an editorial in *America* complained of a lack of character development in the youth.[26] It contended that the church and home did not have control of the children long enough to inculcate in them moral and ethical values. "Further to relegate religious instruction to an hour on Sunday morning, or to assign it to an after-class period, tends to lessen its importance in the mind of the child, and may even arouse his antagonism."[27] This fact then leads the editors to conclude:

> Since the home and the Sunday school are insufficient, we must get back the old American traditions of education and restore religion to its place in the schools. The Fathers of the Republic considered that the diffusion of religion and morality among the people was necessary for the continuance of our free institutions. If their acquiescence in the custom of their day, and their language in the Northwest Ordinance and the Farewell Address report them truly, they thought that the school would ever be an active and effective instrument for the teaching of religion and morality. Some eighty years ago these hopes were blasted by the introduction of a secular system whose first father was Julian the Apostate and whose modern apostles were the French and German secularists of the late eighteenth and early nineteenth century. The typical American school is the religious school. The secular school is an importation from abroad.

In an earlier editorial, *America* had viewed the growing crime wave in the United States and observed that evidence appears to show that mere training in intellect is not sufficient to raise a law-abiding, God-fearing generation.[28] It explained that when religion is excluded from the school or merely tolerated as a task for leisure moments, the pupil cannot help but conclude that it is not a concern of compelling importance. "The result is . . . that the secular school becomes a fosterer of atheism." From this the conclusion is drawn that "after fifty years of secular school control, about six out of every ten Americans have no connection with any religious creed, and 'we are the most lawless people in the world.'"

In the last few years a rash of articles has issued from Catholic sources attacking the lack of religion in public life and in the tax-supported schools. Some have attacked the secular nature of the schools.[29] Others discuss the schools.[30] Several of these have been critical of what they believe to be Protestant tolerance of secularism.[31] Bishop Oxnam, the controversial and much publicized Methodist, is singled out for a scorching attack because of his statement that the Catholics do not believe in a separation of church and state.[32] This is denied by an editorial in *Commonweal,* which gives statements by Cardinal Gibbons and Bishop John Carroll to bear out its contention. However, it is explained that Catholics also believe in the sentiments contained in the Northwest Ordinance — particularly those which state, "Religion, morality and knowledge being necessary to good citizenship and the happiness of mankind, schools and the means of education shall ever be encouraged." The editors conclude that Bishop Oxnam is cutting off his nose to spite his face. For if a complete separation of church and state were instituted in the United States, it would prohibit Protestant influences in the public schools as well as Catholic.

Roman Catholic Reactions to the McCollum Case

The Supreme Court of the United States has come in for its share of criticism by Catholics, particularly because of its decision in the McCollum case, which, many Catholics felt, gave secularism a victory in the public schools.[33] The more recent actions of the Court, particularly in the Doremus and Zorach cases, have been approved by a number of Catholic writers.[34] Interestingly enough, the *Commonweal* even applauded the Court's decision in "The Miracle" case,[35] which disapproved of censorship of motion pictures on the ground of blasphemy.

The majority of these points have been summed up

in the Catholic hierarchy's statement on the condition of religion in America, issued at the conclusion of the Roman Catholic Bishops' annual meeting in New York City, November 15, 1952.[36] Here they explain that religion is our most vital national asset. Not only does man as an individual need religion to "rise above that pessimism, that sense of despair which threatens to engulf the whole of our civilization," but religion is a fundamental need of society as a whole. It is the tie that keeps the family together, and teaches the principles of morals and ethics essential for citizenship. They assert that religious influences have been of great importance in the formation and development of the American tradition. The Bishops are convinced that the founders of this country were deeply conscious of a debt to religion. The long debates over the First Amendment are cited as examples of the deep concern over religion felt by the First Congress. They deny that it was the purpose of these men to eliminate religion's influence on public life. Rather their purpose was "to guarantee to religion its essential freedom."

For these reasons the hierarchy is particularly critical of the growing secularism in the schools, for it ignores the importance of religion in education. The Bishops stress the impossibility of teaching moral and spiritual values divorced from religion, for "without religion, morality becomes simply a matter of individual taste, of public opinion or majority vote." They deny that because they criticize the secular trend of public education they are enemies of public schools. But they point out that since religion is necessary for good citizenship the state should recognize its importance in public education. When the state fails to do this, it is making the task of parents much more difficult.

They were particularly alarmed because some leading educators have criticized nonpublic schools for being divisive. Their statement tartly explained, "Not all differences are divisive, and not all divisions are harmful." They noted that the religious instruction imparted in parochial schools is a "unifying rather than a dividing force." It is for these reasons that the Bishops felt public support should be extended to parochial schools; for secularism has led to materialism, and materialism is closely associated with totalitarianism, and religion is the only effective weapon to counteract this tendency.

Several factors, then, are reasonably clear regarding the attitudes of Roman Catholics toward Bible reading, though there is no single, uniform policy of the hierarchy on the subject. Traditionally they have opposed it because it has usually been associated with Protestant dominance in the public schools. They object first to the fact that the King James Version is the one generally singled out to be read in such programs. Secondly, they have been critical of Bible reading, because they feel public school teachers are not equipped to give instructions on the Bible adequately, and, since the majority of such readings must be done without comment, Catholics feel the effectiveness of the exercises are destroyed. They would appear to prefer a system of tax-supported parochial schools, where religion can be taught by religious leaders of the pupil's denomination. This would provide for instruction in religious ideals and ethical values without offending the religious sensibilities of pupils belonging to different sects. Through such techniques they would overcome the big drawback to religious instruction in public schools.

JEWISH ATTITUDES TOWARD BIBLE READING

A discussion of Jewish attitudes toward Bible reading is made difficult by the essentially congregational nature of their religion. Thus, while it would be incorrect to speak of a Jewish attitude, an attempt will be made to give representative attitudes of Jewish organizations and influential individuals. In general it may be said that Jews have objected to Bible reading because the King James Version is usually chosen for such exercises. Their arguments are similar to those the Catholics use, and frequently, as noted before, the litigation brought seeking to enjoin such programs is instituted jointly by Jews and Catholics.

An example of such cooperation was reported by the New York *Times* some time ago. Here an application by Roman Catholic and Jewish parents for a permanent injunction to prevent distribution of the King James Version of the New Testament in the Rutherford, New Jersey, public schools was denied by a Superior Court judge.[37] The judge ruled that nobody's constitutional rights would be violated since the pupils' acceptance of the Bibles would be voluntary. The Board of Education had stipulated that Bibles would only be given to students who presented slips of approval signed by the parents or guardians. The article notes that Dr. Joachin Prinz, Rabbi of Congregation B'nai Abraham in Newark, and Dr. Isadore Sheim, former Director of the Commission of Community Interrelations and now Professor of Education at New York University, appeared in court supporting the appeal for the injunction.

Since most of the points raised against Bible reading by non-Protestants have already been discussed at length in connection with Roman Catholic objections, they will not be listed here in detail because of their essential similarity. Stokes, however, feels that Jews "on the whole have been less active in their opposition to the reading of the King James Version than the Roman Catholics."[38]

General Reactions

It would appear that Jewish objections to Bible reading in the schools are based on two points. The first is their desire to keep church and state separate, and they feel that Bible reading violates this principle. Secondly, they fear that the Bible's Christological ideas, with which they do not agree, will be taught to their children in the public schools. These sentiments are summed up on pp. 4 ff. in the pamphlet, *Why the Bible Should Not Be Read in the Public Schools,* which was adopted by the Central Conference of American Rabbis from the report of its Committee on Church and State. Though this was issued in 1922, it would still appear to reflect contemporary Jewish sentiment. The pamphlet states:

> No matter which version of the Bible is used, there will always be dissatisfaction. The translation generally used is the King James, or its improved form, the Revised version. But while acceptable to Protestants, this translation is objected to by the Catholics who believe in none but the Douay version. The differences in these two translations reflect some of the vital differences in belief of the faiths that use them. But neither version is altogether acceptable to the Jew. He prefers the Lessar translation with all its imperfections because it is done from a Jewish point of view, and is limited to the Old Testament. While the individual who belongs to no denomination, or is wanting altogether in religious belief, objects to all three versions, on the ground that his views are given absolutely no consideration.

The pamphlet denied that this position is irreligious or unpatriotic and points to a statement of James Madison who said, "Religion is not in the purview of human government. Religion is essentially distinct from government and exempt from its cognizance. A connection between them is injurious to both." It noted there is a great difference between private and public schools, for public schools must insure equal privileges and recognition to all.

Religious instruction of any sort makes such equality difficult or impossible. This prompts the rabbis to state, "Religious exercises in our public schools may please the majority, but they wrong the minority. In plain language they discriminate. . . ." Such exercises might permit teachers to give sectarian instruction, as in the case of a Christian teacher reading selections of specifically Christian truth. Furthermore, since such reading exercises are usually perfunctory and hurried, they hurt rather than help the cause of religious culture.

Rabbi Louis Wolsey has noted how it might be perfectly possible for a teacher to impart sectarian ideals even when reading the Bible without comment to a class. He explained:

> I can well understand how the reading of the Bible without oral comment or exposition, but with the more impressive comment of tonal inflections, postures of the body, gesticulations, the deliberate rising and falling of the voice, and the upraising of eyebrows, might easily help the fundamentalist Christian in the teacher's chair to utilize the public school system for the evangelizing of all the children who do not belong to his particular school of religious thought.[39]

Jewish Groups' Reactions

The American Jewish Committee and the Anti-Defamation League of B'nai B'rith issued a joint memorandum

commenting upon the proposal before the California Legislature seeking to authorize Bible reading in the public
schools of California.[40] After studying the text of the bill,
the organizations concluded it was "ineptly drafted and,
if passed, is likely to cause additional controversy when it
will have to be applied and interpreted." They explained
that the inclusion of authority in the bill for reading the
New Testament makes it objectionable to those who believe only in the Old Testament. They pointed out that
the "authorization that the reading be from 'any recognized translation thereof' puts the public school authorities, an arm of the state, in the position of determining
which translations of the Bible are 'recognized.' Hence, in
a sense the state is required to determine what is and what
is not orthodox."[41]

This memorandum notes that merely because the bill
states in part that such reading is to be carried on "without
sectarian application," sectarian controversies and debates
are not likely to be eliminated. The bill also says that the
State Department of Education has to "publish a syllabus
of graded Bible reading" and to make it "available to all
public schools." These organizations wonder what "competence or constitutional authority" the State Department
of Education has which will permit such action. The memorandum goes on to state:

> Granting unlimited discretion to local school boards to
> 'supervise all arrangements for Bible reading in their dis-
> tricts' and for 'exemption of pupils from such readings'
> opens a Pandora's box. In many communities the result
> will probably be to sharpen religious competition among
> groups to obtain arrangements which favor their sect.
> Much harm can also result from careless or improper
> handling of requests for exemption of pupils from Bible
> reading and the manner of treating such exemptions in
> the classroom.

The American Jewish Committee and the Anti-Defamation League conclude this statement on Bible reading by noting, "The proposed statute highlights the problems raised by any kind of Bible-reading legislation for the public schools."

From conversations with representatives of various Jewish organizations the following views were reflected concerning their attitudes toward religious instruction and Bible reading in the public schools. The Union of Orthodox Jewish Congregations opposes any connection of church and state. It desires complete separation since it considers religion a private matter between man and his God. (Exactly what specific practices were to be included in its conception of "complete separation" was not made clear.) The Rabbinical Council of America (representing the Orthodox position) is also opposed to Bible reading. The Rabbinical Assembly of America (representing the Conservative position) does not consider this problem one it has to face. However, it recommended the view of the New York Board of Rabbis, which also is composed of the Conservative segment. This latter organization has recently adopted a resolution on the subject. It states:

> The New York Board of Rabbis has noted the recent attacks made against public education, particularly in its relation to the moral and spiritual training of our youth.
>
> We have often affirmed that religious training is indispensable to a complete education experience, and that, without it, life is devoid of true meaning or worth. We believe, too, that the American democratic system is founded upon ethical and moral concepts derived from the great religions of mankind, the preservation of which is essential to the fullest realization of the American ideal.
>
> We maintain that the teaching of religion is the proper responsibility of the church, synagogue and home and *not*

of the public school. We strongly approve of the inculcation of ethical and moral values by public school teachers in the course of their teaching of all subjects and in all pupil activities. But we deprecate the introduction of studies or exercises that would involve *formal religion* in any way, as a move that must lead inevitably to sectarian strife and to the deprivation of the protection of youthful pupils from seduction from their parental beliefs.

For these reasons we look with strong disapproval on such divisive practices as daily prayer in the public school classrooms and assemblies, released time, and sectarian religious holiday observances. These threaten the nonsectarian character of our public schools. We urge that all possible avenues be explored by church and synagogue as well as civic, school, parent and other community bodies to effectuate the elimination of such programs where they exist.

In 1925, the Commission on Jewish Education, which is composed of some of the leading Reformed rabbis in the United States, unanimously passed a resolution which, while dealing particularly with suggested programs of "released" and "dismissed time" gives some indication of its general view of religious instruction. It explained:

The Commission on Jewish Education endorses the efforts which are being made to procure more time for week-day religious instruction, and we recommend that for such purposes the public schools reduce their time schedule, schools be closed, and that the time thus put at the disposal of the children be used by the parent for their children as they desire.

Furthermore, we are opposed to any form of religious instruction in the American public school system of education or in public buildings, or to any form of classification of children according to their religious affiliation.[42]

In 1947, the Central Conference of American Rabbis (representing the Reformed position) took essentially the same view in opposing religious instruction in the public schools. But they also objected to any "released time" program. They announced their antagonism to "religious inroads in the public school system," and rededicated themselves to "this struggle for the maintenance of the wall of separation between church and state."[43]

The consistency of the Jewish position was demonstrated when again in 1962, the Central Conference of American Rabbis and the National Community Relations Advisory Council took firm positions against "released time" and "shared time" plans for religious studies in the public schools.[44]

In cautioning against the shared time plan for the joint use of parochial and public schools of tax-supported educational facilities, the Reformed Rabbis warned that such a plan would relieve denominational schools of building their own physical education and manual training facilities. Lewis H. Weinstein, President of the National Community Relations Advisory Council, charged that the shared time program would "impair and vitiate our public school system" and that it would be a "tragic betrayal of our public schools."[45]

Lay Group Views

Leo Pfeffer, an officer of the Commission on Law and Social Action of the American Jewish Congress, concluded an investigation of this field by explaining that the disadvantages and dangers far outweigh the benefits.[46] He believes there are four major objections to such practices: the amount of religious education that can possibly be given is negligible; public school authorities often put pressure upon the pupils to attend such courses; occasionally Jewish children attend Christian classes consistently for fear of disclosing their religious difference; finally, the whole theory of these programs is a threat to the principle of the separation of church and state.

Mr. M. R. Konvitz, onetime Secretary of the American Association of Jewish Education, has also been critical of Bible-reading exercises, since he felt they constitute sectarian instruction. He explained:

> There is no such thing as a non-sectarian Bible. The Catholics use the Douay version; the Jews use the Jewish Publications Society's or some other translation of the Old Testament; the Protestants ordinarily use the King James version. These versions vary sharply. . . . To the non-believer, the differences may seem unimportant, but to the adherents of the various faiths the differences are of great significance. The attack on Bible reading, therefore comes not so much from the Godless groups, but from religious groups who justifiably identify Bible reading with Protestantism.[47]

He went on to explain that it was the multiplicity of sects in the United States that led to the principle of church-state separation. He criticized Protestant attempts to dominate the public schools by explaining, "When Protestants argue that the trend today is away from sectarianism toward unity, they mean intra-Protestant sectarianism." This would in effect, "convert the public schools to Protestant parochial schools." He concluded that if the Protestants succeed in capturing the public schools, other religions will withdraw their children from these schools and set up parochial schools. Then, by consolidating their voting powers, they will pass legislation giving public aid to all parochial schools.

This problem has been thoroughly discussed by another well-known Jewish layman. Will Herberg has pointed out that while the public schools are primarily a Protestant creation, the spirit of the public schools today has changed — it is no longer religious but secular.[48] The schools, in other words, have become neutral in matters of religion. Many people, he noted, believe that this is not a true neutrality but is, in fact, a pro-secularist bias. He felt that the opinions of many churchmen and educators were summed up by President Henry Van Dusen of Union Theological Seminary when he said, "Unless religious instruction can be included in the program of the public school, church leaders will be driven increasingly to the expedient of the church sponsored school."

Religion, Herberg stressed, is always one of the prime objects of public education. Furthermore, he did not think that the "high impregnable wall of separation" between church and state ever existed in the United States. To back this, he cited tax exemptions granted to church groups, chaplains in the armed services as well as in the national legislature, and other examples of indirect governmental aid to religion.

Herberg was deeply concerned over the Jewish position toward religious instruction in the public schools. It was in some ways more secular than the Protestants', he felt. The Jews have frequently objected to any religious programs in the schools, even where a common core of religious precepts has been agreed upon by a great majority of the diverse denominations. He disagreed with the Jewish leaders who have maintained that the place for such exercises is in the home. Since the children spend more time in the schools than in the home, he stated, this institution should also have the responsibility of teaching religious values.

Jewish leaders, he feared, are "out-Blansharding Paul Blanshard" when they hold that American democracy should be made the vehicle of a "common American faith."

The insistence upon the secularization of the public schools by Jewish and Protestant groups, Herberg felt, results from their fear of Roman Catholic domination. As far as the Jews are concerned, he believed, this is a shortsighted view since in the long run "Jewish survival is ultimately conceivable only in religious terms." He went on to stress that "a thoroughly 'de-religionized' society would make Jewish existence impossible." The major reason Jews fear Bible-reading exercises in the public schools is that they believe it will be the Christian Bible that will be read. But Herberg himself believes such programs are ineffectual. He stated, "On the question of teaching religion in the public schools, I have yet to see a plan that seems to me wise or practicable, and perhaps there is none." He concluded with a plea for more understanding and tolerance between the various religious denominations, and a curtailment of the stress placed on fear and hysteria in the discussion of such problems.

PROTESTANT ATTITUDES TOWARD BIBLE READING

Any discussion of Protestant views of a point such as this is extremely difficult because of the great variety of sects involved and the congregational organization of many of these denominations. It would be unwise and misleading to speak of *a* Protestant view, or *a* view of one particular sect of Protestants for that matter. Their very individualism makes generalization impossible. We can present characteristic attitudes enunciated by leading individuals and periodicals representing various Protestant groups. The fact that one important clergyman or Protestant organization expresses an opinion on Bible reading should not necessarily be seen as implying that this is the official dogma of the denomination.

Historically, Protestant groups generally have favored Bible-reading programs and have supported actively the introduction of such exercises in the public schools.[49] This was due primarily to the great stress early Protestant denominations in the United States placed on the Bible as a guide for day-to-day living. But while Protestants in general have favored the practice, at least several Protestant sects have been critical of such programs.

Stokes feels that the Universalists, the Unitarians, and occasionally the Lutherans and Baptists are the only large Protestant groups in which opposition to Bible reading has been noted. The Baptists, in particular, are inclined to make a sharp separation between the sacred and secular.[50] But, as we shall see later, individual clergymen and important lay officials of other Protestant congregations have also been critical of Bible-reading programs and religious instruction in the public schools.

A number of years ago, William Thomas Manning, later Bishop of New York, and one of the leading spokesmen for the Episcopal faith in the United States, summed up what might well be the representative attitude of the Protestants who favor Bible-reading exercises. He explained:

> It is idle to say that religion and morality can be taught in Sunday schools or by parents at home. A religion once a week is not the religion of Christians; neither can men be formed and trained by talk on a Sunday afternoon. It needs the constant and continuous action and influence of parents and teachers, from infancy to the age of reason and from the age of reason to the riper years of youth to form the mind, heart, conscience, will, that is the character of a nation.[51]

One of the most extreme enunciations along this line was uttered almost a century ago by the Reverend Julius H. Seelye, Pastor of the First Reformed Church in Schenectady, New York, and Professor of Moral and Mental Philosophy at Amherst College. He stated:

> We come now to notice the objection from conscience to the use of the Bible in schools. It runs in this way; You may not require that the Bible should be read because the Papist, the Jew, the Mohammedan, the infidel, has conscientious scruples against it. The objection may be very summarily answered. The authority of the state may never be subordinated to the individual conscience.[52]

Deets Pickett, noted for his activities on behalf of the Methodist Board of Temperance, Prohibition and Public Morals, explained a point of view apparently held by a number of influential individuals in the Methodist Church.[53] He believed it was impossible to produce a fully rounded American citizen without instruction in the principles of the Bible. He could see no reason why a book that is used in all courts of the land should not be permitted in the schools. He went on to explain:

> The Bible should be studied in our public schools as the life, laws, and literature of an ancient people, as we study the life, laws, and literature of Greece and Rome. Where shall we find more inspiring ideals than in the Old Testament from which our own political ideals have been largely derived? Where a commonwealth better worth our study than the Hebraic Commonwealth, which forbade all caste and class distinctions, required that all people should be equal before the law, provided against an ecclesiastical aristocracy by making the priesthood dependent for their subsistence upon the contributions of the people; surrounded the monarchy with carefully framed constitutional safeguards; organized the government in three departments, legislative, executive and judicial. . . . Where shall we find a simpler and more compact statement of the spirit which should animate and the principles which should control organized society than will be found in the Ten Commandments. . . . Where shall we find nobler spiritual ideals. Where characters,

thoroughly human in their complexity, more worthy of discriminating a study than Moses, Joshua, David, Isaiah in the Old Testament, and Paul in the New Testament?

Pickett continues by showing the paradoxical policy which permits public school pupils to study the pagan religions of Greece and Rome as well as allowing them to study those which worship power and are grounded on fear, but refuses them the opportunity to study that of the Christians and Jews. Students may study the lives of other great men but are prohibited from studying the life of Him, "whom those who are not His disciples call the greatest of the sons of men." He concludes by stating:

> We should all look forward to and work for the day when ecclesiastical prejudices on the one side and the skeptical prejudices on the other give way and the Bible, the most inspiring book of all literature, ancient or modern, is taught in our public schools as the life, literature, and laws of a great people to whom and through whom has come the great moral and spiritual message of the world's redemption.

In 1953, three widely known Lutheran theologians spoke out against "absolute" separation of church and state. This view appears to have some important applications to the subject at hand, and might carry an implied approval of Bible reading. They felt that life cannot be divided into two neatly separated spheres, one ruled by the church into which the state dare not enter, and one ruled by the state where the church may not trespass.[54] Dr. Herman A. Preus of Luther Theological Seminary, St. Paul, Minnesota, Dr. Jaroslav Pelikan of Concordia Theological Seminary, St. Louis, Missouri, and Dr. George W. Forell of Gustavus Adolphus College were the speakers. The schools are affiliated respectively with the Evangelical Lutheran Church, the

Lutheran Church-Missouri Synod and the Augustana Lutheran Church. They believed that absolute double-standard type spheres of influence will create a double standard of morality and thus, "rob the state of the saving influence of Christian citizens."

Representative Attitudes of Clergymen

While the very structure of the United Church of Christ does not lend itself to any official pronouncements regarding such practices as Bible reading, one influential and well-known clergyman of this faith looks with favor on such programs. The Reverend Albert W. Swan, Pastor of the First Congregational Church in Madison, Wisconsin, when interviewed, stated that in his opinion some of the general elements of the Bible should be included in at least the elementary public schools. He felt that the aesthetic and literary beauties of this book should be a part of every child's education, and every child should be acquainted with the fundamentals of the Judean-Christian religion.[55]

Customs in different sections of the country vary, he noted, for while such exercises are commonly accepted in the eastern part of the United States, the practice never has become as prevalent in the Middle West. As a result of this, he explained, custom and opinion vary also in the United Church of Christ denomination. Reverend Swan admitted that administration of such programs is difficult since the mere choice of a Bible version denotes sectarianism to some people, but he did not feel such difficulties were insurmountable.

Charles Perrin, Educational Director of Christ Presbyterian Church, Madison, Wisconsin, when interviewed, stated that the Presbyterian Church had taken no official stand regarding Bible-reading exercises.[56] He explained that while important churchmen in this denomination wished for some way in which the public schools might impart religious and moral values, they take a dim view of the manner in which Bible-reading religious programs are frequently conducted in the public schools where programs of this nature are legal. Teachers who are indifferent or opposed to such exercises may, when directing them, do more harm than good, and actually subvert the beauty and importance of the Bible in the pupil's eyes. This may be accomplished by using apathetic or sarcastic mannerisms, as well as deliberately choosing controversial passages with an eye toward stirring up sectarian debates.

The consensus among leading Presbyterians, according to Mr. Perrin, seems to favor a type of "dismissed" or "released time" program. This would enable students to learn of the Bible's significance and beauty under tutelage of trained personnel who are members of their own faith. This would not only be a more effective program of religious instruction, but would also avoid injuring any student's religious sensibilities, as general programs of Bible reading and religious instruction in the public schools are wont to do.

C. P. Taft, onetime President of the Federated Council of Churches of Christ, has formulated a series of proposals to meet what he conceives to be a lack of religious instruction in the public schools.[57] He suggests, first, that we pick and train teachers with a personal religion. They would be, in effect, a type of nondenominational chaplain. Secondly, he feels the schools should teach all three of the world's

great religions — Judaism, Christianity, and Islam. All have
as their central dogma the belief in one God. The schools
should include in their nonreligious courses a maximum of
religious material of a noncontroversial nature. This would
be done only after reaching an agreement among the major
faiths regarding the subject matter.[58]

He goes on to voice his opposition to parochial schools
for their divisive influence, and suggests programs of "dismissed time" religious instruction to meet the religious
needs of pupils in the public schools. He concludes by stating that there is a great need for a real process of religious
education in the church school, for he believes they have
not been successful in imparting the importance and beauty
of the scriptures.[59]

In 1949, the meeting of the International Council of
Religious Education had as its major problem for discussion the question of religion and the public schools. While
it was primarily concerned with the consequences of the Mc-
Collum case, some interesting views on religious instruction were also enunciated. The report that emerged from
the conference started out by stressing, "Religion and education are inseparably related and any attempt to separate
them does violence to both."[60] A hope was expressed that
some public educational program could be evolved that
would have at its core an emphasis on the belief in God
as the source of all spiritual values and material goods. The
report concluded by stating that the public schools should
teach ". . . the common religious tradition as the only adequate basis for the life of the school and the personal lives
of the teachers, students and citizens in a free and responsible democracy."

The National Council of Churches' Statements

One of the most important Protestant pronouncements regarding religion and public education was made by the National Council of Churches on December 13, 1952. In a "Letter to the Christian People of America" the National Council warned that unless religion is restored to its rightful place in the social and educational areas of American life, the United States will eventually become a secular state capable of committing "satanic crimes."[61] The Council represents nearly 35,000,000 churchgoers affiliated with thirty Protestant groups and Eastern Orthodox bodies. This message was drafted by the Reverend John A. Mackay, head of the Princeton Theological Seminary. The New York *Times* reports that the message was viewed by many church leaders as similar to the Roman Catholic hierarchy's statement made a month earlier.[62]

A secular state, defined by the "Letter," is one that depreciates religion and exalts irreligion. To prevent this, the Council of Churches suggested that religion play an ever-widening role in education. It was suggested that Christian institutions and teachers should be "challenged to make their contribution toward the formulation of a Christian philosophy of life." Of particular interest to this study was the suggestion that a "reverent reading" of biblical passages in the public schools would go a long way toward deepening the awareness of God in the public schools:

> It is impossible to overemphasize the importance of the Bible in human history and the decisive influence which the popular knowledge of the Book has had on the cultural life of mankind. The decisive difference between religions, as between cultures, is the place which a given religion or culture has accorded the Bible. . . . It is,

moreover, an inspiring fact that the book from which we receive our religious faith is also the chief cultural monument in English letters.

The "Letter" sought a way to make pupils aware of the "heritage of faith upon which the nation was established and which has been the most transforming influence in western culture." The hope was expressed that a constitutional way will be found for the inculcation of the principles of religion either on or off the school precincts. At one point, however, the message took issue with the Roman Catholic Statement of November, 1952. Where the Catholics found the public schools dangerously secularized, this body stated, "It is unfair to say that where religion is not taught in a public school, the school is secular or Godless." It goes on to explain, "The moral and cultural atmosphere in a school and the attitudes, the viewpoints, and the character of the teachers can be religious and exert a religious influence without religion being necessarily taught as a subject." (There are those who might feel that this attitude conflicts with the one mentioned above regarding Bible reading.)

Finally the message emphasized that the state should continue to allow religious bodies freedom to carry on their own schools, but went on to state:

> Those who promote parochial schools should accept the responsibility to provide full support for those schools, and not expect to receive subsidies or special privileges from public authorities. . . . The subsidization of education carried on under religious auspices would both violate the principle of separation of church and state and be a devastating blow to the public school system, which must at all costs be maintained.

The solution to the problem, the "Letter" concluded, lies in loyal support of our public schools and increasing their awareness of God, rather than in state support of parochial schools.

On May 20, 1953, the National Council of Churches issued an official Pronouncement on *Church-State Issues in Religion and Public Education.* A Pronouncement is defined by the National Council of Churches as: "a statement of policy, or an affirmation of conviction formally approved by the General Board or General Assembly. It expresses a substantial preponderance of the General Board opinion that there is a strong weight of ethical, moral, or religious principles in support of the views expressed."

At the outset, the Pronouncement noted with appreciation the organization's general declaration of faith in the public schools. It went on to stress that the home and the school must bear primary responsibility as teachers of religion. It next expressed the conviction that no agency of the state, including the school, "can safely or wisely be entrusted to the task of being a teacher of religion."

Nonetheless, the Pronouncement went on to explain, the public schools have a responsibility with respect to the religious foundations of our national culture. It was emphasized that the nation subsists "under the governance of God and that it is not morally autonomous." The schools, it argued, "can do much in teaching about religion, in adequately affirming that religion has been and is an essential function in our cultural heritage."

The Pronouncement denied that such an approach would violate the separation of church and state, or that it impaired the responsibility of the church and the home in this area. It voiced the belief that as "committed persons teach in or administer the public schools, they can exert religious influence by their character and behavior." Impartial observers might conclude that under this approach, the unbelievers' lot would be an unhappy one.

Some eight years later in its Pronouncement on Public Funds for Public Schools issued on February 22, 1962, the National Council of Churches again offered its heartiest endorsement to the nation's public schools. But it went on to say that: "We stand for the right of all parents, all citizens, and all churches to establish and maintain nonpublic schools whose ethos and curriculum differ from that of the community as a whole."

But, as if to compound the confusion, the next paragraph in the Pronouncement noted: "But we believe that to encourage such a general development (i.e., where the public school system has become inimical to the Christian education of children) would be tragic in its results to the American people."

Understanding of the organization's stand on specific programs is not notably enhanced when the Pronouncement concluded:

> We do not, however, ask for public funds for elementary or secondary education under church control. If private schools were to be supported in the United States by tax funds, the practical effect would be that the American people would lose their actual control of the use of the taxes paid by all people for the purposes common to the whole society. We therefore do not consider it just or lawful that public funds should be assigned to support the elementary or secondary schools of any church.

The Pronouncement suggested that if public funds are used to support elementary and secondary education, other religious groups would be encouraged to establish parochial schools. If this occurred, it would result in the further fragmentation of general education in the United States, the

Council of Churches felt. And this would gravely weaken or even destroy the public school system in the United States.

Some observers might conclude that if the foregoing is a sample of the consensus of a widely based clerical organization toward programs of religious exercises in the public schools, it is small wonder that the Supreme Court of the United States has shied away from putting its stamp of approval on specific programs involving allegedly religious or moral programs in the public schools.

Nonetheless, the organization went on record in this Pronouncement as opposing governmental grants to non-public schools. It further opposed payment of public funds for the tuition of children attending private or parochial schools, and opposed tax credits and exemptions from school taxes for those parents whose children attended nonpublic schools.

OTHER PROTESTANT VIEWS TOWARD CHURCH-STATE RELATIONS

In the past there have been, and there are now, influential Protestant clergymen and laymen who disagree with the general Protestant policy which endorses Bible-reading programs. Their views are not necessarily official pronouncements for their Church as a whole, but in most cases are expressions of personal opinions by men with a great deal of prestige in their field. Thus, while such influence is difficult to evaluate, it cannot be ignored.

Ten years after the Civil War, the Reverend Samuel T. Spear, Pastor of South Presbyterian Church in Brooklyn, and a member of the editorial staff of the liberal religious journal, *The Independent,* explained what he conceived to be the role of the public schools.

> The public school, like the state under whose authority
> it exists, and by whose taxing power it is supported,
> should be simply a civil institution, absolutely secular and
> not at all religious in its purposes, and all practical ques-
> tions involving this principle should be settled in accord-
> ance therewith.[63]

It should be noted that this was written at a period of time
when there was a bitter controversy raging in the United
States over Roman Catholic attacks upon the public
schools.[64]

A number of years later, the Reverend Shailer Mathews
looked unfavorably upon the general practice of Bible reading in public schools. Reverend Mathews was an educator
and clergyman, heading the Federal Council of Churches
of Christ (1912–1916), the Northern Baptist Convention
(1915), as well as being the Dean of the University of Chicago's Divinity School until 1933, and Editor of the *Biblical
World* (1913–1920). He felt that while everyone wishes his
children to learn ethics and morals, it does not follow that
a school teaching Bible reading will achieve this end.[65]
Most schools, Reverend Mathews believed, are incapable of
doing a decent job of Bible study. He explained:

> I can imagine a school in which such instruction could
> be imparted, but I am equally convinced that such a
> school would be exceptional and, as a rule, impossible.
> Something more than a perfunctory reading of certain
> selected passages is implied by such an ideal state of
> affairs. Such a school would be taught by a teacher thor-
> oughly in sympathy with the spirit of revelation, and one
> further possessed of at least the rudiments of training in
> the study and teaching of the Bible.

He went on to point out that teaching the Bible is
quite different from using the Bible for devotional studies.
In the latter case, a reasonably reverent attitude would have
to be adopted by the teacher. To have the Bible taught uni-

versally, he thinks, is to put a premium upon its misuse and would aid in creating false ideas as to its significance. The reasons for this are that some public school teachers do not believe in the Bible. Others have ideas of the Bible that are very crude and their instructions might create a prejudice against the Bible. Finally, the mere choice of one version of the Bible would cause disagreement among citizens of different sects.

Teaching the Bible for literary reasons, according to Reverend Mathews, was worse than not teaching it at all — even though it may be good literature. He thought it was prostituting the Bible to use it to understand Milton or Ruskin. Finally, he demonstrated that in the experience of the countries that have tried Bible reading, such programs were unsatisfactory to all concerned. He concluded by stating that elementary morals may be taught without the use of the Bible. Thus, all of these objections would be avoided, and instruction in the Bible could best be left to the church and the parents.

Herman H. Horne, also writing in the *Biblical World,* opposed Bible-reading exercises in our public schools because they violated the principle of absolute respect for freedom of religious conscience, which is a fundamental doctrine in the United States.[66] The Bible cannot help but be regarded as a sectarian book, Horne believed. To teach sectarian religion in our schools is fatal to the freedom of conscience which our government cherishes. He is forced to conclude:

> Any attempt to formulate a non-sectarian religion of essentials upon which the sects would agree as suitable to teach is impossible; at least, it is what the human ages have been unable to do. Since, therefore, any academic use of the Bible involves religious teaching, and religious

teaching has no place in American public schools, we must conclude that the academic use of the Bible has no place in these schools. Such an academic use is proper, indeed necessary, in all the non-state social organizations, like home and church, and this present widespread interest in Bible reading in the public schools will result in great good, if only to serve to shift the same demand to these other really liable organizations.

Baptist Views

A most significant objection from an organized religious group was issued several years ago by the Baptist General Association of Virginia. Retired Governor John Garland Pollard drafted the memorial, which was duly adopted and presented to the Virginia legislature. Some credit it with defeating proposed legislation which would have compelled public school teachers to read the Bible in school.[67] The statement pointed out that the "Bible is distinctly a religious book, and when properly read is an act of worship which cannot rightfully be enforced by law."[68] It went on to note significant differences between the various versions of the Bible, and explained that the bill tacitly accepted the sectarian nature of the Bible by providing that it must be read without comment and that pupils may be excused from such reading by presenting a written excuse from their parents. "Some argue," the memorial pointed out,

> . . . that the law should compel the reading of the Bible, not as a religious book, but simply as literature. But this is evidently not the view-point of the proponents of the bill for, as if to minimize the wrong done sects who do not accept our Bible, they limit the reading to five verses, prohibit comment, and excuse pupils from attendance upon the reading. . . .

The statement made it clear that the Baptists were in accord with proponents of the bill in their belief in the importance of training our children in the great religious truths taught in the Bible. The only difference was one of method. But it explained, "[T]hat method involves a great underlying principle which is part of our religious as well as our political faith. . . ." It also pointed out that Baptists would suffer no direct injury if the bill were passed, but Baptists knew from history what discrimination against their religion was, and were not anxious to extend discrimination against other sects today. The memorial closed with an exhortation to the legislature to keep intact the historic wall of separation between church and state.[69]

It was noted previously that the Baptist Joint Committee on Public Affairs criticized the Roman Catholic hierarchy's statement of November, 1952, which urged an increase in religious instruction in the public schools. The Baptist group believed that such practices would violate the Constitutional mandate for the separation of church and state. In a discussion with this writer, the Reverend George L. Collins, of the Baptist Student Center of the University of Wisconsin, also agreed that Baptists generally are opposed to the practice of Bible reading and religious instruction in the public schools.[70] He did not feel, however, that criticizing such programs as sectarian was justified by the facts. Nor did he believe that a given version of the Bible is necessarily sectarian when read to public school students belonging to a variety of denominations.

His objection to such exercises was directed to the type of teacher who frequently is called upon to conduct these programs. A teacher who is opposed or apathetic toward such instruction may create in the students a dislike or a thorough misunderstanding regarding the truths and literary beauty of the Bible.

In June of 1962, C. Emanuel Carlson, Executive Director of the Baptist Joint Committee on Public Affairs, made public the fact that this organization had placed the problem of proper religious expression in the public schools on the agenda for its October, 1962, meeting.[71] In the meantime, while making it clear he spoke only for himself, Mr. Carlson felt constrained to make some general comments on the subject. At the outset he observed that the true friends of "genuine prayer experience must obviously be cautious about the devising of prayers by governmental agencies." He thought it unfortunate that all too frequently the issue emerging out of discussion over the Supreme Court's decision in the Engel case was mistakenly the question of whether one is for prayer or against it.

"When one thinks of prayer as a sincere outreach of a human soul to the Creator," Mr. Carlson explained, " 'required prayer' becomes an absurdity." He felt that all too frequently those who insist that prayer recitation is "morally uplifting," fail to recognize that "hypocrisy is the worst of moral corrosion." Moreover, he replied to those who feel our national heritage is in danger, they fail to realize that the distinctive quality of our heritage is not legislated prayer, but rather a people praying in freedom under the guidance of their church and of the Spirit of God.

Mr. Carlson called attention to the paradoxes in the present debate, when many of the people who are crying for "less government" are the same ones who publicly defend a governmentally formulated prayer. He is emphatic in his hope that the Supreme Court will continue to defend both the "Establishment of Religion" and the "Free Exercise of Religion" clauses of the First Amendment. In conclusion he said: "The issues of our day, including the problems of Communism and secularization, will not be solved by the prayer formulas set up by official agencies. As Americans we must go deeper than legislation and conformity in order to meet the call of God upon us in our day."[72]

It seems fair to conclude that the Baptists, more than any other Protestant group, have a reasonably definite program of opposition to Bible reading and religious exercises in the public schools.

Presbyterian Views

During the last decade the Presbyterians have manifested a considerable interest in church-state relations especially as they affect the public schools. During this period, this denomination has revealed a notably consistent point of view on the subject and has produced several noteworthy documents dealing with the problem.

In 1957, the 169th General Assembly of the Presbyterian Church issued an official statement called "The Church and the Public Schools." In the portion dealing with "Religion in the School Curriculum," the statement objected vigorously to the "unwarranted criticism" heaped on the schools because some people allege they are Godless.[73] Such criticism resulted from an inadequate understanding of the position of public schools in our society, it was thought. Furthermore, the statement insisted, we must remember that "the inclusion of an overt religious observance of religion does not necessarily provide any institution with a dynamic religious character."

It goes on to express doubt as to whether the public schools can really do a proper job of teaching religion, because of the fundamentally sectarian nature of religion. Thus, "the Presbyterian Church along with those of other persuasions must supply their own instruction in the areas of revelation and grace." It goes on to warn that "Protestants must always be on guard against what might happen if sectarian teaching were imposed upon the schools of America." It cautions Presbyterians not to betray the "genius of the public schools, nor yet be mesmerized by the fatal assumption that the church can delegate its responsibility to any institution in order to make up for the prevalence of religious illiteracy."

Moreover, in a comment which might be applied to general prayer programs in the schools similar to those that the Supreme Court held unconstitutional in New York State, the Presbyterian statement noted: "While we neither expect nor desire any teacher to indoctrinate any form of sectarianism, neither do we countenance the teaching of a devitalized 'common faith' as a proper substitute for highly specific religious belief." On the other hand, the statement makes it clear that the church is not suggesting eliminating references to the religious backgrounds of our heritage.

An especially noteworthy and thoughtful report was submitted in 1962 to the 174th General Assembly of the Presbyterian Church by its special committee on Church and State. Entitled "Relations Between Church and State," its section dealing with suggested ground rules for members of the church to follow when becoming involved in discussions or debates over church-state relations might well serve as a guide-book for all persons concerned with the field of human relations. While not purporting to be an authoritative statement of the church's position, the report suggests that its major purpose is "to indicate a sense of direction for further study by United Presbyterians and others, and to provide certain guidelines for study and action on issues of urgent import to our church and society."[74]

Although dealing with a great variety of subjects, the Report has some specific recommendations on the subject of Bible reading in the public schools. It recognized that the public schools can justify their existences solely in terms of their usefulness to the whole society. Moreover, it is pointed out that the public schools should neither be hostile to religious beliefs nor act in any manner which tends to favor one religion or church over another. On this basis the Report goes on to recommend:

> Religious observances should never be held in a public school or introduced in the program of the public school. Bible reading (except in connection with courses in literature, history, or related subjects) and public prayers tend toward indoctrination or meaningless ritual and should be omitted for both reasons.[75]

Methodist Reactions

The position of Methodists toward Bible reading and related exercises in the school is not completely clear. The most authoritative statement of their views on the general area of religion and the public schools is found in Paragraph 2028 of the *Doctrines and Disciplines of the Methodist Church* (1960).

This section provides that the church is committed to the public schools as the "most effective means of providing common education" for all children. And, while recognizing the public schools as essential to democracy, it is also noted that "our public schools are hard pressed." The paragraph then explains why: "Public tax funds, in increasing sums, are diverted to sectarian schools. Opponents of the public schools call the schools 'Godless' while at the same time legal restrictions are placed upon the recognition of religion in the schools."[76]

This section suggests that there is no ambivalence in this church's position toward the parochial school: "We are unalterably opposed to the diversion of tax funds to the support of private and sectarian schools. In a short time, this scattering process can destroy our American public school system and weaken the foundations of national unity."

Undoubtedly, some people will view the next section of this paragraph as somewhat paradoxical when compared to the above statement concerning sectarian schools. It announces:

> We believe that religion has a rightful place in the public school program, and that it is possible for public school teachers, without violating the traditional American principle of separation of church and state, to teach moral principles and spiritual values. We hold that it is possible, within this same principle of separation of church and state, to integrate religious instruction with the regular curriculum — for example, teaching religious classics in courses in literature, and in social studies showing the influence of religion upon our society.[77]

While agreeing that the home and church must bear the chief responsibility for nurturing faith, this paragraph insists that the home and church need the support of the school. It is up to our society, it is concluded, to discover the techniques within the principle of separation between church and state by which this support can be accomplished.

From this provision, one would have difficulty concluding, with any degree of definiteness, whether the Methodist Church actually supports programs of Bible reading in the schools.

Bishop G. Bromley Oxnam of the Methodist Church, when discussing the role of religion in the public schools, has been particularly critical of the Roman Catholic attitudes on the subject. He believes the Catholics, through the use of the term "secularism," have created a smokescreen behind which they operate in their endeavors to destroy the American principle of separation of church and state.[78] It is in this manner, he explains, that the Catholics seek to draw off public funds for parochial schools and thus weaken and destroy the public schools which they vehemently oppose. He quotes Paul L. Blakely, S. J., as saying a Catholic's first duty to the public schools is not to pay taxes to them. Bishop Oxnam stresses that the public schools are the bulwark of democracy, for people of all faiths may attend. Furthermore, he denies the Catholic contention that tax-supported schools have banned religion. He points out that there is:

> . . . no constitutional prohibition of the study of religion in the public schools. The difficulty stems rather from denominational differences and insistences upon a particular emphasis. The place of religion, of all religion in history, sociology, art, music, literature must be known by all educated men and women. To rear youth without knowledge of the place of religion in life is to educate but partially. But church and synagogue do more than study religion as a subject; they seek commitment to it as a faith. This is not the function of the school.

Bishop Oxnam views with favor the American Council of Education's report on "The Relation of Religion to Public Education" which states that the school should seek to teach the importance of the role of religion in our history and culture. He concludes by stressing that the place

of religion in the public schools could be worked out demo-
cratically without difficulty if it were not for sectarian
strife.[79]

Methodist Bishop Corson, however, in an address to
the Biennial Christian Education Convention of the Methodist Church in Grand Rapids, Michigan, in December of
1949, stated that the public school had ceased to be an
ally of the church.[80] He felt that the present educational
system was actually an obstacle to adequate religious education, whereas until recently the public school was an important factor in the communication of religious knowledge.

The Christian Century's Viewpoint

For these sentiments, Reverend Corson was taken to
task by an editorial in the *Christian Century*.[81] The editors
felt the Bishop was in error at every point. They explained:

> In the first place the free public school is an ally of the
> church, even though it is rightly prevented from becom-
> ing the tool of any church. Its objective of helping the
> child to know the truth is essentially religious. Its cul-
> tivation of the free intellect and its program of character
> education are strong counterparts of what the church in
> its own sphere should try to do. The 'exclusion and sepa-
> ration' which the Bishop regards as an 'obstacle' to Chris-
> tian education were forced on the public schools by the
> differences between the churches. In spite of this, the
> schools are still capable of communicating and are com-
> municating the factual basis about religion in literature,
> history and other fields. An obstacle to Christian edu-
> cation much bigger than these fancied failings of the
> public schools is an attitude on the part of Protestant
> church leaders which refuses to recognize how great a
> stake Protestantism has in the preservation and extension
> of the public school system.

In 1952, the *Christian Century* was also critical of the
New York State Board of Regents' proposed nonsectarian
prayer to be used in the New York public schools (See Engel

case).[82] The editorial noted that the American Civil Liberties Union and the American Jewish Congress had voiced opposition to such a plan. These organizations felt this program would be ineffective in practice, wrong in principle, and dangerous in its implications. Furthermore, they believed, it would infringe on religious liberty and the historic American principle of the separation of church and state. The editors of the *Christian Century* did not share the fears of the previously mentioned groups that such a program would violate the United States Constitution. But they agreed with the American Jewish Congress,

> . . . observance of this sort is likely to deteriorate quickly into an empty formality with little if any significance. Prescribed forms of this sort, as many colleges have concluded after years of compulsory chapel attendance, can actually work against the inculcation of vital religion. This is one of the reasons (among others) why this paper has never had any sympathy for attempts to reproduce in American schools classes in religious education patterned after European models. . . . There are few places where it is more true than in school religious exercises that 'the letter killeth but the Spirit giveth life.'

A later editorial devoted to this same proposal in New York noted the problems religious groups encountered when attempting to agree upon a type of prayer acceptable to all.[83] Since these organizations were unanimously opposed to the prayer suggested by the regents, a compromise was finally reached whereby it was agreed to have students recite the last stanza of "America."

> Our Father's God to Thee
> Author of Liberty,
> To Thee we sing:
> Long May our Land be bright
> With Freedom's Holy Light:
> Protect us by Thy Might,
> Great God our King.

The editors objected to this proposal, wondering, "But when youngsters are induced to pray to God on the assumption that they are sharing in a patriotic exercise, what is the religion that is being exalted? Nationalism?"[84]

Finally, the attitudes of one more group of Protestants who take an unfavorable view toward the inculcation of religion in the public schools should be noted. The Protestants and Other Americans United for the Separation of Church and State have not only bitterly assailed Catholics for suggesting there is no historical basis to the theory of church-state separation, but they also objected to Protestant groups who attempted to violate the principle by favoring "released time" and other religious programs in the public schools.[85] This organization feels that when the Protestant denominations engage in these activities, they are simply following a mistaken notion of their theological dogmas. But the Catholics, they believe, are serious and consistent in their desire to have the public schools teach religion. It is this group's sincere belief that the churches must stay out of the schools. They are "opposed to a union of church and state wherever it appears and by whomever it is sponsored, whether by Protestants, Catholics or Jews."

From the foregoing survey, it is clear that while Protestants historically have been primarily concerned with sponsoring Bible reading and other programs of religious instruction in the public schools, today there is no clear-cut consensus in their attitudes on such programs. All agree that the imparting of religious and moral values is important, but there is no agreement on how this is to be done and whether or not the public school is the proper vehicle for such instruction.

CLERGY'S RESPONSE TO THE SCHEMPP CASE

The reactions of religious leaders to the Schempp decision were, as might be expected, mixed. The responses of a majority of spokesmen for religious groups, the New York *Times* found, were in favor of the decision.[86] Again it is well to recall that most often the comments of an important clergyman on matters of this sort cannot necessarily be construed to constitute the official position of his church. In some instances the church, in fact, may have no official position. In general, however, it can be said that Protestants and Jews tended to support the court's position while Roman Catholic spokesmen deplored it.

For the most part, Roman Catholic leaders tended to view the Schempp ruling with alarm. Three of the five American Roman Catholic Cardinals, in a statement from Rome where they were attending the Ecumenical Council, vigorously opposed the Supreme Court's position. In a joint statement, Cardinal Spellman of New York, Richard Cardinal Cushing of Boston, and James Francis Cardinal McIntyre of Los Angeles took the court sharply to task for the Schempp ruling.[87] Also in Rome, at the same time, and in an interview for the New York *Times,* Albert Gregory Cardinal Meyer of Chicago had "no immediate comment," and Joseph Cardinal Ritter of St. Louis was not available for comment.

Msgr. John J. Voight, Secretary for Education of the Roman Catholic Archdiocese of New York, observed that the ruling came as no surprise and asserted: "I deeply regret the court action. I say this for two reasons: one, because it will bring about the complete secularization of public education in America, which to me represents a radical departure from our traditional and historical religious heritage, and, two, because it completely disregards parental rights in education and the wishes of a large segment of America's parents who want their children to participate in these practices in the public schools."[88]

The Archbishop of Washington, D.C., the Most Reverend Patrick O'Boyle said: "The Supreme Court's decision is disappointing. It is obvious that little by little it is discarding religious traditions hallowed by a century and a half of American practice."[89] In the Middle West, however, Msgr. Edmund J. Goebel, Superintendent of Schools of the Milwaukee Roman Catholic Archdiocese described his position as "not outright critical, but fearful of the results it might have." He said: "Every effort should be made to retain the teaching of God in all our schools, public and private. This decision of the Court might interfere with that. If God is completely ignored, we will go into complete secularism. That would have its effect on our growing youth."[90]

Although a preponderance of Protestant spokesmen and groups tended to support the Supreme Court's position, some were sharply critical. The New York *Times* concluded that "conservative Protestants, members of small fundamentalist bodies or minority groups in the large denominations, deplored the Court action."[91] In what the *Times* called a surprising reaction, Methodist Bishop Fred Pierce Corson, President of the World Methodist Council, took issue with the Schempp ruling. He declared that it "penalized" the "religious people who are very definitely in the majority in the United States." Bishop Corson went on to predict that the decision would mark the beginning of a "new movement among Protestants and Catholics for parochial education simply to protect their children from a growing secularism which now seems to have invaded the courts."[92]

Another example of a representative of a major Protestant group who was critical of the court's stand was Bishop Donald H. V. Hallock of the Milwaukee Episcopal Diocese. He said of the Schempp decision: "I don't agree with it and I don't like it, but it cannot be denied that this is the next logical step in the direction the Court has been going." He concluded with the observation, "one of these days, no doubt, 'In God We Trust' will go off our coinage."[93]

Representatives of the mainstream of Protestant thinking, however, hailed the Schempp ruling. The National Council of Churches, which reflects this consensus, asserted that the decision served as a reminder to all citizens that "teaching for religious commitment is the responsibility of the home and the community of faith (such as church or synagogue) rather than the public school." The council also noted that "neither the church nor state should use the public school to compel acceptance of any creed or conformity to any specific religious practice."[94] Furthermore, the Council of Churches had noted somewhat earlier that "neither true religion nor good education is dependent upon the devotional use of the Bible in public school programs."[95]

Another point of view in the Methodist Church is reflected by the position taken by the Board of Christian Social Concerns of the New York East Conference of the Methodist Church which is diametrically opposed to the position of Bishop Corson, noted earlier. In supporting the court ruling the Board's statement said: "Increasingly in the section of the country where we serve, there are no public schools which are homogeneous in respect to religion to the degree that religious observance of any sort would not offend the taste or violate the conscience of some individual."[96]

A high-level statement of the Episcopal Church was given by the Right Reverend Arthur Lichtenberger, Presiding Bishop of the Episcopal Church. He emphasized: "it should be understood that the Court's action is not hostile to religion." He went on to note that the decision reflects "the Court's sense of responsibility to assure freedom and equality to all groups of believers and non-believers as expressed in the First Amendment of the Constitution."[97]

In an action consistent with their church's position outlined several years earlier, two leaders of the United Presbyterian Church strongly supported the Schempp decision. The Reverend Doctor Eugene Carson Blake and the Reverend Doctor Silas G. Kessler, moderator, in a joint statement noted that the court's ruling had "underscored our firm belief that religious instruction is the sacred responsibility of the family and the Churches."[98] In the Middle West, the Reverend Edgar G. Bletcher, minister of the West Granville Presbyterian Church and stated clerk of the Presbytery of Milwaukee of the United Presbyterian Church, read a statement of the General Assembly of that denomination which said: "Bible reading and prayers as devotional acts tend toward indoctrination of meaningless ritual and should be omitted for both reasons." Reverend Bletcher concluded, ". . . whenever the same prayer is offered every morning in a school, it tends toward meaningless ritual, and where there are students of non-Christian religions present, it can be considered an affront to their beliefs."[99]

Lutheran spokesmen tended to be consistent in support of the court's action. The Reverend Oscar J. Nauman, President of the Wisconsin Evangelical Lutheran Synod, which maintains an extensive parochial school system of its own, strongly endorsed the court ruling. He said, "It has long been our position as a synod that the exercise of any religious function — and prayer and Bible reading are to us a religious function — falls within the province of the family and church and is not the concern of the state as such."

A representative of another Lutheran body, The Lutheran Church of America, the Reverend Doctor Theodore E. Matson, President of the Wisconsin-Upper Michigan Synod expressed similar sentiments. "Personally," he observed, "I cannot get excited about prohibiting the reading of the Bible or praying the Lord's Prayer in public schools." Although expressing his concern about the "increasing climate of secularism," Dr. Matson noted that the court decision "serves as a reminder to the churches to take seriously their responsibility in regard to solid Christian education." He went on to make a most interesting observation. "Schools," he said, "must also make sure that they do not impose upon the time of children and youth with the result that the churches are placed at a real disadvantage." He concluded, "The time may come when the Supreme Court may have to rule on how much of the time of the children and youth the schools can command."[100]

The opinion of Jewish religious leaders was overwhelmingly favorable to the Schempp ruling. The Synagogue Council of America, representing Orthodox, Reform, and Conservative Judaism, through its president, Rabbi Uri Miller, said: "We fervently believe that prayers, Bible reading and sectarian practices should be fostered in the home, church and synagogue, that public institutions such as the public school should be free of such practices."[101] The New York *Times* reported that a host of other Jewish groups hailed the decision. These included: The Rabbinical Council of America, the American Jewish Committee, the Central Conference of American Rabbis, the Union of American Hebrew Congregations, the American Jewish Congress, and the United Synagogue of America.

7

Educator Attitudes

THE VIEWS OF EDUCATORS are as widely divergent as those presented by religious spokesmen. It would be impossible, without the benefit of a super-poll, to obtain exact statistics on the percentage of American educators who favor or oppose such practices. An attempt is made here simply to present a representative sampling of the various attitudes expressed in a variety of journals and periodicals. Prior to the 1840's and the rapid influx of Catholic immigrants, few public school teachers could object to reading the King James Version of the Bible for reasons of conscience, since the majority were Protestants.[1]

Characteristic of the attitude of early teachers' organizations was that of the Western Literary Institute and College of Professional Teachers. This group, which had great influence in the Midwest, favored from the beginning (1829) religious education in the public schools, with the Bible as a reading book "from the infant school to the University." It was this group's policies and proposals that Bishop Purcell objected to in 1873. From approximately this time on there were increased efforts by legislatures and school boards to eliminate sectarian instruction, although many did not consider Bible reading and related religious exercises as sectarian. It is, of course, because many people do not regard Bible reading as sectarian instruction that so much controversy has arisen over this point.

VIEWS OF UNITED STATES COMMISSIONERS OF EDUCATION

It was in the last decade of the nineteenth century that debate among educators on the efficacy of Bible reading and religious instruction in the public schools really began. This has since become one of the major points of discussion at teachers' conventions and educational association meetings.[2] The United States Commissioners of Education allowed themselves to get drawn into this controversy during this period. In 1889, Austin Bierbower pointed out that it is unnecessary to teach religion in the public schools because there are abundant opportunities elsewhere for such instruction.[3] The Sunday school, church, and home were the places to instill religious instruction. If the schools attempted to teach religious principles, such practices woud invariably lead to sectarian disputes. The Commissioner explained:

> There is no occasion for even using the Bible in the schools. While it might be used without any influence whatever, good or bad, it can be read elsewhere abundantly, and is read in the family, in the Sunday schools, and in the churches almost daily, and is constantly discussed and quoted, so that people are not left in ignorance of it. With an open Bible everywhere the Protestants ought not to insist on forcing it into the schools to the irritation of Catholics, Jews and unbelievers. . . . The fact that some regard it as a revelation from God does not justify them in forcing it on others who do not so regard it, or who believe it can not be safely read by the people. Protestants who think the Bible is not sufficiently read can

teach it more at home, and in church. . . . There is not enough to be gained from Bible reading to justify the quarrel that has been raised over it.

Finally he believed that the influence of the Bible would not be diminished if it were excluded from the school. He flatly denied that this would make the school Godless, for it was not the duty of public schools to teach religion. "One might as well call insurance companies or banks 'Godless' because they have nothing to do with religion, or to speak of 'Godless' kite-flying or musical festivals." He concluded by stressing that since all religions teach the same virtues — truth, honesty, purity, etc. — and since all men agree on these, it logically followed that schools could effectively teach moral and ethical values without engaging in religious instruction and exercises.

A number of years later, William P. Harris, who was then United States Commissioner of Education, agreed that it was inadvisable to attempt to have religious instruction in the public schools.[4] The techniques necessary for this instruction were inconsistent with those used in the public schools. He stated:

> The principle of religious instruction is authority; that of secular instruction is demonstration and verification. It is obvious that these two principles should not be brought into the same school, but separated as widely as possible . . . . Even the attitude of a mind cultivated in secular instruction is unfitted for the approach to religious truth. Religious instruction should be surrounded with solemnity. It should be approached with ceremonial preparations so as to lift up the mind to the dignity of the lesson received.

Harris also believed that almost every type of religious instruction was a form of sectarian instruction. "Even the doctrine of the existence of God implies a specific conception of Him, and the conception of the divine varies from that of the finite deities of animism to the infinite deity of East Indian pantheism and the Holy Bible." He finished by explaining that only the church has learned the proper method of religious instruction, and this was accomplished only after long ages. It is able to elevate the sense-perception through solemn music addressed to the ear and works of art which represent to the eye the divine self-sacrifice for the salvation of man. "It clothes its doctrines in the language of the Bible, a book sacredly kept apart from other literature, and held in such exceptional reverence that it is taken entirely out of the natural order of experience."

At least one United States Commissioner of Education took a more favorable view of religious exercises, and Bible reading in particular. A. P. Peabody felt that asking the American people to exclude the Bible from public schools would be "garbling and truncating history."[5] He believed that the Bible is very important in teaching not only Jewish history but general history. Since he felt that "Christianity is the most important factor in the history of mankind" and "Jesus Christ . . . is so far the most influential personage that ever appeared in the history of the world," omitting Bible study would in effect omit these things from the schools. It would be as bad to omit Christ as it would be to ignore Washington, Franklin, and Adams.

Peabody noted that in other departments of education the Bible is no less essential than in history. "If moral philosophy is to be taught at all, I suppose that none would deny that it is distinctly Christian ethics in which our children are to be trained." (This is, of course, the main reason non-Christians object to Bible reading and religious instruction.) The best place to obtain Christian ethics is not from modern theorists who may distort or misrepresent them, Peabody believed, but from the Bible which is the inspired work of the Divine Teacher. In addition to this, he stressed that the Bible is of great literary worth, and should also be studied for that reason. He concluded rhetorically:

> We are by profession a Christian people. We recognize the great principles of religion, of Christianity in the devotional services in our legislatures and our courts of justice, and in the use of oaths in every department of public administration. Shall our children be trained as citizens without the inculcation of those fundamental religious ideas which will impress upon them the significance of prayer and the dread solemnity of an oath?[6]

On the other hand, Dr. Sterling M. McCurrin, United States Commissioner of Education in 1962, when commenting on the Supreme Court's decision declaring unconstitutional programs of prayer in the public schools (the Engel case), said, "I believe it is no loss to religion but may be a gain in clarifying matters. Prayer that is essentially a ceremonial classroom function has not much religious value."[7]

TEACHING RELIGION FOR THE SAKE OF RELIGION

There is, however, a considerable group of educators, as well as religious leaders, who feel the schools should impart religious values, because by themselves these are important.[8] It is true most of these writers do not suggest the teaching of sectarian religion in the schools. Rather they feel there is some central core of general religious ideals that the schools should impart. Some think Bible reading without comment is admirably suited for this task since the Bible can speak for itself.[9] Others feel that if the school does not impart religious instruction many children will never learn of these values at home. This was explained by E. J. Goodwin.[10] He pointed out:

> The number of irreligious and unreligious homes in this broad land is as countless as the trees of the forest. . . . The appalling fact is that those classes of our population which most need religious instruction and training do not attend church and do not come within the influences of church organizations. . . . If we affirm that religious instruction is an essential part of true education and assume that under present conditions the home and church can not or do not encompass and accomplish it, why is it that the American people do not seriously protest against the exclusion of religious teaching from the public school, which is the only place where all the children can be taught?

These views are heatedly attacked by a host of other writers on the subject.[11] Some point out that our public schools are not to blame for, and should not be charged with, the responsibility for correcting the present world-wide religious crises.[12] Others think that what advocates of such programs want is not religious education but religious indoctrination.[13] Several writers believe that religious instruction would breed prejudice and intolerance.[14] The New York *Times*, commenting editorially on this point stated:

> A state giving welcome to all creeds cannot in its public schools, which it taxes all to support and which it wishes the children of all to enter, impose any religious teaching without contravening the very principle of freedom that is at the foundation of this republic. Even if such teaching could be given without doing violence to this principle, there would be danger in many communities of engendering hatreds which might outweigh or defeat all the good sought by the compulsory reading of the Bible.[15]

This led the editors to conclude, "It was through the teachings of the homes and Sunday schools that the Bible came into its dominant place in early American life. Everything was not left to the public schools. It need not be now."[16]

Norman Cousins, editor of the *Saturday Review*, has commented on some of the negative influences of religion on the schools.[17] He objected to a decision by the New York State Board of Regents to omit from high school examinations questions relating to the germ theory of disease. This was done to avoid offense to believers in Christian Science, although it should be noted that the Christian Science Church carefully avoided any pressure to impose its views on education. The question he raised, while not specifically aimed at Bible-reading programs, might well be used by those who oppose such exercises.

> But if religion becomes the yardstick for other courses of study what happens when the yardsticks clash? Isn't it likely that the moment the school doors give way to outside pressures the strongest pressure will prevail? Isn't there danger that the religion of the majority would become dominant in education over the minorities? Our constitutional guarantees of freedom of worship are based not so much upon the need to protect religion from nonbelievers in or out of government, as upon the need to protect religions from one another.

THE BIBLE AS HISTORY AND LITERATURE

Controversy among educators over studying the Bible for its historical and literary qualities is strong. Several of the typical opinions on both sides of this debate will be noted here.

Lyman Abbot, the noted clergyman and editor, explained he would not advocate Bible reading and the use of prayer in the public schools if anyone objected, because this is "worship, and it is not the function of the state to conduct worship, certainly not to conduct compulsory worship, whether the worshippers are little children or grown men."[18] However, he went on to state:

> I do advocate the use of the Bible in the public schools as a means of acquainting our pupils with the laws, the literature, and the life of the ancient Hebrews, because the genius of the Hebrew people pervading their laws and their life and their literature was a spiritual genius. The United States is more intimately connected with the Hebrew people than with any other ancient people. Our literature abounds with references to the literature of the ancient Hebrews; they are probably more frequent than the references to the literature either of Greeks or Romans. No man can read the great English or American poets or authors understandingly unless he knows something of his English Bible. Historically we are more closely connected with the Hebrew people than with the Greeks. Our free institutions are all rooted in the institutions of the Hebrew people, have grown out of them as the result of the long conflict between their political principles and those of pagan imperialism. A man is not a truly educated man who knows nothing of the sources and foundations of our national life, and they are found in the Bible.

Professor William Lyon Phelps of Yale particularly lauded the literary quality of the Bible.[19] He explained that if he were appointed a "committee of one" to regulate the much-debated question of college entrance examinations in English he would,

> . . . erase every list of books that has been thus far suggested, and I should confine the examination wholly to the authorized version of the Bible. The Bible has within its pages every single kind of literature that any proposed list of English classics contains. It has narrative, descriptive, poetical, dramatic, and oratorical passages. . . . Priests, atheists, skeptics, devotees, agnostics and evangelists are all agreed that the Bible is the best example of English composition that the world has ever seen. It contains the noblest prose and poetry with the utmost simplicity of diction.[20]

Nicholas Murray Butler, then President of Columbia University, was concerned because he felt a knowledge of the Bible was passing out of the life of the younger generation.[21] This would result in a disappearance of any acquaintance with the religious element which has shaped our civilization from the beginning. He explained:

> The neglect of the English Bible incapacitates the rising generation to read and appreciate the masterpieces of English literature, from Chaucer to Browning, and it strikes out of their consciousness one element, and for centuries the controlling element in the production of your civilization. . . . My own feeling is that what has come to pass can only be described by one word, shameful!

He did make one important qualification that must be noted. He stressed:

> I want to make it perfectly clear that I am not talking about religious teaching in school, that I am not talking about theological influence in education, but that I am only protesting against sacrificing a knowledge of our civilization to theological differences.

He did not, however, clarify how it would be possible to read the Bible in schools without getting involved in sectarian disputes.

Reactions to President Butler's Views

Shortly after this, an editorial in the *Independent* took Dr. Butler to task for these sentiments.[22] It explained that not as literature, but for religious purposes, is the Bible wanted in schools by those who favor its restoration. It went on to state:

> Indeed, President Butler laments that the decay of the religious sentiment has followed the giving up of Bible

reading, and it is to recover this religious spirit that he wants it restored. But this is not the business of the public school.

Continuing on this theme, a later editorial praised the Supreme Court of Nebraska for prohibiting Bible reading.[23] It stressed that it is the business of the church, not the state, to teach religion. "[F]or the church to confess its incompetence, and to ask the state, through such miscellaneous teachers as we have, to supplement its lack of service, is humiliating and shameful."[24] In keeping with these views, the editors objected to public schools' requiring Jewish children to sing Christmas carols.[25] They went on to claim that those who wish to use the Bible only as a literary work use this argument only as a pretense to get the Book's religious views across to the students. If it is really literature these people are concerned with, the editors wondered, why has no one suggested exercises in which *Paradise Lost* and the *Iliad* are read? They concluded:

> But it is not as literature that we chiefly value the Bible. It is degrading to it to lower it to that level and make it a lesson of style or story. It is not the Beautiful Bible, but the Holy Bible. It is impossible to put it on any other basis. Call it literature, if you will, but it will be considered and treated as a religious book, and that will be the real reason for introducing and teaching it. We do not want to smuggle the Bible into the public schools under a false pretense. It is our one great book of religion, and as such let it be treated, the Churches' sacred Book.[26]

H. W. Horwill, writing in the *Atlantic Monthly,* noted some of the inadequacies and difficulties inherent in any scheme to study the Bible as literature or history. He explained:

> Owing to the religious implication of the Bible it is impossible to teach it even as literature or history without

becoming involved in questions of acute controversy. It is a thin and ineffectual criticism which concerns itself only about an author's manner to the neglect of his matter, and any teaching of literature which limits itself in the same way is equally unprofitable. But the moment the matter of the Bible is seriously considered, strife is inevitable. Nay, in these days it is more difficult than ever before to treat even the manner of the sacred writer without provoking an acrimonious religious discussion.[27]

He also explained that the religious advocates of Bible study in the schools will not be happy with the type of teaching that satisfies its literary advocates. He saw little purpose of a religious nature served by research into now obsolete Biblical words and expressions, or by comments in the Psalms on natural phenomena. "So far from promoting religious culture, it is to be expected that an exclusively literary and historical treatment of the Bible will actually impair its moral impressions on the young.[28]

Essentially the same sentiments were expressed by H. H. Horne, speaking before the annual convention of the Religious Education Association.[29] He said:

> To ask that the Bible be used as a text book in morals or even literature would be good for morals and literature no doubt, but not for religion, whose interest it is the prime function of the Bible to serve. The teaching in the public school, under any guise, of the book upon which all the religious sects are founded would end inevitably in sectarian interpretations. It would also tend to reduce to the level of an ordinary text book that volume of the Christian religion whose sacredness is regularly held to be essential.

Others have pointed out the impossibility of studying the Bible as literature because of the way it has become entangled in the religious emotions of the people. This is particularly true in the case of young and immature minds.[30] J. H. Blackhurst, in an article in the magazine *Education*, agreed with these sentiments and presented an additional argument of importance. He explained:

> As in the case of its literary merits, it is here also to be regretted that the Bible cannot be used more freely in moral training. I believe, however, that the loss is not as great as we are at first inclined to think: for those moral principles have been so diffused through literature and moral philosophy that they are the common property of all and can be taught with little or no reference to their origin. Then, too, modern psychology is beginning to point out that successful moral instruction is not so much a matter of directing the child's reading and thinking about moral principles as it is a matter of guiding the child's activities along lines which are in keeping with those principles.[31]

BIBLE READING AND CRIME

We now turn to a major point, made by its advocates, that Bible reading and religious instruction will cut down on crime and juvenile delinquency because they develop good citizenship.[32] One of the most outspoken proponents of this view was W. S. Fleming. Writing in *Nation's Schools* he contended that when Cincinnati shut the Bible out of her schools in 1869, she lit the flame that "soon burned to death the character building function of our public education."[33] This he felt, was one of the major explanations for the increased crime rate in the United States.

To prove this he quoted statistics revealing that there were a higher number of arrests than eighty years ago when Bible reading was a generally recognized function of the schools.[34] He believed that true religious liberty would allow giving religious instruction in the schools, with each child permitted to accept or reject that which he chose.[35] Using Cincinnati as an example of a city which has erred, he concluded that if the town fathers had allowed the Bible to be read in the schools, "her crime rate would be far less today."

A number of years before, Dr. Luther A. Weigle, Professor of Religious Education at Yale, eloquently announced that the absence of religious education in the public schools accounted for the "pagan lustfulness of a world that is drifting away from God and good."[36] Speaking before the final session of the Forty-Ninth Annual Convention of the Kings County Sunday Schools, he explained:

> The desire of folk to do what they please, when they please, and where they please finds supposedly scientific backing, and sanction in the behavioristic psychology of John B. Watson, the psychoanalytic mythology of Sigmund Freud, and the free love philosophy of Bertrand Russell. This pseudo-scientific materialism and pagan ethics find fit expression in the sex fiction and shady verse, the indecent shows and raucous jazz, which have so largely taken the place once occupied by literature, art and music. And then we blink our eyes and shake our heads and ask despairingly, 'What ails our youth? What is the matter with our young people of today?' We forget that youth holds a mirror to middle age. There is nothing the matter with young people today except that they are reacting in perfectly natural ways to the stimuli offered them by the pagan lustfulness of a world that is drifting away from God and good.

(If John Dewey and his disciples had been included in the above-mentioned triumvirate, even effusive William E. Buckley, Jr., who has been critical of the secularist tendencies of Yale,[37] might find himself in agreement with at least a onetime professor at his alma mater.) Dr. Weigle pointed out that the movement to remove religion from the schools was not the work of infidels and atheists, but of "folk who spoke and acted in the name of religion." He concluded that if the schools continue to ignore religion, the perpetuity of those moral and religious institutions which are most characteristic of American life would be endangered. "It imperils the future of the nation itself."

There is substantial disagreement, however, on whether religious instruction really aids in the development of better citizens.[38] After analyzing prison records, and finding that prisoners claiming some religious affiliation far outnumber those who are unaffiliated, Lamar T. Beman, in his book, *Religious Teaching in the Public Schools,* concluded:

> The claim that absence of religious instruction and worship from the public schools is the cause of the crime conditions in this country, fails to consider certain painful realities. In every school some pupils do not make progress; some of them can not, or will not, or at least do not learn so as to measure up to the standards of the school. Many cities have a special school for unruly or disorderly boys. . . . Most of our crime is committed by young people, much of it by boys. That any school or any system of instruction fails to interest or to educate one hundred per cent of its pupils is not a reproach, for no school and no system has as yet done so. This is true even of those schools which have the best possible system of religious instruction and worship. . . . Criminals, as a rule, are not bright or intelligent people. Many, perhaps most, of them are the kind that could not have been changed by any system of education, or made better by any instruction in religion.[39]

Joseph Lewis, in an article in *Teachers College Journal* objecting to statements that religious instruction and Bible reading will reduce crime, told of the results of a survey conducted by Professor Hightower of Butler University.[40] Professor Hightower concluded, after administering examinations of various kinds to 3,300 children, that the students who participated in Bible-reading exercises were found to be less honest than those who did not take part. This led Lewis to conclude that the "mere knowledge of the Bible itself is not sufficient to insure the proper character attitudes." He thought the crowning irony of religious instruction was that its supporters feel that it is all right to teach children principles and theories which later in their life they may find to be incorrect. He suggested this is analogous to teaching a child the wrong principles of grammar under the assumption that as he grows older he will realize the inaccuracies and correct them himself.

STUDIES TESTING THE EFFECTS OF RELIGIOUS INSTRUCTION

A number of surveys have been made which attempt to test the efficacy of Bible reading and religious instruction. While it might be perfectly possible to quarrel with the testing techniques, as well as the results, several of them should be noted here. Franzblau found in a study of 701 Jewish children that "character responses manifest a slight tendency to be higher among children who affirm the foregoing beliefs than among those who deny them."[41] Bartlett studied the beliefs and action patterns of 1056 pupils in grades six through eight.[42] Nearly 600 of the students averaged five semester hours of weekday religious instruction in church schools. The remaining pupils were without such teachings. Bartlett concluded after measuring all of them by a variety of tests that the former knew considerably more about the Bible than the latter, but showed no greater degree of Christian motivation in conduct.

Hartshorne and May have done some of the major studies in the field of character education.[43] They have concluded that religious education as then conducted did not result in improvement of character, nor did the indoctrination of children in a religious ideology result in a significant increase in approved behavior. They explain that a moral trait such as honesty or truthfulness is not a unified trait of character. On the contrary, it is "a series of specific responses to specific situations."[44]

Thus, if a social situation appears to make honesty easy, or evokes honesty as an appropriate response, the child tends to be honest. If the opposite is true, the child will be dishonest. These authors see no carry-over from one situation to another, or from religious teachings to tested behavior unless the two situations are essentially similar. It is the common elements which appear to facilitate transfer. Cook, commenting on these findings, stated:

> The authors do not contend that honesty as a generalized trait cannot be developed, they show that, for the children tested, religious idealism has not been taught so as to carry over into conduct. In view of this conclusion, the value of the church's traditional work with children is a debatable question.[45]

Critics of religious instruction in the school might ask how a public school teacher, untrained in the art of religious instruction, might succeed in an area where there is an indication that even churches have failed.

POLLS OF TEACHER ATTITUDES

Several surveys of teacher attitudes toward the advisability and effectiveness of Bible reading and related exercises have been undertaken. These are presented merely as indications of the various views held, rather than as a final answer. The magazine *Nation's Schools* conducted such a study in 1945.[46] In a questionnaire sent to 500 school administrators, 220, or about 44 per cent of them answered. On the question, "Do you believe that public schools can give religious instruction which is wholly nonsectarian in nature," 49.1 per cent replied in the affirmative and 40 per cent answered negatively. Finally, in answer to the query, "Whose responsibility is it to train children in religion?" 1.4 per cent thought it was a job solely for the church, 54.5 per cent felt it was the duty of the church and the home, while 44.1 per cent believed such training was up to the church, home, and school.

Two studies of a similar nature have more recently been completed by California educators. The inquiries were related to a proposed bill before the California legislature which would require daily reading of the Bible in public schools "without comment." It is noted that:

> Both studies concluded that the controversy likely to be generated by the practice would create disturbances out of proportion to the values which such a program could secure. The California Curriculum Commission, which made one of the studies, found that reading the Bible, without comment, 'does not represent the recommendations of the general public,' and that, 'religious groups and religious leaders do not reveal common faith in and support of,' the proposed legislation. Both reports reveal the existence of serious and widespread doubts as to whether Bible reading without comment has any educational value or would contribute importantly to the teaching of moral and spiritual values.[47]

The study done by the California State Curriculum Commission was requested by the California State Board of Education which was seeking to determine potential results of the proposed Bible-reading bill. The other study was made by a Committee of Moral and Spiritual Values in Education, appointed by Dr. H. M. McPherson, Superintendent of Schools of Napa, California. It was asked to "analyze opinions on how the local school system could transmit moral and spiritual values, and to give special attention to Bible reading as a device to attain this goal."[48]

The Curriculum Commission, whose hearings were held

in Los Angeles, in what it called an "atmosphere of controversy," left these hearings, "with a deeper appreciation of the wide divergence and points of view, and of the deep and sincere convictions of their proponents." Its inquiry was limited to the educational value and psychological soundness of Bible-reading exercises and it sought information from educators as to how such practices would fit into the curriculum and affect local administration.

Its investigations disclosed the following factors. Because of overcrowding, the handling of those pupils who would be dismissed from such exercises for reasons of conscience would prove a serious administrative problem. Forty-two per cent of those who replied felt that the reading would be "ineffective without explanation or comment," while an additional 40 per cent thought a "refusal to answer pupil questions regarding any curricular activity is not educationally sound." Twenty-five of the 348 school districts that replied felt that by denying teachers the opportunity to explain, pupils would get the idea that something is "hidden or wrong." Twenty-six more said that such an arrangement made it impossible to motivate pupils to learn anything from the Bible. Still others felt it was a "major contradiction of accepted pedagogy" to require the same textbook for children in kindergarten through junior college. This was particularly true since no comment could be made on the portions of the Bible read.

The Commission drew the following conclusions: (1) The Bible-reading proposal is controversial and includes unreconciled difficulties. (2) Administration of the bill would be difficult because of inadequate facilities and insufficient teachers. (3) The method of instruction is pedagogically unsound. (4) The vocabulary and concept difficulty is above the general level of the elementary school. (5) The bill might result in the church's and home's shifting the burden of religious instruction to the school. (6) Some teachers would be required to read selections that conflict with their personal convictions. (7) The State Board of Education would be faced by an enormous problem in having to classify, evaluate, and select Bible content for the program. (8) Conflict would result, not only among parents, but also among children over excusing children whose parents requested it. (9) Present programs of teaching moral and ethical values are much more effective than is the proposed plan. (10) Additional work can be done along these lines which would not involve the schools in religious controversies or in the use of "educationally unsound techniques."[49]

The Napa study included teachers from elementary schools through college, thus viewing the problem on all school levels. Fifty-three elementary teachers, 27 high school teachers and 34 college teachers were included in the survey. Ninety-eight per cent of the teachers questioned thought the school ought to transmit moral values, while 93 per cent felt the school should transmit spiritual values. Seventy-eight per cent believed the school should be responsible for transmitting these values, and 95 per cent thought there should be greater emphasis on these values in the curriculum. Interestingly enough, the highest proportion of the 22 per cent who took a negative view of the school's transmitting of religious instruction were elementary teachers, and the lowest proportion was among the college teachers.[50]

Fifty per cent of the teachers stated they had made efforts to include moral and spiritual values, while only 10 per cent said they had not. Twenty-five per cent said this was a goal in all their work and was integrated in all activities. Nine per cent of these said they taught such values by teaching about religion. One per cent said they did so by encouraging Sunday school attendance. It is significant that 65 per cent of the teachers were not certain that they could deal with the facts about religion in an unbiased manner." On the proposed Bible-reading bill, only 15 per cent felt that no unfavorable results would flow from it, while 49 per cent believed conflicts would develop. Forty-seven per cent thought the negative effects of Bible reading would outweigh the positive, while only 26 per cent believed the positive results would be greater. From this the Napa Committee concluded that "Bible reading does not have the endorsement of religious education, it creates the danger that animosities will develop, and there are probably better educational ways of teaching moral and spiritual values than through Bible reading."[51]

Following the completion of these studies, the California State Board of Education issued its recommendations on the California Bible-reading proposal. It suggested that if any legislation of this nature were adopted it should leave the question of beginning each school day by reading the Bible for each school district to decide.[52]

EFFECTS OF THE SCHEMPP CASE

There is no doubt that the Supreme Court's decision in the Schempp case had a profound impact on educational practices throughout the nation. For example, Fred M. Hechinger, writing in the New York *Times,* noted that the court decision would require a change in a majority of state educational systems.[53] Moreover, his analysis concluded that the Schempp ruling would materially affect practices in 41 per cent of the nation's school districts. This finding, of course, is predicated on the assumption that states and their local school districts would comply with the court's decree.

In point of fact, however, early evidence in 1963 suggested a substantial reluctance on the part of top state educational administrative agencies to alter practices involving Bible reading and related exercises in the public schools. In August of 1963, some two months following the Schempp decisions, Louis Cassels surveyed the national scene for United Press International and concluded that prayer and Bible reading would continue in many public schools.[54] Indeed, he found only a few states which previously had religious exercises in their schools which had issued explicit orders for their discontinuation. Many state educational officials said they were still "studying" the matter.

At that time the survey found only two states — Pennsylvania and California — which were taking positive action on the court's suggestion that it is perfectly acceptable for public schools to engage in "objective" study of the Bible as history or literature. This fact alone would seem to underline the high level of public misunderstanding and emotionalism which followed the court's ruling.

As might be expected, the greatest amount of opposition and even open defiance of the Schempp ruling occurred in southern states. In the South, and in other parts of our country, no politician stands to lose many votes by attacking the Supreme Court while at the same time defending the Bible.

In Alabama, on August 6, 1963, the State Board of Education openly defied the court and made Bible reading part of the required curriculum of the public schools. The state board's resolution denounced the decision as a "calculated effort to take God out of the public affairs of the nation."[55] Governor Wallace, who has had other disagreements with the Federal Government, introduced the resolution before the State Board of Education and said if the courts ruled out the practice in a specific Alabama school, "I'm going to that school and read it myself." Alabama law already required daily Bible reading in state-supported schools, but the resolution went a step further in making it part of the course of study.

The reactions of other southern states were somewhat similar though less volcanic. South Carolina's State Superintendent of Public Instruction, Jesse Anderson, publicly notified teachers in his state that they may "feel free" to continue classroom religious exercises.[56] In Kentucky, the State Board of Education issued a directive to local school boards to "continue present practices" with regard to devotional exercises. Kentucky's State Superintendent of Public Instruction, Wendell P. Butler, advised school officials to "Continue to read the Bible and pray until someone stops you."

In Florida the state legislature passed with only one dissenting vote a measure which allows each county school board to decide what it will do about religion in public schools. The bill's sponsor pointed out that since Florida has sixty-seven counties it would take sixty-seven different court suits to eliminate religious practices in the state's schools. On June 2, 1964, the United States Supreme Court reversed the Florida high court's decision which had defied the ruling of the Schempp case by upholding Bible reading and prayer programs in the Miami public schools.[57]

A much more mixed reaction was found in northern states in the period immediately following the Schempp decision. In New Jersey, the State Department of Education acting on the advice of State Attorney General Arthur J. Sills, officially notified all local school boards that religious exercises must be discontinued. Nonetheless the school board of Mahwah, New Jersey, voted 5–4 to continue Bible reading and recitation of the Lord's Prayer.[58]

In Delaware, the Attorney General on August 15, 1963, ruled that Bible reading and related exercises would continue in Delaware's public schools.[59] He took the position that the Schempp decision applied only to Pennsylvania and Maryland — the states involved in the litigation. The state law requiring Bible reading and recitation of the Lord's Prayer in Delaware's public schools, he said, "is still the law in Delaware and will remain so until repealed by the General Assembly or declared by a court to be violative of the state or federal constitution."

In Massachusetts, shortly after the court's ruling in *Schempp,* the State Commission of Education formally advised all school districts that the Supreme Court ruling clearly means that "the Lord's Prayer may not be recited, nor may there be a reading of the Bible for devotional or religious purposes."[60] However, the superintendent of at least one town — Montague — spurned this notice and recommended that religious exercises be continued in the schools of his district. But on May 28, 1964, the Massachusetts Supreme Court noted that such practices were unconstitutional in the state's public schools and counsel for the school board indicated the board would not continue the legal battle.[61]

In Iowa, which has a law permitting, but not requiring Bible reading, the State Superintendent of Public Instruction in a general way urged compliance with the decisions of the Supreme Court. A survey of school districts of that state compiled by the Iowa Civil Liberties Union in the spring of

1964 indicated that the state superintendent's advice was not followed universally in that state. With 72 per cent of the local school superintendents replying to the questionnaire, it was found that 15 per cent admitted that organized prayers were said during school hours, but the great bulk of this activity occurred in only a few rather than a majority of the classes in each of these schools. There was no reported instance where students were required to participate in programs of organized prayer.

In many cases, the Iowa study indicated that where prayers were being said, only a few teachers — usually in the lower grades or in kindergarten — were responsible, and this was not school policy. One Iowa superintendent indicated that no prayers were authorized, but added that he could not be sure that "no prayers are bootlegged into the school."

The Iowa survey also revealed that Bible reading during school hours occurred in 10 per cent of the schools, with slightly over half this number indicating that the Bible was studied as literature. About 30 per cent of the superintendents indicated that hymn singing occurred during school hours, but in almost all instances this was noted as constituting part of the vocal training program of the school. Of particular interest, in light of the Supreme Court's decision in the McCollum case banning such practices, is the response indicating that approximately 5 per cent of the schools have released-time programs of religious instruction which take place inside the school building.

THE AASA COMMISSION REPORT

In 1964, a commission appointed by the American Association of School Administrators released a published study supporting the Supreme Court's decision on prayers and

Bible reading in the public schools.[62] In addition, the commission sought to provide a set of guidelines for those who frame local school policy and those who administer and teach within such policy when confronted with problems arising from practices involving religion and the schools. This group emphasized, however, that such guidelines were not intended to be infallible. On the contrary, some may be subject to constitutional challenge in the future.

In voicing their support of the Supreme Court decisions on prayers and Bible reading the educators said:

> Along with government and all its agencies, the schools must be neutral in respect to the religious beliefs of its citizens. There is no threat to the individual, to religion, or to the common good in the removal of religious exercises from the schools.

On the other hand, the study called for better public school instruction in the literary and historic aspects of religion. The commission pointed out that the history of western civilization cannot be understood "without some understanding of the great religious and church influences reaching back to the earliest of recorded times." The commission also recognized religion "as one of the greatest influences in man's history." Moreover, the report recommended that school calendars, personnel policies, and extracurricular activities all should be adapted to accommodate a diversity of religious backgrounds and practices.

In a related area, however, this study urged that high school baccalaureate services be left to individual churches and synagogues. The public schools should not require attendance at such programs, the commission recommended.

The report also dealt with Christmas programs in the public schools and suggested methods of handling exercises of this nature. The schools should eliminate the religious emphasis in their observances of Christmas, it noted. Christmas should be presented as one of many contributions to the American heritage which has been created by many religions. "A public school, whatever the feeling of its constituents, may not observe Christmas as though it were a church or combinations of churches," the report said.

"The non-Christian is not a guest in a Christian school — he is a fellow citizen in a public school which includes a good many Christian members," the report emphasized. The basic law seems clear, the commission noted. It is that "under the Constitution, the public schools may not sponsor a religious service . . . whether it be for a single or multi-denominational group. Neither may public schools support the Christian religions, Christian churches, nor distinctively Christian doctrines."

Concerning such Christmas programs, the study recommended a "policy that encourages reasonable recognition of Christmas in the public schools in the spirit of exposition of the differing rites and customs of families, cultures and creeds — each with deep meaning for its adherents and in sum revealing that many different religions, philosophical and cultural practices and beliefs are held by Americans."

The report concluded with a good statement of the role of the public schools and the position of religion in this relationship:

> The power of the public school is in the opportunity it provides for the creative engagement of differences — differences in physical and mental capacities and characteristics, differences in background and culture, differences in the creeds men live by. This is a power not always understood, not uniformly supported, nor invariably exercised effectively. Concern over the role of religion in the

public school that leads to a lessening of that power weakens the very institution that serves a diverse society so faithfully. Concern that leads to improvement in the methods, materials and competence with which the school deals with the role of religion is constructive. The Commission has earnestly tried to respond to this latter concern.

PUBLIC OFFICIALS AND THE BIBLE

Observers of practicing politicians might conclude that the Bible occupies as haloed a place in their speeches as does motherhood and democracy. It is of interest to note here expressions by several public officials; but they must be regarded simply as illustrative and not as a comprehensive survey.

One governor's conscience compelled him to veto a compulsory Bible-reading bill. A. V. Donahey, Governor of Ohio, explained this action in his veto message of April 30, 1925. He stated:

> It is my belief that religious teaching in our homes, Sunday schools, churches, by the good mothers, fathers, and ministers of Ohio is far preferable to compulsory teaching of religion by the state. The spirit of our federal and state constitutions from the beginning have [sic] been to leave religious instruction to the discretion of parents. Under existing Ohio law, as upheld by our supreme court, when the people of local communities desire or demand it, boards of education in their discretion may require the reading of the Holy Bible in the schools. In other words, we now have home rule in this respect and there is no necessity for this bill establishing state dictation in the matter of religion.[63]

The idea of a "Bible Week," somewhat related to this study, has been commended by several governors in recent years.[64] An example of this is the rather interesting proclamation issued in 1942 by the then Governor of Massachusetts Leverett Saltonstall. He encouraged daily Bible

reading by the citizens "as a patriotic religious exercise."
He noted that in the present world crisis, "We need to be
reminded not only that the deepest needs of our day remain spiritual, but also that the best things in American
life are traceable to the Scriptures."[65]

Today the Bible is not usually read at the opening of
Congress, since a prayer is generally used. Government
officials, however, have frequently urged the public to engage in more Bible reading.[66] President Wilson, for example, made a public appeal for funds to give the Scriptures to all servicemen during World War I. In his message
in behalf of Universal Bible Sunday, President Franklin
D. Roosevelt said, "We know that the ancient truths of
the Bible will prevail over all error because they constitute
the teachings of God."[67] The reticent President Coolidge
remarked in a letter to E. E. Thompson in March, 1927,
that:

> The foundations of our society and our government rest
> so much on the teachings of the Bible that it would be
> difficult to support them if faith in these teachings should
> cease to be practically universal in our country.[68]

These are, of course, general sentiments and it cannot
necessarily be deduced from them that these men would
favor Bible reading in the public schools.

President Theodore Roosevelt, for one, specifically opposed such exercises. In a letter to a New York legislator
in 1915 he noted:

> I see you appeared against the bill making compulsory
> the reading of the Bible in the public schools. If I were in
> the legislature or governor, I should vote against or veto
> that bill, because I believe in absolutely non-sectarian
> public schools. It is not our business to have the Protes-
> tant Bible or the Catholic Vulgate or the Talmud read in

those schools. There is no objection whatever, where the local sentiment favors it, for the teacher to read a few verses of the ethical or moral parts of the Bible, so long as this causes no offense to anyone. But it is entirely wrong for the law to make this reading compulsory, and the Protestant fanatics who attempt to force this through are playing into the hands of the Catholic fanatics who want to break down the public school system and introduce a system of sectarian schools. . . .[69]

It is clear from the foregoing that substantially no more agreement exists among public officials regarding questions of Bible reading and religious instructions than exists among educators or religious groups.

8

The Court, The Becker
Amendment, and Congress

THE CLERGY AND THE BECKER AMENDMENT

CERTAIN LEADING CLERGYMEN and religious groups, rather
than being passive in their presentation of views concerning
the Schempp ruling, were willing to fight for these views in
the political arena. By May of 1964, more than one hundred
and forty-five proposed constitutional amendments had been
introduced into the House of Representatives to overcome
the effects of the court's decision. Representative Emanuel
Celler, Chairman of the House Judiciary Committee, reluctantly yielded to relentless organized pressure and held hearings on the Becker Amendment, which seemed to have the
most support. Mr. Celler indicated that he was in no hurry
to rush an amendment out. "The nature and importance of
the subject," he said, "require that the committee have the
best thinking of all schools of thought in its consideration of
the pending resolution."[1]

The amendment was proposed by Representative Frank
J. Becker, a Republican from Nassau County, New York. It
sought to permit reading of prayers or biblical selections in
public schools and other governmental institutions, "if par-

ticipation therein is on a voluntary basis." The latter qualification suggests that dissenting children would be permitted
to leave the classroom if they wished to during such programs.

From the first it seemed clear that while individual
clergymen might disagree with the Schempp ruling, the
torrent of mail that descended upon congressmen in early
1964 stemmed not so much from formalized religious sects
as from *ad hoc* organizations bearing religious titles. For
example, The Committee of Christian Laymen, Inc., of
Woodland Hills, California, circulated a printed form at-
tributing the drive against religious exercises in the public
schools to "the American Civil Liberties Union and the
Communist Party." A detachable section of this form was
designed to be sent to congressmen. It read: "We are organ-
izing a door to door campaign to let our fellow Americans
know the names of those Congressmen who have not yet
signed the discharge petition" [a parliamentary device to take
the proposed amendment out of the hands of the committee
and place it on the floor of the House of Representatives for
consideration].[2] A number of congressmen privately confided
to this author that if the discharge petition had been successful the amendment would have passed the House of Representatives since many members of the House felt it was impossible politically to oppose the amendment despite personal views to the contrary.

After surveying the testimony of a multitude of religious
spokesmen which appeared before the House Judiciary Committee, several generalizations can be made. Representatives
of the National Council of Churches, and of the Baptists,
Lutherans, Presbyterians, Seventh Day Adventists, Unitarians, the United Church of Christ, and the Jewish faith,

unanimously opposed the amendment and supported the Supreme Court's position.³ Indeed, on one day, April 30, 1964, churchmen representing more than thirty Christian denominations were shown to be unanimously in support of the Supreme Court's position.⁴ This is not meant to suggest that these official or semiofficial statements are necessarily concurred in by every individual minister or layman within the denomination. The House Judiciary Committee received a variety of letters similar to the one that said, "I am one Baptist they do not represent."⁵

Other major American religious sects were not as consolidated in their views as those mentioned above. Spokesmen for Roman Catholics, Episcopalians, and Methodists differed among themselves over support of the Becker Amendment.⁶ Representatives of fundamentalist sects normally tended to support the amendment.

Dr. Carl McIntire, President of the International Council of Christian Churches, who was identified by Representative B. F. Sisk of California as a leader of "somewhat extremist" groups opposing the Supreme Court's decision, gave particular support to the Becker Amendment. Arguing that the amendment would not erode the First Amendment or compromise the separation of church and state, Dr. McIntire indicated he had supported the Engel decision of the Supreme Court because it struck down state-composed prayer. His opposition developed, he said, when, in the Schempp case, the court struck down "the prayer composed by Jesus Christ 2,000 years ago, the Lord's Prayer as it is called." From this he concluded, "It was clear that the issue was God and prayer, per se."⁷

A leading Roman Catholic, Bishop Fulton J. Sheen, in testimony before the House Judiciary Committee was critical of the Schempp decision but urged Congress not to try to override it by amending the Constitution. Emphasizing he was speaking as an individual and not as a spokesman for his church, he argued that the Supreme Court had exceeded its competency in ruling against prayers and Bible reading in the public schools. The court's decisions, he insisted, were based upon a myth — that there was a wall of separation between church and state. Bishop Sheen suggested, however, that there was real danger that the guarantees of the First Amendment would be destroyed by adding a few words. "We have disestablishment written into the First Amendment," he said. "We do not want it disturbed." In answer to a committee member's question as to who should compose the prayer if an amendment overrode the court's decision, Bishop Sheen answered, "I would suggest the prayer that every member is carrying with him in his pocket—'In God We Trust.' "[8]

Another Roman Catholic clergyman, the Reverend Robert G. Howes, a professor at Catholic University of America on leave from his parish in Wooster, Massachusetts, supported adoption of the amendment and was much more critical of the Supreme Court. Speaking for the Massachusetts Citizens for Public Prayer, an organization, he said, that represented many faiths, Father Howe told the committee: "What the prayer decisions do clearly is to explode a bomb with deadly fall-out. From these decisions, unless we now reverse them emphatically, must develop an irradiation which goes to the very marrow of the bones of those long traditions of public reverence which have for so many decades distinguished our people."[9]

A quite different Roman Catholic attitude is reflected in the editorials of the influential Jesuit magazine *America,* submitted to the Judiciary Committee in its hearings. A May 25, 1963, editorial argued that the "thinking behind some of the Court's decisions is bad political philosophy, bad history and bad constitutional law." On the other hand, it pointed out, the court had often changed its mind when it became evident that it had "departed too far from the sense of the people." Urging caution to American Catholics because of the commonly heard accusation that they pay only lip service to the principle of church-state separation, the editorial warned: "In the atmosphere of suspicion that still surrounds us, we should gain little and lose much by identifying ourselves with an effort to change the text of the First Amendment, however good our motives or sound our interpretation of religious liberty."

A later editorial took an even more clear-cut position by noting, ". . . we are opposed to any amendment of the First Amendment." It noted, however, that, "we have never thought that the practices mentioned were an establishment of religion in the Constitutional sense." But the editorial argued that there is an additional reason not to support the proposed amendments. "All that their amendment would do would be to reverse the Supreme Court's school prayer decisions. It would not solve the basic question of the relationship of religion and education in this country. . . . Indeed, the adoption of the prayer amendment might freeze the Court's church-state doctrine as it now stands."[10]

Another example of attitudes represented by religious spokesmen who were critical of the Supreme Court and supported the Becker Amendment in testimony before the House Judiciary Committee is reflected by the views of Dr. Robert A. Cook, representing the National Association of Evangelicals. He noted that from the inception of the public schools, where ministers were the teachers, it had been "a tried and proven" custom to have prayer and Bible reading in many of them. "While the good that has come from the practice cannot be measured," he admitted, "we believe that it has been considerable and provided a stabilizing influence greater than many realize. The adverse effects have been insignificant. We know of none," Dr. Cook concluded.[11]

The sharp controversy the Becker Amendment caused in some religious denominations is revealed by the spirited debate which occurred at the 1964 Annual Convention of the Episcopal Diocese of New York. There the Episcopal leaders of that state took a strong stand against the amendment and in favor of the Supreme Court's views, when by a wide margin they defeated a resolution backing moves to negate the court's ruling. During the thirty-five-minute, heated debate on the resolution, various Episcopal leaders, including the Reverend Benjamin Minifie, the Reverend Fredrick C. Grant, who had represented the church at the Vatican Ecumenical Council, and Clifford B. Morehouse (who, as President of the House of Deputies, is the highest ranking Episcopal layman in the country), took the rostrum to warn against the "militant forces of atheism that are trying to lock God out of the schools."[12]

Opposing the resolution in support of the Becker Amendment, the Reverend Miller Cragon, Director of the diocesan Department of Christian Education, argued, "I do not believe we can legislate God into the classroom or legislate him out of it." Another supporter of the Supreme Court in this dispute was Judge Thurgood Marshall of the United States Court of Appeals and an active Episcopal layman. Judge Marshall said he was "bitterly opposed" to the resolution supporting a constitutional amendment. Bishop Donegan, who presided, took no stand on the issue, but he did not demur when one speaker claimed that the court's decisions had the Bishop's support.[13]

Less than a month after this debate, the National Council of the Episcopal Church at its quarterly meeting in Greenwich, Connecticut, formally supported the Supreme Court in its decisions on prayer and Bible reading. This action closely coincided with the stand taken by the United Churches of Christ in opposing the Becker Amendment or any other constitutional alteration designed to permit voluntary devotional exercises in the public schools.[14] Somewhat earlier, the United Presbyterian Church meeting in its 176th General Assembly reaffirmed opposition to Bible reading and prayer in the public schools as devotional exercises and contended that religious indoctrination was the task of the home and the church.[15]

The testimony of clergymen and others (much of it favorable) before the House Judiciary Committee fills three hefty volumes or 2,774 printed pages.[16] Space limitations here prevent little more than the presentation of a representative sample of the reactions. Speaking for an *ad hoc* committee of Episcopalians, Baptists, Jews, Presbyterians, and members of the United Church of Christ, the Reverend Arthur C. Barnhart of the Pennsylvania Episcopal Diocese, told the committee early in its hearings: "We see nothing in the decisions which prevent a youngster praying — before school, in school, after school, in his home or in his church or synagogue. We see nothing which prevents schools from studying the Bible or the role of religion as part of our cultural heritage." In fact, he concluded, "we see these decisions, which the resolutions before your committee seek to negate, as clarifying the respective roles of government and religion."[17]

The same day, Rabbi Irvin M. Blank, representing the Synagogue Council of America, told the committee that a truly nonsectarian prayer for school use would be impossible to compose. "Such a prayer as advocated by proponents of a constitutional amendment," he pointed out, "would of necessity be so devoid of any real spiritual content that it would come dangerously close to irreverence and blasphemy." The concept of voluntary participation in school prayer programs is meaningless, he contended. "For children, voluntary participation is an illusory concept and for parents it imposes a responsibility which should not be imposed," he said.[18]

In somewhat the same vein, Rabbi Maurice N. Eisendrath, President of the Union of American Hebrew Congregations, later urged the Judiciary Committee to weigh its conscience instead of its constituents' mail before recommending a constitutional amendment. Tampering with the First Amendment, he explained, could "unravel the historic fabric of the Bill of Rights. Prayer," he noted, "must come from the heart and not the school board." Moreover, he pointed to the danger of "an American public school religion" consisting of a set of "meaningless, watered-down, nonsectarian platitudes" that would not be religion at all. Some of the committee members, apparently nettled by his comments about mail, tartly pointed out during the two hours they questioned the Rabbi, that there had been an increase in constituent request to leave the Constitution alone.[19]

Rabbi Harry Halpern representing the United Synagogue of America, the Rabbinical Assembly, the National

Women's League and the National Federation of Jewish Men's Clubs opposed the proposed amendment before the Judiciary Committee. "If this effort is successful," he said, "what is there to prevent any well-organized group from agitating for further amendment of the Bill of Rights whenever it is in disagreement with a Supreme Court decision?"[20]

Rabbi Halpern spoke to the point often made by Justice Oliver W. Holmes — that the key reason for the Bill of Rights is to protect the minority. The majority can look after itself since it should normally control the political branches of government. In taking this position, the Rabbi presented an opposing line of reasoning to that presented to the committee on a number of occasions. This was exemplified in the testimony of Dr. Charles Wesley Lowry, head of the Foundation for Religious Action in the Social and Civil Order when he argued in support of the amendment, "It is a calamity and not straight thinking to convert legitimate radical dissent into public policy and impose it on the overwhelming majority of American people."[21]

Early in the hearings the Reverend Edwin Fuller, Chief Executive Officer of the American Baptist Convention spoke also for the National Council of Churches of Christ and opposed passage of the amendment. "The leadership of the major Protestant churches," he said, "are not convinced by and large, that God desires an attenuated and conventional worship administered in public school classrooms." Moreover, the leadership of the major Protestant churches, he explained, "are opposed to jeopardizing our long-cherished freedom to worship God as conscience dictates by tampering with the First Amendment." Such an amendment, he concluded, would be dangerous to the freedom of nonbelievers and a threat to the religious well-being of believers.[22]

Appearing the same day and concurring with Dr. Fuller, were the Reverend Eugene Carson Blake, stated clerk of the United Presbyterian Church, and the Reverend William A. Morrison, General Secretary of the Board of Christian Education of that church. Dr. Blake noted that his church had been against governmental involvement in religion for one hundred and eighty years. "I take alarm at this experiment on our liberties," he said. "The Bill of Rights should remain unamended for the rights are inalienable."

Dr. Morrison noted: "If the form and content of religious exercises in the public schools derive from some kind of syncretism or blend or only those elements of several religious traditions that are acceptable to everyone, then the result, as in the Supreme Court case of the Regents' prayer in New York State, can only be seen as a theological caricature at best or a theological monstrosity at worst."

The New York *Times* in its coverage of the testimony of these clergymen noted that "the witnesses underwent extended questioning by Committee members, who obviously disagreed with their testimony."[23]

A key Methodist Church leader, Bishop John Wesley Lord, Head of the Methodist Church in the Washington, D.C., area, saw in the Supreme Court decisions an opportunity and a challenge to give objective religion a rightful place in classrooms within the framework of the Constitution. "I believe it possible," he told the committee, "for public school teachers, without violating the traditional American principle of separation between church and state, to teach moral principles and spiritual values by precept and example." He also explained his belief in the possibility and the necessity within the principle of church-state separation to "integrate objective religious instruction with the regular curriculum, for example, teaching religious classics in courses of literature and in social studies showing the influence of religion upon our society."[24]

This approach was concurred in by the Right Reverend William F. Creighton, Episcopal Bishop of Washington, D.C. Before the committee he explained that "Many of us have . . . rejoiced at the possibility of rescuing religious concern from its confinement in a brief period of Bible reading and prayer, and of making it an integral part of the education process." This view was shared by the Right Reverend J. Brooke-Mosely, Episcopal Bishop of Delaware, who said that both prayer and Bible reading had been "debased" by the ways some schools handled them. Some schools, he added, even broadcast prayers through loudspeakers.[25]

Some notion of the general consensus against the proposed amendments by major religious groups may be seen by scanning the names of those testifying in favor of the court decisions in a typical day — May 29, 1964. These spokesmen included C. Emanuel Carlson, Executive Director of the Baptist Joint Committee of Public Affairs; James F. Cole of the Public Affairs Committee of the Louisiana Baptist Convention; Daniel Neil Heller, National Commander of the Jewish War Veterans of the U.S.A.; and the Reverend Robert L. Zoerheide, representing the Unitarian Universalist Association and the Fellowship for Social Justice.

Testimony was not, however, restricted to regularly recognized religious groups. For example, on June 4, 1964, the Judiciary Committee hearings were interrupted by a protest from Kenneth F. Klinkert of Menomonee Falls, Wisconsin, that no atheists had been invited to testify. At Chairman Celler's suggestion, Mr. Klinkert left with the committee a statement of his position which said, "In the first place, no such thing as a personal 'God' exists. Therefore, uttering an untruth or forcing children to utter an untruth is harmful morally, psychologically and emotionally." Mr. Klinkert suggested that this was similar to "false or untrue advertising on the air or in the newspapers."[26]

The committee also heard Tolbert H. McCarroll, Executive Director of the American Humanist Association, who opposed any amendments in this area. In supporting the Supreme Court's position, he noted: "If a religious or political bias finds its way into a public school, some Americans will inevitably be deprived of the democratic right to live their lives and bring up their children in accord with their own beliefs." Furthermore, he explained, "Those most likely to suffer the immediate deprivation of this basic right are atheists, agnostics, humanists and religious liberals." He also pointed out that the proposed amendments would create, by law, many minorities — Christian children in the public schools of Honolulu, Roman Catholic children in the public schools of Salt Lake City, or Jewish children in the schools of rural western Pennsylvania. The role of the public schools is not to create minorities, but to build an informed population, attentive, among other things, to minority opinion, Mr. McCarroll concluded.[27]

Also opposing the Becker Amendment was Dr. Francis J. Brown, Chairman of the National Association for Personal Rights, an organization centered primarily in Chicago. Arguing that nonsectarian religious instruction in public schools was a logical impossibility, he explained that it was "one thing to tax for the public benefit of academic content and quite another thing to tax for the support of private educational philosophies."[28]

The committee hearings reveal that there occurred early in 1964 a torrent of mail initiated by various well-organized, *ad hoc* groups with names bearing religious overtones. Concerned by this avalanche of mail, which some veteran congressmen privately confided exceeded the amount of mail they had ever received on any subject, the Judiciary Committee not only felt impelled to hold hearings, but for a time in the spring of 1964, it appeared the committee was apt to jump its traces, override the views of its chairman, Representative Celler, and others who insisted on a calm, thorough review of all sides in the dispute, and vote the Becker Amendment out for passage.

It was only in late April and early May, when many of the major congregations began to appreciate the real threat to the First Amendment posed by the organized minority, and began to take official stands publicly and before the committee against the amendment, that the issue was placed in its proper, public perspective. When this occurred, the revisionist tide was stemmed. Future historians may well regard this almost belated action as one of the finest hours in organized religions' programs of social action. To paraphrase Mr. Dooley, if the Supreme Court follows the election returns, this experience suggests that in some instances, at least, Congress follows the churches.

EDUCATOR ATTITUDES TOWARD THE BECKER AMENDMENT

Many educators representing a variety of school systems, colleges, and universities appeared before the committee. In

general it can be said that the testimony of those from public schools and universities and from private nondenominational institutions of learning overwhelmingly opposed the
Becker Amendment and supported the Supreme Court.
There were, of course, those who disagreed.

David A. Robertson, Supervising Principal of the New
Cumberland, Pennsylvania, joint school system told the
committee that his school district had continued programs of
Bible reading after the Supreme Court decisions. When
threatened with an injunction, he said, the devotional exercises were abandoned "reluctantly." He asked for a constitutional amendment to permit their resumption.[29]

Moreover, the Pittsburgh Board of Education came up
with a plan to solve the problem of retaining religion in the
public schools without violating the Supreme Court ban.
On May 19, 1964, the board approved a 168-page guide containing a program of morning exercises which contained
passages from the Bible and references to God in excerpts
from literature, poetry, songs, and student compositions. To
be used first on a one-year trial basis, it was designed to be
a permanent replacement of the former reading of ten Bible
verses.[30]

Sometime earlier, the Pittsburgh Superintendent of
Schools, Sidney P. Marland, Jr., appeared before the Judiciary Committee to oppose the Becker Amendment and to
support the Supreme Court. He contended that pupils could
be taught brotherhood of man, ethics, and integrity without ritual scripture reading or prayer.[31] Mr. Marland served
also as the Chairman of the Commission on Religion and
the Schools established by the American Association of
School Administrators which was later in its published report to strongly support the Supreme Court and to suggest

to public school officials throughout the nation legally acceptable methods of dealing with questions of ethics and morals in the public schools. (This report is discussed at length in Chapter 7.)

Several state school administrators supported amending the Constitution as proposed by Representative Becker. Thomas D. Bailey, Florida State Superintendent of Public Instruction, in favoring the amendment, argued that, "To be silent about religion and the contribution of God-centered religious thought to the growth and development of our nation may be, in effect, to make the public schools an anti-religious factor in the community."[32] In the interests of accuracy it should be pointed out that the Supreme Court rulings by no means require public schools to be "silent about religion."

Mr. Bailey's position, nonetheless, was supported by the Florida Education Association in a resolution adopted on April 25, 1964, and filed with the House Judiciary Committee. The resolution said: "We affirm our faith in Almighty God and our belief that this faith is the chief cornerstone upon which our religious heritage is founded. Therefore we urge the passage of an amendment to the U.S. Constitution to permit the practice of non-sectarian devotions in the public schools. . . ."[33]

The Reverend Robert G. Howes of Catholic University of America called the committee's attention to the fact that state legislatures in Maryland, Michigan, Kentucky, Mississippi, South Carolina, New Jersey, Louisiana, and Massachusetts supported proposals to amend the Constitution to overrule the Supreme Court's decision. He submitted for the record, in addition, fifteen resolutions from school boards and local governing bodies in Massachusetts urging adoption of an amendment in this area. Most of them were almost identical in wording to that of the Gloucester School Committee which stipulated "That the Gloucester School Committee express itself as favoring legislation that is necessary to restore prayer and Bible reading in the public schools . . . on the same basis as prevailed prior to the Supreme Court ruling. . . ."[34]

The typical point of view of denominational school leaders opposing the Supreme Court decision and supporting the need for amendment was given the committee by the Reverend Vincent F. Beatty, S. J., President of Loyola College, Baltimore, Maryland. He argued that the "prayer decisions have inflicted a deep and dangerous hurt in the nation." Furthermore, he felt that unless these decisions were nullified they would "destroy every other practice of public reverence among us." In rejecting the argument that the proposed amendment would weaken the First Amendment, he noted that this had already occurred because of the court's decisions and, in fact, "we are indeed the real defenders of the Bill of Rights."[35]

The preponderant opinion among public school boards as reflected by public statements during this period, however, is exemplified by the Policy Statement of the Wichita, Kansas, Board of Education presented to the Judiciary Committee during its hearings. It said:

> The Board of Education holds that the relationship between religion and the state as expressed in the First Amendment of the Constitution is one of the most distinctive features of American political and religious life. The Board endorses and supports the doctrine of separation of church and state as interpreted by the Supreme Court of the United States . . . the Board hereby commits itself to a position of neutrality with respect to religion. . . .[36]

This view was shared by Thomas W. Braden, President of the California State Board of Education. Mr. Braden said that the question was whether "Government in the United States may force or coerce or embarrass children into prayer."[37]

Reflecting the sentiment of another highly populated area, Frederick C. McLaughlin, Director of the Public Education Association of New York City, testified that the proposed amendment would undermine the integrating function of the public schools. No single prayer would be satisfactory, he said, to win a substantial majority. He also contended, moreover, that a routine devotional exercise was neither good religion nor good education.[38]

A most significant presentation to the House Judiciary Committee came in the form of a statement opposing the Becker Amendment signed by two hundred and twenty-three leading constitutional lawyers and professors of law. The law professors represented all the leading law schools in the country, private and public, denominational and secular.[39] The statement recognized that Supreme Court decisions have, on occasion, been controversial and subject to strong criticism, in some cases, perhaps, even by a majority of Americans. It was too early, however, to determine whether the decisions in question here were in that category, the statement noted. In any event, it argued, it would be far wiser to accept the decisions than to amend the Bill of Rights.

The statement acknowledged that it was, of course, constitutionally possible to amend the Bill of Rights. It pointed out, however:

> American liberties have been secure in large measure because they have been guaranteed by a Bill of Rights which

the American people have until now deemed practically unamendable. If now, for the first time, an amendment to 'narrow its operation' is adopted, a precedent will have been established which may prove too easy to follow when other controversial decisions interpreting the Bill of Rights are handed down.

In conclusion it noted, "Whatever disagreements some may have with the Bible-Prayer decisions, we believe strongly that they do not justify this experiment."

Individual testimony against the amendment came from professors of law from highly diversified law schools. These included, for example, Jefferson B. Fordham, Dean of the University of Pennsylvania Law School; William G. Katz, University of Wisconsin Law School; James C. Kirby, Jr., Vanderbilt University Law School; Phillip B. Kurland, University of Chicago Law School; and the Reverend William J. Kenealy, Boston College Law School.

Father Kenealy told the committee that he did not agree at numerous points with the court's decisions, but he did agree with the results.[40] Ritual prayers and Bible reading, the Jesuit priest insisted, violated the constitutional and personal right of free exercise of religion. This personal right he explained was "independent of political controversies, subject to no primaries or elections, above popular passions and majority votes, and beyond the power of state officials and school boards, guaranteed by our Constitution and entrusted by it to the protection of our courts."

All available evidence suggests that the preponderant majority of educators on all academic levels and from public and private schools alike, supported the Supreme Court and opposed the Becker Amendment or similar devices to alter the First Amendment.

REACTION OF CONGRESS TO THE SCHEMPP CASE

When the news of the Supreme Court's action in the Schempp case first reached Congress, the initial reactions of most of the members willing to be quoted tended to be more restrained than critical. Senate Democratic leader Mansfield said only: "The Supreme Court has its function — we have ours." Asked if the Senate would drop its opening prayer, he replied quickly: "No Sir!"[41]

Senator Aiken (Rep., Vt.) said: "If it is illegal to quote the Bible or read the Lord's Prayer in the public schools it's illegal in Congress, too." He went on to point out, however, that the Supreme Court decision could be changed by a constitutional amendment.[42]

Senator Carlson (Rep., Kans.) who headed the International Christian Leadership movement also was unhappy. "Prayer and religious services are fundamental in the nation's history, and I regret to see a decision that in any way lessens the need for sound principles that are so basic."[43]

Although initial reactions in the Congress were not enthusiastically in support of the court's decision, they did lack the vitriol and rancor of the later reactions of some politicians both in Congress and out.

POLITICS, PRESSURE, AND THE BECKER AMENDMENT

As on most key issues, the division of opinion on the Becker Amendment did not split according to strict party lines. It appears rather that a coalition reaction resulted similar to that apparent in congressional behavior on other major issues. Southern Democrats and "conservative" Republicans tended to favor the amendment, while northern Democrats and "liberal" Republicans tended to oppose it.

There were, however, some notable exceptions to this generalization.

Two months before the House Judiciary Committee began its hearings, House Republican leaders endorsed the amendment. Representative John W. Byrnes of Wisconsin, Chairman of the House Republican Policy Committee, informed the press that this group went on record February 18th in support of the proposal. While not specifically saying so, the context in which this announcement was made suggests it was the hope of House Republican leaders that their members would sign the discharge petition initiated by Representative Becker, thus removing the proposal from the Judiciary Committee.[44]

An example of congressional opinion supporting the Becker Amendment can be seen from the first day's testimony before the House Judiciary Committee when twenty-four members of the House of Representatives appeared, all supporting the amendment. Of this total of twenty-four, twelve represented southern or border states, eight came from the Middle West, while only four came from the states with major metropolitan areas on the east coast. During the first day of hearing fourteen of the twenty-four testifying for the amendment were Republicans and ten were Democrats. But of the Democrats nine came from southern or border states.

The relatively restrained approach of the House Republican Policy Committee opposing the Supreme Court's decisions and supporting the amendment was not the one followed by all Republican congressmen when discussing the issue. A letter from Congressman George A. Goodling (Rep., Pa.) to R. H. Edwin Espy, General Secretary of the National Council of Churches of Christ, was made part of the Judiciary Committee's record. The congressman took Mr. Espy to task because in the congressman's judgment the elected leaders of the National Council of Churches in opposing the amendment did not represent or speak for forty million church members. If Mr. Espy believed that the leadership reflected its membership's views, Congressman Goodling wrote, ". . . you simply don't know what you are talking about." If Mr. Espy would come down from his "exalted" position, the congressman thundered, "You will discover . . . that the chiefs and the Indians are in violent disagreement." Furthermore, Congressman Goodling asserted, ". . . if ever any organization aided, abetted and gave comfort and encouragement to atheists, your organization would head the list."[45]

The impact of his constituents' mail was also alluded to by Congressman Goodling in his letter to Mr. Espy. He pointed out that during the week of April 26, his office had received more than five thousand communications "with more coming in daily." While in no way attempting to minimize the torrent of organized mail sent to congressmen on this subject, it seems clear that it varied from one congressional district to another. Somewhat earlier, Representative Otis Pike (Dem., N.Y.) said that since the mail campaign began several months before, his office had received a total of about four thousand pieces of mail favoring the amendment and perhaps fifty against it.[46] Congressman Paul B. Dague (Rep., Pa.), in his testimony supporting the Becker Amendment, reiterated the experience of some of his colleagues by noting "that no single issue arising in the last 17 years has elicited such a reaction from my constituents as has the Court's decision in the *Schempp* and *Murray cases*."[47]

There is little doubt that from the first, Chairman

Emanuel Celler of the Judiciary Committee was less than enthusiastic about proposals to amend the First Amendment and made it clear that neither he nor the committee was going to be stampeded into rushing an amendment out for floor debate.[48] From the mail and cries of anguish of some congressmen, he concluded even before the hearings began, that one thing was already obvious — that there are eighty-three different religious sects in this country with fifty thousand members or more.[49] In this, Representative Celler was accurately analyzing the high degree of religious pluralism in this country, a fact that seemed to have escaped other congressmen who apparently saw a homogeneity of religious attitudes which does not exist.

Before and during the hearings Mr. Celler was supported by other members of the committee who insisted that whether the Congress or the courts were in favor of religion per se was not the issue in this debate. Congressman Roland Libonati (Dem., Ill.), for example, pointed out repeatedly that the Becker Amendment would cancel the "Freedom of Religion" Clause and "Establishment of Religion" Clause of the First Amendment by superseding it as a later reflection of constitutional policy.[50]

Representative James C. Corman of California, another member of the committee, noted that critics of the committee feared it would take "either a negative attitude or that we would be reaching an un-American decision . . . if we should decide that those who propose amendments are unable to improve on the works of Madison and the First Amendment." While he urged members of the committee to be patient in hearing opposing views, he concluded, ". . . I have impatience with those who would be changing Madison's work."[51]

Representative Corman and Representative Robert Kastenmeier of Wisconsin, as well as Chairman Celler, pointed to the possibility that the amendment, if adopted, would override those state court decisions and statutes prohibiting Bible reading and prayer in the public school. The amendment would preempt the field and force major changes upon a number of states. "Those who are asking that we get back to where we have been, are trying very desperately to take some of us along a road which we have never been, which would be state administration of religious activities," Mr. Corman observed.

Following these comments by northern Democrats, Representative Whitney of North Carolina, a supporter of the amendment, commented dryly, "I know some of us welcome these three colleagues of ours on the states rights bandwagon." And Representative William Cramer (Rep., Fla.) sharply disagreed with the view that the amendment would override state practices prohibiting such programs.[52]

Representative Charlotte T. Reid (Rep., Ill.) complained to the committee that, as a result of the court's decisions, "the malleable student cannot avoid the impression that his Government is, somehow, Anti-God."

This prompted a sharp response from Representative John V. Lindsay, a New York Republican. "We will be taking testimony for weeks," Representative Lindsay said, "and we should require that witnesses address themselves strictly to the constitutional question we face. We should not," he insisted, "permit this to become mixed up with morality and emotionalism. We are not anti anything . . . ," he concluded.[53]

STATE GOVERNORS
AND THE BECKER AMENDMENT

Only two state governors appeared before the Judiciary Committee during its hearings on this subject. Both were from the South and both supported the amendment. Governor Farris Bryant of Florida contended that compulsory attendance at public schools and a barring of prayers from classrooms formed a combination unfair to the pupils. "By what right," he inquired, "can they be required by the federal government or any government, to live most of their waking hours during most of their youth in an environment from which an acknowledgment of prayer to God is artificially restricted?"[54]

The peripatetic Governor Wallace of Alabama also strongly supported the Becker Amendment or something similar to it in his testimony before the Judiciary Committee. His appearance before the committee coincided with that of Bishop Sheen. Some observers felt that Bishop Sheen's position was not enhanced noticeably by this juxtaposition, inasmuch as the two men's names tended to be merged in the headlines of newspapers covering the story.[55]

Governor Wallace told the committee that the court decisions were "part of the deliberate design to subordinate the American people, their faith, their customs and their religious traditions to a Godless state." The Supreme Court, he pointed out, had made "a hollow mockery of the guarantees of the Bill of Rights and sounded the death knell to the democratic institution of local schools controlled by local elected school officials." Nonetheless, the Governor insisted, no school prayers should be made compulsory. When such prayers were used, he contended they should be composed by "decent local folks," who would know just what should be said.[56] The Governor, of course, ignored the fact that in the world of reality which spawned these disputes, the "decent local folks" could not agree on whether such practices were proper, let alone which prayer should be repeated in the public schools.

INTEREST GROUP REACTIONS

In addition to the activities of religious groups and educators who were immediately concerned with the issues involved in the Becker Amendment, a number of major national-interest groups took an active role in the debate. Their particular positions should come as no surprise to anyone familiar with the political polarization of the mid-1960's. If anything, they help bear out the fact that the debate over the court's decisions on prayer and Bible reading was not isolated from the political crosscurrents of the day.

In May of 1964, the American Legion came out in support of an amendment similar to that sponsored by Representative Becker. This organization, claiming three million members, stated that if the court's decisions were not modified, "there will arise from the grass roots a cry of indignation which war veterans and their families will not only support but lead and which will exceed the protests already registered in Congress."

Daniel J. O'Connor, Chairman of the Legion's National Americanism Commission, however, told the Judiciary Committee that his organization while opposing these decisions did not share the criticisms of the Supreme Court, "which would make the judiciary a whipping post for extremists." But he went on to argue that the decisions were coercive and despite arguments to the contrary, interdicted all prayers, whether voluntary or under school, city or state supervision.[57]

A spokesman for the American Farm Bureau Federation, which claimed to represent over 1,628,000 farm and ranch families, said this group not only opposed the court's decisions but supported an amendment to the Constitution overriding them. Mrs. Haven Smith, Chairman of the Women's Committee, testified before the Judiciary Committee and argued that the court's decision "created a great fear among our people. . . . The vast majority of American farmers and ranchers," she explained, "do not believe that religion should be confined to one day of the week, or to the church, or to the home."

Mrs. Smith went on to state "there is a present and pressing need to establish clearly that our Constitution does not make antagonists of religion and government." Furthermore, she advanced the belief that the rationale of those initiating actions seeking to enjoin prayer and Bible reading "has not been an effort to neutralize public education in regard to religion, it has instead appeared to be an effort to outlaw and censor traditional religious references and activities in our public school system."

Students of interest-group behavior should see some significance in the fact that under questioning by Chairman Celler, Mrs. Smith admitted that the policy position supporting a constitutional amendment had not emanated from the grass-roots membership as she had said earlier. Instead, it had been adopted by the American Farm Bureau Board of Directors in executive committee. The resolution of the membership adopted at its national convention stated merely: "We believe the decisions of the Supreme Court in prayer and Bible reading cases constitute an erroneous departure in constitutional interpretation."

Congressman Celler quickly called this discrepancy to the attention of Mrs. Smith. He pointed out:

> It is quite a different thing when you are discussing a matter of such paramount importance as a constitutional amendment to say that resolutions which have been adopted, *which do not even mention a constitutional amendment* [emphasis added], can be construed to favor a constitutional amendment. . . . I don't care what executive board says so, it cannot possibly be so when the original source of power comes from the original resolution passed by the Farm Bureau Federation which, in turn, says nothing about a constitutional amendment. . . . Maybe that is what the executive board wanted or desired, but it is certainly not a part or parcel of the resolution originally adopted.[58]

Months before this, however, other groups less well known but highly active had begun a concerted drive to bring pressure on Congress to negate the court decisions. Testimony before the House Judiciary Committee reveals that as early as October 17, 1963, groups such as the International Christian Youth of the U.S.A., and its subsidiary, "Project America," launched the "Return the Bible to the Schools Campaign." Their goal was to obtain one million signatures and petitions to congressmen in support of the Becker Amendment.[59] They did not stand alone.

The John Birch Society was active in their behalf as is revealed in the John Birch Society Bulletin of March 2, 1964. This document briefly summarized the background of the Becker Amendment and the problem faced by its supporters in obtaining enough signatures on a discharge petition to remove it from the Judiciary Committee of the

House. The importance of the discharge petition to the success of the amendment is stressed. "It is almost certain that
the Bill will be passed if it can be brought to the floor of the
House," the bulletin reported. "This would start the wheels
rolling," it predicted, "for almost certain ratification of the
amendment by the required 38 legislatures."

This publication of the John Birch Society went on to
emphasize the significance of passing the amendment. It explained: "This forced reversal of the winds blowing atheistic
communism in, as the official 'atmosphere' of our country,
would be a body blow to the morale of all the pro-Com-
munist bellows behind those winds — which means most of
the liberal establishment."

The bulletin concluded by urging members to write to
their congressmen and to the "Americanism Committee . . .
or to the International Christian Youth — U.S.A., Collings-
wood, New Jersey, or to both. They will give you the information and guidance to do a really effective job."[60]

Testifying before the committee in this connection were
Carl Thomas McIntire, National Chairman of the International Christian Youth of the U.S.A., accompanied by Larry
Miller, National Director of that group's "Project America"
and "Return the Bible to the Schools Campaign." Under
careful questioning by members of the committee, especially
Congressman Senner (Dem., Ariz.), these young men admitted that the International Christian Youth of the U.S.A.
was in fact a part of the International Council of Christian
Churches (which they defined as composed of conservative
Protestant congregations), although in these two programs,
they said, they sought support from youth of all denominations.

They took credit also for their organization's action in

circulating thousands of post cards to be sent by individuals to their congressmen urging passage of the Becker Amendment. But they denied that their "Project America" was the same one referred to in the *Liberty Letter* of May, 1964, distributed by the Liberty Lobby. The purpose of the *Liberty Letter* is clarified in that issue to correct any wrong ideas that subscribers may have. It explained:

> They think that its purpose is to inform liberals and do-nothings about the communist conspiracy. Or they think that its purpose is to tickle their intellect, like a crossword puzzle or a book by Bill Buckley.
>
> But LIBERTY LETTER is neither a philosophical treatise nor an exposé. LIBERTY LETTER is written to Conservatives who already 'know the score' and want ACTION.[61]

This issue of the *Letter* irritated committee members for a number of reasons. Not only did it invite people to an old-fashioned political rally where "the distinguished columnist Westbrook Pegler" would "lower the boom" on the White House crew and its pinko friends, the *Letter* contained also a sharp attack on Chairman Celler of the Judiciary Committee. After warning its readers not to be deluded into the belief that "Manny [Celler] has suddenly 'got religion'" because he had scheduled hearings on the Becker Amendment, the *Letter* noted:

> Celler knows that if the Becker Resolution ever reaches the floor of the House it will be passed by an overwhelming majority and sent on its way to the Senate and the individual states to certain victory. To prevent this savage slap at the Warren Court, Arch-secularist Celler will pull out all stops to tie the Becker Amendment into endless knots of red tape until the Congress adjourns for this summer's political conventions.

The two young men who appeared before the committee to represent the International Christian Youth of the U.S.A., insisted under questioning that the various phases of its operation were in no way connected to the Liberty Lobby or similar groups, despite the similarity of the post cards designed to be sent to congressmen which emanated from the several organizations. But Mr. Miller replied to Congressman Corman that he was happy the congressman had read into the record the endorsement of their project by the John Birch Society.

Their prepared statement to the committee said, "We believe that you must move with great haste to guard our Constitution which provides three distinct branches of Government, *taking away from the Judicial branch the final authority over all legislation* [emphasis added] and asserting the power properly vested in you, and only you." Despite the seemingly clear-cut recommendation to abolish the power of judicial review contained in this testimony, Mr. Miller under questioning from Representative Rogers insisted that nothing in the statement was meant "to imply that we would be taking away anything from the judicial branch."[62]

TURNING OF THE TIDE

By mid-May, 1964, it would appear from the Judiciary Committee hearings and from press reports, that the issues and forces involved in the movement for the Becker Amendment had come to be better understood in Congress and throughout the country. When this occurred, it seems to this writer that much of the impetus behind the drive in favor of the amendment was lost.

Several reasons explaining this phenomenon stand out. First, during April and May of 1964, many religious organizations and leaders went on record as opposing the amendment, with most of them also formally supporting the Supreme Court's decisions. Secondly, the action of the Judiciary Committee itself was extremely important in clarifying and delineating group responses and attitudes toward the proposal and pinpointing the organized nature not only of the mail campaign on Congress, but the organized nature of much of the resistance to the Supreme Court itself. This is one instance where the classic role of congressional hearings to inform both Congress and the public of countervailing forces in the society seems to have been realized.

The actions of Representative Robert L. Leggett (Dem., Calif.) are illustrative of the change in congressional reactions as the hearings progressed. Mr. Leggett, who had been one of the first members of Congress to sponsor legislation to override the Supreme Court's decisions, appeared before the Judiciary Committee on May 20, 1964, and urged that the First Amendment be left unchanged.[63] He told the committee that a constitutional amendment in this area could result in religious upheavals, intolerance, and the persecution of minorities. He noted that the hearings had demonstrated that the leadership of the National Council of Churches, Baptist, Quaker, Jewish, Lutheran, Presbyterian, Seventh Day Adventist, Unitarian, and United Church of Christ groups all opposed amendatory action. Moreover, he reminded the committee, Roman Catholics, Episcopalians and Methodists were divided among themselves over support of such an amendment.

Mr. Leggett also alluded to the absence of an understanding of facts which characterized some who supported the amendment. For example, he said that several thousand of his constituents were still pressing him to keep fighting for a return of prayers to California public schools. What these people failed to realize, he explained, was that there have been no public school prayers in California for sixty-two years because the state constitution bans them.[64]

During the same day the committee heard Representative Paul C. Jones (Dem., Mo.) complain that misinterpretations of the First Amendment, the focal point of the court's decisions, were causing widespread and dangerous confusion. He did not excuse members of the court from contributing to this state of affairs. Mr. Justice Douglas' concurring opinion in the Engel case had declared "in advance," Mr. Jones thought, that many of the religious aspects of government ceremonial and financial operations were unconstitutional. According to the congressman, these ranged from the prayers of congressional chaplains to the motto "In God We Trust" on coins and bills. Rather than concentrating on possible amendments, Mr. Jones said, Congress should repudiate such interpretations "and let the world know we believe in God."[65]

At this time the New York *Times* was reporting that the Judiciary Committee's mail which at first was heavily in favor of an amendment was now running heavier in opposition.[66] The paper noted that "a similar trend was reported from the offices of individual members, including sponsors of some of the pending 147 overriding resolutions."

Shortly afterward, the sponsor of another proposal to change the First Amendment suggested a compromise to the Judiciary Committee. Representative Cornelius E. Gallagher (Dem., N.J.) asked the committee to convert his proposed amendment into a simple congressional expression in favor of his plan. His plan would have set aside a few minutes at the beginning of each school day for silent prayer or meditation. Mr. Gallagher told the committee that "This requires no prescribed prayer, it requires no one to pray. It eliminates the need for excusal provisions and the harsh stigma of nonconformity."

Despite the fact that he introduced an amendment on the subject, Mr. Gallagher told the committee he agreed with the court decision that banned school prayer composed and ordered by school management. He expressed the belief that the Bill of Rights needed no amendment, but argued that some action was now required by Congress.

The New York *Times* reported that the Judiciary Committee showed "immediate and cooperative attention." Chairman Emanuel Celler observed later, the newspaper noted, that this or a similar measure might serve to get sponsors of many of the pending one hundred and forty-seven resolutions calling for constitutional amendments "off the hook."[67]

The Judiciary Committee hearings were concluded June 3, 1964, with the committee taking no action on any of the proposed amendments then or later and Congress was to adjourn without acting either upon a discharge petition or upon the substantive proposals. The tide of public reaction seemed to turn as churches, Congress, and many other groups, by clarifying the significance of the court's rulings and their scope, placed matters in a clearer perspective and stemmed one of the most powerful onslaughts upon basic constitutional guarantees in the history of the United States.

9

Where We Stand

THIS PROBLEM does not submit to generalities and even attempts at summarization must be made with a great deal of caution. I do so here. There is no question, however, that the Supreme Court's decisions banning state-sponsored prayer and Bible reading in the public schools profoundly affect state laws and educational programming in many states.

At the time the Schempp case was handed down, the Constitution and statutes of various states reflected an abiding desire to keep public funds from supporting sectarian institutions of any type. All states but Vermont had constitutional provisions prohibiting the expenditure of public funds for sectarian purposes. In addition to this, twenty-four states had statutes prohibiting sectarian instruction in the public schools. But these enactments did not spell out what practices constituted sectarian instruction. As a result, Bible reading and religious exercises of the sort outlawed by the court in the Engels case and the Schempp case, had not been regarded as sectarian in many of the states.

At the time the Supreme Court acted in this area, thirty-seven states permitted Bible reading in their public schools.

Mississippi was the only state which had a constitutional provision which permitted such an exercise. (No state constitution specifically prohibited programs of this type.) Twelve states had statutes which required Bible reading in the public schools. Five other states had statutes which permitted, but did not require, Bible reading. Five states, in addition to the above, had court decisions in the absence of statutory provisions, which permitted Bible reading and, prior to the Supreme Court action, were equally binding. Furthermore, fourteen states permitted Bible reading in the absence of any provisions whatsoever, and this practice had never been challenged in the courts of those states.

In only eleven states was Bible reading considered sectarian instruction prior to the court's decision in the Schempp case. In eight of those states, this conclusion had resulted from judicial decisions of the states' high courts. In the remaining three states, educational policy formulators had looked at the state constitutions and statutes and had concluded that Bible reading in the public schools was illegal. Montana, Hawaii, and Alaska are not included in any of the foregoing categories because of an absence of any evidence regarding their policies. Clearly then, while most states opposed sectarian instruction in the public schools, there was real disagreement as to what practices were sectarian prior to the Supreme Court's actions in 1962 and 1963 clarifying this matter.

Prior to the Schempp decision, the high courts of twenty-one states plus a federal district court in Pennsylvania had ruled on the legality of Bible reading in the public schools.

The highest courts of fourteen states had specifically upheld Bible-reading practices. Essentially the same argu-

ments were used by all these courts. Their major conclusion was that the Bible is not a sectarian book. Moreover, they denied that the King James Version of the Protestants was sufficiently different from the Douay Version of the Catholics to require its being classed as a sectarian book. Christianity is so interwoven in the fabric of our government, these courts noted, that it would violate our historic tradition to prohibit such a practice as Bible reading in the schools. Furthermore, they refused to accept the contention that such exercises constituted a public expenditure for sectarian purposes because the Bible was not sectarian in their judgment. They stressed that the Bible contained moral instruction common to all religions and emphasized that moral instruction is an important part of public education. They also believed that Bible reading was important for an understanding of literature and history. They stated that the power of curriculum planning rests with the state legislatures and the school boards. Courts had no right to dictate educational policy, these courts argued. However, most of the courts which upheld Bible reading prior to the Schempp case stressed that such reading must be done without comment and attendance could not be made compulsory.

Prior to the action of the Supreme Court in 1963, the high courts of seven states and a federal district court in Pennsylvania had concluded that Bible reading in the public schools was illegal. State courts reached this conclusion because they sincerely regarded the Bible as a sectarian book. There could be little doubt, they explained, that such exercises violated the religious sensibilities of non-Christians as well as nonbelievers. They noted that these practices violated the American tradition of church-state separation since they constituted governmental preference of one religion over others. Furthermore, they pointed out, since it was the King James Version that was usually chosen for these exercises, this violated the religious freedom of Roman Catholic and Jewish children. The King James Version lacks the Apocryphal books upon which are based the theory of purgatory and other points of dogma important to Roman Catholics. Jews object to the Christology of the New Testament and prefer the Lessar translation or other similar translations of the Old Testament.

The courts which held Bible reading unconstitutional prior to the Supreme Court's action in the Schempp case were concerned with keeping the public schools open to children of all religions. The only way this could be accomplished, it appeared to them, was to prevent the teaching of the schools from injuring any student's religious beliefs. Finally, they stressed, it made little difference that these exercises were conducted without comment or that a child might be excused from them by presenting a request from his parents. Such exclusion stigmatizes the student in the eyes of his fellows, they pointed out, since he was leaving because of apparent hostility to a book which was revered by those students who remained. Thus the democracy of the classroom was destroyed. Several of the lower courts noted in conclusion that the free enjoyment of religious worship included the right not to worship.

At this juncture, there may be some merit in summarizing the arguments on both sides of this controversy.

The individuals and groups who advocate Bible reading and related exercise in the public schools generally base their arguments on the following points: Their major premise seems to be that present conditions in the United States and in the world demand religious exercises in the schools. They explain that it has been only recently that our public schools have been "secularized," since historically the public schools have always been deeply concerned with religion. Not only were religious exercises conducted every day in the schools, but there was systematic Bible study in the upper grades. During the early days of our history, the churches affiliated and cooperated with the public schools.

In the middle of the nineteenth century, the public schools gradually became secularized because of the infiltration of large numbers of immigrants belonging to the Roman Catholic and Jewish faiths. This period also saw the multiplication of Protestant sects. The change to a secular public school system was gradual but complete.

Many of the proponents of Bible reading feel that the few states which kept up the empty formality of Bible reading without comment, prior to the Supreme Court's decisions, were maintaining a practice which probably did more harm than good. Today, while the public schools have become totally separated from all church influence, there exists in the United States a lack of religious instruction and understanding, these groups point out. Those who favor such programs note that the majority now receives no systematic religious instruction.

They go on to stress that in the one hundred years in which the change to a secular public school was effected, America has been slowly but surely losing its ideals and moral standards. Early Americans, they note, whether Puritan, Cavalier, Calvinist, or Quaker, were devoutly religious and insisted upon religious education and training for their children. Today, they argue, crime conditions are worse than in any other state or leading nation in the world. (This statement is followed by a host of statistics seeking to bear out such a contention.) Furthermore, they note, our literature is generally unwholesome and some of it is vulgar, obscene, and immoral. Newspapers and magazines stress the sensational and sordid, while movies and TV pollute the minds and morals of our youth. Politics has degenerated to a new low in the subterranean abyss of corruption. Public apathy has increased to a point where today a majority of people do not vote, with the result that professional politicians control the government of almost every state and city. Finally, they conclude, feeble-mindedness, insanity, and suicide are increasing rapidly.[1]

Those who favor Bible reading and religious instruction believe that such programs will go a long way toward remedying these conditions. They stress that morals and ethics cannot be taught apart from religion, and it is education and moral training that distinguishes a cultured man from a barbarian or criminal. Moreover, a majority of children cannot be reached for the inculcation of moral and religious values except through the public schools.

In addition, they put forth several other reasons why it would be desirable to maintain programs of religious instruction in the public schools: It will bring the lofty ideals and beautiful lessons of Christianity to all the children in our land. This will aid greatly in the improvement of the developing generation, and, while such improvement will be gradual, it will be continual. American ideals will thus be restored and elevated. Furthermore, such a plan is a practicable remedy for our ills, they believe. It is truly American, having worked well in this land for over two hundred years, and is required by law today in a substantial number of states. Programs of this nature have been and are now successfully being used in many countries of the world. It is not necessary, they insist, to teach sectarian dogmas in these exercises, but merely the fundamentals upon which nearly everyone agrees.

Those who oppose religious instruction and Bible reading agree essentially that such programs are unnecessary and unwise. They state that our public schools are now doing a very satisfactory job of educating our young, and they present material which illustrates that public schools are better than parochial and private schools. The public schools are no more godless, they explain, than are the executive, legislative, and judicial branches of our government. While everyone agrees public schools are not perfect, it is clear that they are being constantly improved.

The opponents of Bible reading in the public schools stress that crime conditions in the United States are not due to the absence of religious teaching in the public schools. They note that no real evidence has been presented which proves that crime is caused or increased by the absence of such programs, in spite of the many people who keep making such assertions. It is pointed out that crime is not perceptibly less in those states which have Bible reading and religious instructions in the schools. Because of better methods of communication, crime is much more publicized today than it was in the past. This creates an impression that more crime exists, which does not necessarily follow. Moreover, this group cites statistics which illustrate plainly that the great majority of criminals have had religious instruction in their youth, and are Christians with church affiliations. They note that criminologists attribute the prevalence of crime to other causes, such as the breakdown of the American home, poor environments, and bad companionship.

Ignorance of the Bible, they believe, does not result from the fact that many public schools do not give religious instruction. Whereas one hundred years ago the Bible was the only book in most homes from which the children might learn to read, today there are thousands of children's books to develop youthful reading. It is the duty of the church and the home to teach religious and moral values. This is the only way each child may be taught the religion of his parents' choice. If the public schools were required to have programs of this nature, they could not help but injure the religious sensibilities of some students. Furthermore, while the school can teach moral and ethical truths without resorting to religious instruction, if such instruction is given it will offend the religious beliefs of some students, thus making the moral and ethical instruction ineffectual.

Those who oppose Bible reading believe that admitting these programs into the public schools would be an unfortunate backward step. The mere reading of several biblical passages without comment, they note, can do no good but may do considerable harm. In the first place, some teachers might seize this as an opportunity to proselyte. Secondly, parts of the Bible are not suited for reading to young children. Thirdly, since students are inquisitive, it is unwise pedagogically to read them anything which the teacher may not explain. Finally, the Bible by its very nature is sectarian, for even within the Christian faith Catholics and Protestants disagree as to which version is correct. Such programs, it is also pointed out, disregard the rights and deny religious liberty to freethinkers and nonbelievers. The

American tradition of separation of church and state would be violated by such exercises, and examples are given to illustrate that church control of education has always been bad for education.

Lastly, the opposition believes it is impracticable to have Bible-reading and related exercises in the public schools. People have never been able to agree on the fundamental religious tenets that might be included in programs of this sort. There is even disagreement over whether it should be read for its literary and historic value or for its moral teachings. They go on to point out that not only is the average public school teacher unqualified to teach religion, but programs for compulsory religion have always proved ineffective regardless of the teacher's training. It should also be remembered that some public school teachers are nonbelievers; this would certainly affect their method of directing these programs. Such exercises, it is concluded, are certain to create violent dissension which will impair and often disrupt the work of the public school.

THE CONTEMPORARY SCENE

This writer is convinced that the Supreme Court was correct in its constitutional interpretation of the state-sponsored prayer and Bible-reading cases, and clarified in its interpretation an important area of public policy which had for long been lacking in explicitness. These cases rank in prominence and controversial nature with the court's decisions outlawing racial discrimination in the public schools and its action designed to curtail malapportionment in state legislatures and congressional districts. Moreover, it appears to this writer that, if possible, more public misunderstanding resulted from the Supreme Court's decisions on religion in the public schools than in either the race relations cases or the apportionment decisions. This may account for the fact that the most thorough attack to undercut the Supreme Court through constitutional amendment occurred in this area.

Bible-reading and related programs stirred increased resentment in the mid-twentieth century in part because of the mushrooming metropolitan areas characteristic of the United States today. The megalopolis represents a polyglot of economic, social, political, and religious attitudes. Today it is increasingly more difficult to find in any community the uniformity and homogeneity of religious views which characterized the United States when it was largely an agriculturally oriented society.

Thus, practices such as Bible reading aroused little or no controversy when the community was, for example, predominantly Protestant (and in many instances composed of members of one or two Protestant denominations). Today, however, such programs cause considerable restiveness where the population represents a variety of religious faiths. Second, there is discernible a growing willingness of large numbers of Americans, as reflected in the 1960 American presidential campaign, not only to recognize but to insist on respecting the religious sensibilities of divergent religious faiths. This willingness may result from the fact that in the last twenty years large numbers of Americans have served or visited in foreign lands with vastly different religious customs. In matters of this sort, it appears that familiarity breeds respect.

It is true, nonetheless, that the Supreme Court's action in the Engels and Schempp cases brought forth vicious attacks upon that body in some circles. There are a number of possible reasons for this. Many people did not really study the court's opinions, and were thus easy victims for those who chose to distort their scope. Furthermore, the public is probably less informed concerning the intricacies inherent in the workings of the judiciary than the other branches of government and the coverage by the mass media is also less thorough.

In addition, persons and groups critical of the court for other reasons, sought to capitalize upon the prominence of this issue, and, by distorting the court's ruling, to marshall major public opposition to the court and to the entire principle of judicial review. Thus many well-intentioned laymen were convinced that the court had completely banned the Bible from the school. They did not realize that the Supreme Court, in both the Engels and Schempp cases, specifically pointed out that its decision did not prohibit the use of the Bible in the study of history or of literature. The decisions said merely that the Bible could not be used as a devotional tool.

One of the more disturbing revelations growing out of the opposition to the court's decisions was that a great many people, some in governmental positions of prominence, do not clearly understand the nature of contemporary American society. Or, if they do, they are attempting to escape its complexities, and crave the quick, easy answer. It is clear from some of the comments quoted in earlier pages, that many critics of the court do not understand the pluralism elemental to the United States and reflected especially in the proliferation of religious sects. It was this religious pluralism, already obvious in the nation's formative years, which, after all, prompted the First Amendment.

Another factor which helps to explain the bitter attacks upon the Supreme Court is the unfortunate fact that many

Americans do not really understand the purpose of the Bill of Rights. That purpose is, of course, to protect minorities of one type or another and to post some things as off-limits to majorities regardless of how sincere and morally motivated the majority may be. Nothing is more personal than an individual's relationship between himself and his God, and thus, in one sense, every man is his own minority in this area. It was not by accident that our founding fathers placed as the very first provision of the Bill of Rights, the prohibition against establishing a religion and next, the provision protecting the freedom of religion. Moreover, it is quite possible to see the public, rote, religious, or devotional exercises discussed here as actually a manifestation of religiosity rather than religion.

Moreover, too few Americans appreciate that the public schools, more perhaps than any other agency, are the meeting place and focus of American pluralism. Individuals, irrespective of race, creed, color or wealth, are brought together in the public schools as the faculty and student body. They include more Roman Catholic children than all of the Catholic schools on every level combined; they include more Protestant children than all the Protestant schools combined; and they include more Jewish children than all the Jewish schools combined. Of all institutions in our democracy, the public school is probably the most religiously tolerant and functionally cognizant of the plural nature of our society.

The key power of America's public schools resides in the opportunity they provide for the creative engagement of differences. Such differences include not only mental and physical capacities, but, even more importantly, differences in culture and background and differences in the creeds men live by. Those concerned with pushing governmentally sanctioned religious exercises in the public schools, knowingly or unknowingly would lessen this power of the schools and weaken the very institution which has served our heterogeneous society so well.

Notes

CHAPTER 1

1. Leo Pfeffer, "Religion, Education and the Constitution," 8 *Lawyers Guild Review* 387 (1948).
2. In Peter G. Mode, *Source Book and Bibliographical Guide for American Church History*, (1921), pp. 78–79.
3. Butts, *American Tradition in Religion and Education*, (Beacon Press, Boston, 1950), p. 113. See also: D. J. Boorstin, *The Americans*, (New York, 1958), pp. 17–19; C. H. Dodd, *The Authority of the Bible*, (New York, Harper Torchbook, 1958), pp. 173–76.
4. M. Curti, *The Growth of American Thought*, (Harper & Brothers, New York, 1951), pp. 53 ff.
5. Curti, *op. cit.*, p. 53.
6. Pfeffer, *op. cit.*, p. 391.
7. Nathan Schachner, *Church, State and Education*, reprinted from *The American Jewish Year Book*, Vol. 49 (1947–48), American Jewish Committee, (New York, 1947), p. 11.
8. *Ibid.*
9. Sherman Smith, *The Relation of the State to Religious Education*, (New York, 1926), p. 71.
10. E. P. Cubberley, *Public Education in the United States*, (Houghton Mifflin Co., New York, 1934), p. 41.
11. Curti, *op. cit.*, p. 54.
12. M. G. Hunt, "Bible Study in Public Schools," *Peabody Journal of Education*, 23:156, Nov., 1945.
13. Curti, *op. cit.*, p. 55.
14. C. H. Moehlman, *School and Church*, (Harper & Brothers, New York, 1944), p. 28.
15. *Ibid.*
16. Curti, *op. cit.*, pp. 57–58.
17. Quoted in Moehlman, *op. cit.*, p. 27.

18. A. P. Stokes, *Church and State in the United States,* (Harper & Brothers, New York, 1950), Vol. I, pp. 470–71.
19. *Journal of the American Congress, 1774–1788,* (Washington, 1823), II, pp. 261–62.
20. *Ibid.,* XIX, p. 221. For a full account see, Robert Dearden, Jr., and Douglas Watson, *The Bible of the Revolution,* (San Francisco, 1931), p. 16; Stokes, *op. cit.,* Vol. I, pp. 470–72.
21. See for example, Butts, *American Tradition in Religion and Education,* (Boston, 1950); Konvitz, "Separation of Church and State," 14 *Law and Contemporary Problems* 55 [1949; Justice Rutledge's dissenting opinion in Everson v. Board of Education, 330 U.S. 1 (1947)].
22. See for example, E. S. Corwin, "The Supreme Court as National School Board," 14 *Law and Contemporary Problems* 3 (1949); James O'Neill, *Religion and Education Under the Constitution,* (New York, 1949); L. Pfeffer, "Religion, Education and the Constitution," 8 *Lawyers Guild Review* 387 (1948).
23. Stokes, *op. cit.,* Vol. II, p. 53.
24. Sherman Smith, *The Relation of the State to Religious Education in Massachusetts,* (New York, 1926), p. 104.
25. Stokes, *op. cit.,* Vol. I, p. 310. For a summation of Washington's writings on the Bible and religion see: N. Cousins, *In God We Trust,* (New York, 1958), pp. 44–73.
26. "Washington's Farewell Address," C. R. Gaston, ed., in *Standard English Classics.*
27. *U.S. Stat. at Large,* Foreign Treaties, VIII, 155.
28. Jared Sparks, *The Works of Benjamin Franklin,* (1847), V. 153, quoted by Moehlman, *op. cit.,* p. 52. For a summary of Franklin's writings on the Bible and religion see: Cousins, *op. cit.,* pp. 16–43.
29. From S. Padover, *The Complete Jefferson,* (New York, 1943), p. 1049, by permission of Duell, Sloan & Pearce, Inc. For a summation of Jefferson's views on religion and the Bible see: Cousins, *op. cit.,* pp. 114–216.
30. Padover, *op. cit.,* pp. 669–70.
31. Butts, *op. cit.,* p. 121. See also R. J. Honeywell, *The Educational Work of Thomas Jefferson,* (Harvard University Press, Cambridge, 1931), pp. 200–256; and J. F. Constanzo, "Thomas Jefferson, Religious Education and Public Law," 8 *Journal of Public Law* 81 (1959).
32. Padover, *op. cit.,* p. 1104.
33. Butts, *op. cit.,* p. 126.
34. Honeywell, *op. cit.,* p. 249.
35. From *James Madison: Nationalist, 1780–1787,* by Irving Brant, pp. 353–54; copyright (c) by The Bobbs-Merrill Co., Inc., used by special permission of the publishers. See also: Cousins, *op. cit.,* pp. 295–325.

36. I. James D. Richardson, *Messages and Papers of the Presidents,* (1896), pp. 489–90.
37. See Konvitz, *op. cit.,* p. 56.
38. 7 Pet. (U.S.) 243 (1833).
39. 3 How. (U.S.) 589 (1845).
40. Cantwell v. Connecticut, 310 U.S. 296 (1940).
41. State ex rel. McCollum v. Board of Education 333 U.S. 203 (1948).
42. Pfeffer, *op. cit.,* p. 391.
43. A. Schlesinger, Jr., *The Age of Jackson,* (Little, Brown and Co., Boston, 1945), p. 355.
44. Butts, *op. cit.,* p. 115. Some observers might disagree with this view.
45. For a thorough discussion of this see: R. A. Billington, *The Protestant Crusade, 1800–1860,* (New York, 1938); also Stokes, *op. cit.,* Vol. I, pp. 833–38.
46. J. L. Blau (ed.), *Cornerstones of Religious Freedom,* (Boston. 1949), p. 160.
47. Sherman Smith, *op. cit.,* pp. 61–62.
48. Stokes, *op. cit.,* Vol. II, p. 56.
49. R. B. Culver, *Horace Mann and Religion in the Massachusetts Public Schools,* (Yale University Press, New Haven, 1929), p. 193.
50. Culver, *op. cit.,* p. 170.
51. Stokes, *op. cit.,* p. 56.
52. *Ibid.,* p. 57.
53. Culver, *op. cit.,* pp. 230–31.
54. Butts, *op. cit.,* pp. 132–33.
55. *Laws of New York,* 1842, 65 Session, C. 150.14.
56. H. S. Randall, *Decision of the State Superintendent of Common Schools, on the Right to Compell Catholic Children to Attend Prayers,* (Dept. of Common Schools, Albany, Oct. 27, 1853), pp. 5–8.
57. Lewis v. Board of Education, 157 Misc. 520, 285 NYS 164 (1935), *appeal dismissed,* 276 N.Y. 490, 12 N.E. 2d. 172 (1937).
58. See Billington, *The Protestant Crusade;* and Stokes, *op. cit.,* Vol. II, Chapt. XIX, 4, Vol. III, Chapt. XXIII, 1.
59. For reproductions of some of these cartoons, see Stokes, *op. cit.,* Vol. II, (Illus. inserts).
60. Stokes, *op. cit.,* p. 68.
61. Pfeffer, *op. cit.,* p. 142.
62. *Ibid.*
63. Pfeffer, *op. cit.,* p. 392.
64. Butts, *op. cit.,* p. 144.
65. C. Zollman, *Church and School in the American Law,* (Concordia Publishing House, St. Louis, 1918), p. 8.
66. H. Beale, *A History of Freedom of Teaching* (New York, 1941), p. 214.

67. *Ibid.,* p. 215.
68. See Moore v. Monroe, 64 Iowa 367, 20 N.W. 475 (1884); Pfeiffer v. Board of Education, 118, Mich. 560, 77 N.W. 250 (1898); Spiller v. Inhabitants of Woburn, 12 Allen (Mass.) 127 (1866); all upholding Bible reading; and, Board of Education v. Minor, 23 Ohio St. 211 (1872); State ex rel. Weiss v. Dist. Board, 76 Wis. 177, 44 N.W. 967 (1890), prohibiting such programs.
69. *U.S. Stat. at Large,* 29:411 (June 11, 1896).
70. National Educational Association Research Bulletin, "The State and Sectarian Education," February, 1946, p. 36.

CHAPTER 2

1. Leo Pfeffer, "Religion, Education and the Constitution," 8 *Lawyers Guild Review* 387 (1948); Butts, *American Tradition in Religion and Education,* (Boston, 1950), p. 142.
2. 221 U.S. 559 (1911).
3. Wisconsin Const., Art. I, Sec. 18.
4. *Ibid.,* Art. X, Sec. 3.
5. For fuller discussions of the state constitutions mentioned in this section see F. N. Thorpe, *The Federal and State Constitutions, Colonial Charters, and Other Organic Laws of the States,* (Washington, 1909), Vols. I–VII; and A. P. Stokes, *Church and State in the United States,* (New York, 1950), Vol. I.
6. Thorpe, *op. cit.,* Vol. IV, p. 2454. For the text of this section see Ch. 2, p. 45, *infra.*
7. Stokes, *op. cit.,* Vol. I, p. 424. For J. Adams' views on religion and the Bible see the Jefferson-Adams letters, as selected in N. Cousins, *In God We Trust,* (New York, 1958), pp. 217–94.
8. J. C. Meyer, *Church and State in Massachusetts, 1740–1833,* (Cleveland, 1930), pp. 234–35.
9. Stokes, *op. cit.,* Vol. I, p. 432. For the text of this elaborate article see Thorpe, *op. cit.,* Vol. VI, pp. 3255–57.
10. Swart v. South Burlington Township School District, 167 A. 2d. 514 (1961).
11. For a thorough discussion of the battle in Virginia, see for example, Stokes, *op. cit.,* Vol. I, pp. 366–97.
12. Thorpe, *op. cit.,* Vol. I, pp. 544–45.
13. *Ibid.,* Vol. III, pp. 1274–76.
14. N.E.A. Research Bulletin, "The State and Sectarian Education," February, 1946, p. 10.
15. Cooley, *A Treatise on Constitutional Limitations,* 8 ed., (Little, Brown and Co., Boston, 1927), Vol. II, Ch. XIII, "On Religious Liberty," p. 966.
16. But Vermont does have a constitutional provision guaranteeing the free exercise of religion; Vt. Const. c. I, Art. 3.
17. See "Public Aid to Establishments of Religion," 96 *Univ. of Pa. L. Rev.* 230 (1947); "Catholic Schools and Public Money," 50 *Yale L. J.* 917 (1940); David Fellman, "Separation of Church and State," 1950 *Wis. L. Rev.* 443–44.

18. See 96 *Univ. of Pa. L. Rev.* 230 (1947).
19. Constitutions of: Ariz. Art. II, sec. 12; Calif., Art. IV, sec. 30; Colo., Art. V, sec. 34, Art. IX, sec. 7; Fla. Declaration of Rights, sec. 6; Ga. Art. I, sec. 1, par. XIV; Idaho Art. IX, sec. 5; Ill. Art. VIII, sec. 3; Ind. Art. I, sec. 6; La. Art. IV, sec. 8; Mich. Art. II, sec. 3; Minn. Art. I, sec. 16; Mo. Art. II, sec. 7; Mont. Art. V, sec. 35; Nev. Art. XI, sec. 10; N. H. Art. 82; Okla. Art. II, sec. 5; Ore. Art. I, sec. 5; Pa. Art. III, sec. 18; S. Car. Art. XI, sec. 9; S. Dak. Art. VI, sec. 3; Tex. Art. I, sec. 7; Utah Art. I, sec. 4; Wash. Art. I, sec. 11; Wis. Art. I, sec. 18; Wyo. Art. I, sec. 19.
20. Constitutions of: Ala. Art. XIV, sec. 263; Ariz. Art. IX, sec. 10; Calif. Art. IX, sec. 8; Del. Art. X, sec. 3; Fla. Art. XII, sec. 13; Ky. sec. 189; La. Art. XII, sec. 13; Minn. Art. VIII, sec. 3; N. Mex. Art. XII, sec. 3; N. Y. Art. IX, sec. 4; N. Dak. Art. VIII, sec. 152; Pa. Art. X, sec. 2; S. Dak. Art. VIII, sec. 16; Tex. Art. VII, sec. 5; Wash. Art. IX, sec. 4.
21. Constitutions of: Ala. Art. IV, sec. 73; Ark. Art. XIV, sec. 3; Calif. Art. IX, sec. 8; Idaho, Art. IX, sec. 5; Kans. Art. VI, sec. 8; Me. Art. VIII; Mass. Amend. XLVI; Mo. Art. XI, sec. 11; Mont. Art. XI, sec. 8; Neb. Art. VIII, sec. 11; N. Mex. Art. XII, sec. 3; Utah, Art. X, sec. 13; Va. Art. IX, sec. 141; Wyo. Art. VII, sec. 8.
22. Ala. Const. Art. XIV, sec. 263; Ohio Const. Art. VI, sec. 2.
23. Constitutions of: Ark. Art. XIV, sec. 3; Conn. Art. VIII, sec. 2; Del. Art. X, sec. 4; Idaho, Art. IX, sec. 3; Ind. Art. VIII, sec. 3; Iowa, Art. IX, par. 2, sec. 3; Kans. Art. VI, sec. 3; Neb. Art. VIII, sec. 9; N. J. Art. VI, sec. 6, par. 6; N. Car. Art. XI, sec. 4; Okla. Art. XI, scc. 3; R. I. Art. XII, sec. 4; Tenn. Art. XI, sec. 12; W. Va. Art. XII, sec. 4.
24. This arrangement may be found in "Catholic Schools and Public Money," 50 *Yale L. J.* 917 (1940) along with the appropriate citations to the state constitutions at 920–21. See also Fellman, *op. cit.,* at 444.
25. 29 Stat. 411 (1896), D.C. Code, sec. 32–1008 (1940).
26. See Hale v. Everett, 53 N.H. 9 (1868); Glover v. Baker, 76 N.H. 408 (1912).
27. Hale v. Everett, 53 N.H. 9 (1868).
28. Warde v. Manchester, 56 N.H. 509 (1876).
29. "Model State Constitution," Fourth Edition, 1941, reprinted in W. Brooke Graves, *American State Government* (Boston, 3d. ed., 1946), p. 1028.
30. Const. of Kansas, Art. VI, sec. 8.
31. 69 Kans. 53, 76 Pac. 422 (1904).
32. Ariz. Code Anno. 1939, c. 54, sec. 1006; Calif. Ed. Code (Supp. 1941), sec. 3.52; Code of Ga. Anno. 1951, tit. 32, sec. 708; Idaho Code Anno. 1932, Vol. 2, tit. 32, sec. 2204; Burn's Indiana Stat. Anno. (1933 Supp. 1953), Vol. 6, tit. 28, sec. 601; Kans. Gen. Stat. Anno. (1935 Supp. 1947), c. 72, sec. 1722 and 1819; Ky. Rev. Stat. (1942 Supp. 1948), tit. XIII, sec. 158.190; Anno. Code of Md. 1951, Vol. 3, Art. 77, c. 10, secs. 139 and 197; Rev. Stat.

of Me., 1944, Vol. I, c. 37, sec. 127; Anno. Laws of Mass. (1932 Supp. 1953), Vol. II A, tit. XII, c. 71, sec. 31; Miss. Code, 1942, tit. 24, sec. 6672; Rev. Code of Montana 1947, Vol. 4, c. 20, sec. 75–2002; Nev. Compiled Laws, 1929, Vol. 3, sec. 5754; Rev. Laws of N. H. 1942, c. 135, sec. 26; New Mex. Stat. Anno. 1941, Vol. 4, c. 55, sec. 1102; N. J. R.S. Cum. Supp. (1937 Supp. 1953), tit. 18, sec. 14–78; N. Dak. Rev. Code of 1943, tit. 15, sec. 2507; Okla. Stat. Anno. 1941, tit. 70, sec. 495; Code of Laws of S. Car. 1952, Vol. 3, tit. 21, sec. 21–23; S. Dak. Code (1939 Supp. 1952), Vol. 1, tit. 15, sec. 3103; Utah Code Anno. 1953, Vol. 5, sec. 53–1–4; Wis. Stat. 1951, tit. VI, sec. 14.57; Rev. Stat. of Wash. Anno., (1932 Supp. 1949), Vol. 6, tit. 28, sec. 4693.

33. Kans. Gen. Stat. Anno. (1935 Supp. 1947), c. 72, sec. 1819.
34. Nev. Comp. Laws, 1929, sec. 5754.
35. N.E.A. Research Bulletin, *op. cit.,* p. 12.
36. Butts, *op. cit.,* p. 189.
37. For a most thorough expression of this point of view see Butts, *American Tradition in Religion and Education,* p. 103.
38. Const. of Miss., Art. III, sec. 18.
39. Code of Ala., 1940, tit. 52, sec. 542; Ark. Stat. Anno. 1947, Vol. 7, sec. 80–1616; Rev. Code of Del. 1935, c. 71, sec. 2758; Fla. Stat. Anno. 1943, tit. XV, sec. 231.09; Code of Ga. Anno. 1951, tit. 32, sec. 705; Idaho Code Anno. (1932 Supp. 1947), Vol. 6, sec. 33–2705; Ky. Rev. Stat. 1948, tit. XIII, sec. 158.170 & 158.990; Rev. Stat. of Me. 1944, Vol. I, c. 37, sec. 127; Anno. Laws of Mass. (1945 Supp. 1950), Vol. 2, tit. XII, c. 71, sec. 31; N. J. Rev. Stat. (1937 Supp. 1952), c. 18, sec. 14–77; William's Tenn. Code Anno. (1934 Supp. 1943), Vol. 2, tit. 7, sec. 2343 (4). To these might be added the Rev. Code of Del. 1935, c. 71, 136, which deals mainly with Bible reading and the Lord's Prayer, but refers to no other religious instruction.
40. Schempp v. School District, 177 F. Supp. 398 (1959) and Schempp v. Abington School District, 201 F. Supp. 815 (1962).
41. 374 U.S. 203 (1963).
42. Code of Ala., 1940, tit. 52, sec. 542.
43. Ark. Stat. Anno., 1947, Vol. 7, sec. 80–1606.
44. Butts, *op. cit.,* p. 192.
45. See, for example, Vollmar v. Stanley, 81 Col. 276, 255 Pac. 610 (1927) and Wilkerson v. City of Rome, 152 Ga. 763, 110 S.E. 895, 20 A.L.R. 1535 (1921), Murray v. Curlett, 179 A. 2d. 698 (1962).
46. Stevenson v. Hanyon, 7 Pa. Dist. R. 585 (1898).
47. For a thorough yet humorous discussion of some of the essential differences of the various Bibles see Moehlman, *School and Church,* (New York, 1944).
48. Stevenson v. Hanyon, *op. cit.,* pp. 590–91.
49. See Konvitz, "Separation of Church and State," 14 *Law and Contemporary Problems,* 55 (1949); Brant, *James Madison: Nationalist, 1780–1787* (1948), pp. 353–54.

50. Burn's Indiana Stat. Anno. (1935 Supp. 1948), Vol. 6, tit. 28, sec. 5101; Iowa Code, 1950, tit. XII, sec. 280.9; Kan. Gen. Stat. Anno. (1935 Supp. 1947), c. 72, sec. 1722, 1819; N. Dak. Rev. Code, 1943, tit. 15, sec. 3812; Okla. Stat. Anno. 1941, tit. 70, sec. 495; Laws of Pennsylvania (1959) Act 700.
51. State ex rel. Finger v. Weedman, 55 S.D. 343, 226 N.W. 348 (1929).
52. Indiana Stat. Anno. (1933 Supp. 1948), Vol. 6, tit. 28, sec. 5101.
53. Iowa Code, 1950, tit. XII, sec. 280.9.
54. Colorado, Connecticut, Maryland, Michigan, Minnesota, Missouri, New Hampshire, New Mexico, North Carolina, Oregon, Rhode Island, South Carolina, Texas, Utah, Vermont, Virginia, West Virginia, Wyoming, and New York.
55. Arizona, California, Illinois, Louisiana, Nebraska, Nevada, Ohio, South Dakota, Washington, and Wisconsin.
56. N.E.A. Research Bulletin, *op. cit.*, p. 36.
57. Rev. Code of Ariz. 1928, sec. 1044.
58. N.E.A. Research Bulletin, *op. cit.*, p. 36.
59. Calif. Const., Art. 8, sec. 9.
60. Calif. School Code, sec. 3.52 (Supp. 1941).
61. N.E.A. Research Bulletin, *op. cit.*, p. 36.
62. Evans v. Selma High School, 193 Cal. 54, 222 Pac. 801 (1924).
63. The American Jewish Committee and The Anti-Defamation League of B'nai B'rith, *Joint Memorandum*, "Proposed Bible Reading Legislation in California," February 20, 1953.
64. *Ibid.*, p. 1.
65. Nev. Const., Art. II, sec. 9 and sec. 10.
66. Nev. Comp. Laws, 1929, sec. 5754.
67. A. W. Johnson and F. Yost, *Separation of Church and State in the United States*, (Univ. of Minnesota, 1948), p. 65.
68. N.E.A. Report, *op. cit.*, p. 36.
69. Const. of Montana, Art. V. sec. 35.
70. N.E.A. Report, *op. cit.*, p. 35.
71. *Ibid.*, p. 35.
72. State ex rel. Dearle v. Frazier, 102 Wash. 519, 293 Pac. 1000 (1930).
73. Rev. Code of Del. 1935, c. 71, sec. 2758; Rev. Stat. of Me., 1944, Vol. I, c. 37, sec. 127; N.J. Rev. Stat. Anno. (1937 Supp. 1952), tit. 18, sec. 14 and sec. 78.
74. Miss. Code, 1942, tit. 24, sec. 6672; N. Dak. Rev. Code, 1943, tit. 15, sec. 4710.
75. Moehlman, *op. cit.*, pp. 110–11.
76. See, for example, L. A. Cook, *Community Backgrounds of Education*, (McGraw-Hill Book Co., New York, 1938); Sidney Hook, "Moral Values and/or Religion in the Schools," *Progressive Education*, 23:256–57, May, 1946.

CHAPTER 3

1. Moore v. Monroe, 64 Iowa 367, 20 N.W. 475, 52 Am. St. Rep. 444 (1884); Hackett v. Brooksville Graded Dist., 120 Ky. 608, 87 S.W. 792, 69 L.R.A. 592, 117 Am. St. Rep. 599 (1905); Billard v. Board of Education, 69 Kan. 53, 76 Pac. 422, 66 L.R.A. 166, 105 Am. St. Rep. 148 (1904); Murray v. Curlett, 179 A. 2d. 698 (1962); Pfeiffer v. Board of Education, 118 Mich. 560, 77 N.W. 250, 42 L.R.A. 536 (1898); Kaplan v. School District, 171 Minn. 142, 214 N.W. 18, 57 A.L.R. 185 (1927); Spiller v. Inhabitants of Woburn, 12 Allen 127 (Mass. 1866); Donahoe v. Richards, 38 Me. 379, 61 Am. Dec. 256 (1854); Lewis v. Board of Education, 157 Misc. 520, 285 N.Y. Supp. 164 (1935), *appeal dismissed,* 276 N.Y. 490, 12 N.E. 2d. 172 (1937); Doremus v. Board of Education, 5 N.J. 435, 75 A 2d. 880, 342 U.S. 429 (1952); Church v. Bullock, 104 Tex. 1, 109 S.W. 115, 16 L.R.A. (n.s.) 860 (1908); People ex rel. Vollmar v. Stanley, 81 Col. 276, 255 Pac. 610 (1927); Wilkerson v. City of Rome, 152 Ga. 763, 110 S.E. 895, 20 A.L.R. 1535 (1921); Carden v. Bland, 288 S.W. 2d. 718 (1956); Schempp v. Abington School District, 177 F. Supp. 398 (1959).
2. Pfeiffer v. Board of Education, 118 Mich. 560, 77 N.W. 250, 42 L.R.A. 536 (1898).
3. People ex rel. Vollmar v. Stanley, 81 Col. 276, 255 Pac. 610 (1927).
4. Colo. Const. Art. V, sec. 34; Ga. Const. Art. I, It. 14; Mich. Const. Art. II, sec. 3; Minn. Const. Art. I, sec. 16, Art. VIII, sec. 3; N.Y. Const. Art. XI, sec. 4; Tex. Const. Art. I, sec. 7; Tenn. Const. Art I, sec. 3.
5. Code of Ga. Anno. 1951 tit. 32, sec. 708; Kan. Gen. Stat. Anno. c. 72, sec. 1722 & 1819 (1935 Supp. 1947); Ky. Rev. Stat. 1948, tit. XIII, 158.190; Rev. Stat. of Me. 1944, Vol. I, c. 37, sec. 127; N.J. Rev. Stat. (1937 Supp. 1952), c. 18, sec. 14–78; Md. Code (1957) Art. 57, sec. 203.
6. Code of Ga. Anno. 1951, tit. 32, sec. 705; Ky. Rev. Stat. 1948, tit. XIII, sec. 158.170 & 158.990; Rev. Stat. of Me. 1944, Vol. I, c. 37, sec. 127; N.J. Rev. Stat. (1937 Supp. 1952), c. 18, sec. 14–77.
7. Kan. Gen. Stat. Anno. (1935 Supp. 1947), c. 72, sec. 1722 and 1819.
8. Anno. Laws of Mass. 1945 (1950 Supp.), Vol. 2, Title XII, Ch. 71, sec. 31; Tenn. Code Anno. sec. 49–1307 (4).
9. Iowa Code 1950, tit. XII, sec. 280.9.
10. 47 Am. Jur. 448.
11. State ex rel. Weiss v. District Board, 44 N.W. at 973.
12. Church v. Bullock, 109 S.W. at 117.
13. *Ibid.,* 109 S.W. at 118.
14. 255 Pac. at 616.
15. 285 N.Y. Supp. at 170.
16. F. Swancara, "The Colorado Bible Case," 21 *Lawyer and Banker* 164 (1928).
17. 110 S.E. at 899.
18. 109 S.W. at 117.

19. *Ibid.* at 118.
20. 214 N.W. 19.
21. *U. S. Stat. at Large,* Foreign Treaties, VIII, 155.
22. 214 N.W. at 19.
23. People ex rel. Ring v. Board of Education, 92 N.E. at 253; Board of Education v. Minor, 23 Ohio St. at 239 and 245.
24. 77 N.W. at 252.
25. *Ibid.,* at 254.
26. *Ibid.,* at 262.
27. 20 N.W. at 476.
28. *Ibid.,* at 476.
29. 285 N.Y. Supp. at 167.
30. *Ibid.,* at 168.
31. 12 Allen (Mass.) at 129.
32. 61 Am. Dec. at 272.
33. West Virginia State Board of Education v. Barnette, 319 U.S. 624 (1943).
34. 61 Am. Dec. at 267.
35. McGowan v. Maryland, 366 U.S. 420 (1961); Gallagher v. Crown Kosher Super Market, 366 U.S. 617 (1961); Braunfeld v. Brown, 366 U.S. 599 (1961); Two Guys from Harrison-Allentown, Inc. v. McGinley, 366 U.S. 582 (1961).
36. 87 S.W. at 794.
37. 61 Am. Dec. at 265.
38. 110 S.E. at 904.
39. 214 N.W. at 22–23.
40. 214 N.W. at 23.
41. Swancara, *op. cit.*
42. 81 Col. 276, 255 Pac. 610 (1927).
43. Swancara, *op. cit.,* p. 166.
44. 12 Allen (Mass.) at 128.
45. 76 Pac. at 423.
46. 214 N.W. at 18.
47. 157 Misc. 520, 285 N.Y. Supp. 164 (1935).
48. 76 Pac. at 423.
49. 12 Allen (Mass.) at 129.
50. Nessle v. Hum, 1 Ohio N.P. 140 (1894).
51. 61 Am. Dec. at 258.
52. *Ibid.,* at 271.
53. 109 S.W. at 118.
54. Hart v. Board of Education, 2 *Lanc. Law Rev.* at 351, (1885).
55. 285 N.Y. Supp. at 174.
56. 87 S.W. at 794.
57. 61 Am. Dec. 270.
58. 255 Pac. at 616.
59. Evans v. Selma High School, 193 Cal. 54, 222 Pac. 801, (1924).
60. 222 Pac. at 802.
61. 77 N.W. at 257.
62. *Ibid.,* at 255.
63. 104 Tex. 1, 109 S.W. 115, 16 L.R.A. (n.s.) 860 (1908).
64. 81 Col. 276, 255 Pac. 610 (1927).

65. 255 Pac. at 614.
66. 214 N.W. at 22.
67. 255 Pac. at 618–20.
68. *Ibid.,* at 618.
69. 214 N.W. at 22.
70. Wilkerson v. City of Rome, *op. cit.*
71. Doremus v. Board of Education, 5 N.J. 435, 75 A. 2d. 880, 342 U.S. 429 (1952).
72. 159 Wash. 519, 293 Pac. 1000, 284 U.S. 573 (1931).
73. N.J. Rev. Stat. (1937) 18:14–77.
74. 5 N.J. 435, 75 A. 2d. 880 (1951).
75. 75 A. 2d. at 882 ff.
76. 343 U. S. at 312.
77. *Ibid.,* at 313.
78. *Ibid.,* at 435.
79. *Ibid.,* at 435.
80. 262 U.S. 447, 486 (1923).
81. 343 U.S. at 316.
82. Tudor v. Board of Education of Rutherford, 14 N.J. 31 (1953).
83. For a detailed discussion evaluating the rationale of the court in the Tudor case and comparing it to that in the Doremus case, see: R. F. Cushman, "The Holy Bible and the Public Schools," 40 *Cornell L. Rev.* 475 (1955).
84. Carden v. Bland, 288 S.W. 2d. 718 (1956).
85. 288 S.W. 2d. at 719.
86. Article I, Section 3 of the Tennessee Constitution provides:

    "That all men have a natural and indefeasible right to worship almighty God according to the dictates of their own conscience; that no man can of right be compelled to attend, erect, or support any place of worship or to maintain any minister against his consent; no human authority can in any case whatever, control or interfere with the rights of conscience; and that no preference shall be given by law to any religious establishment or mode of worship."

87. 288 S.W. 2d. at 724.
88. 245 Ill. 334, 92 N.E. 251 (1910).
89. Murray v. Curlett, 179 A. 2d. 698 (1962).
90. *Ibid.,* at 699.
91. *Ibid.,* at 700.
92. *Ibid.,* at 701.
93. *Ibid.,* at 702.
94. 81 S. Ct. 1680.
95. 74 S. Ct. 686 (1954).
96. 179 A. 2d. at 704.
97. 179 A. 2d. at 708.
98. 366 U.S. at 441–42.

CHAPTER 4

1. People ex rel. Ring v. Board of Education, 245 Ill. 334, 92 N.E. 251, 29 L.R.A. (n.s.) 442 (1910); Herold v. Parish Board, 136 La. 1034, 68 So. 116 (1915); State ex rel. Freeman v. Scheve, 65 Neb. 853, 91 N.W. 846 (1902); Board of Education v. Minor, 23 Ohio St. 211 (1872); State ex rel. Finger v. Weedman, 55 S.D. 343, 226 N.W. 348 (1929); State ex rel. Clithero v. Showalter, 159 Wash. 519, 293 Pac. 1000 (1930); State ex rel. Dearle v. Frazier, 102 Wash. 369, 173 Pac. 35 (1918); State ex rel. Weiss v. District Board, 76 Wis. 177, 44 N.W. 967 (1890); Schempp v. School District of Abington, 177 F. Supp. 398 (1959).
2. 276 N.W. 348 (1929).
3. Research Bulletin of the National Education Association, *The State and Sectarian Education*, Vol. 24, No. 1, 1946, p. 26.
4. 76 Wis. 177, 44 N.W. 967 (1890).
5. 92 N.E. 251, at 252–53.
6. State ex rel. Dearle v. Frazier, 102 Wash. 369, at 370.
7. 23 Ohio St. 211, at 247.
8. 92 N.E. 251, at 256.
9. 23 Ohio St. 244.
10. 44 N.W. 981.
11. *Ibid.,* 976.
12. *Ibid.,* at 981.
13. 23 Ohio St. 239.
14. *Ibid.* at 245.
15. 92 N.E. at 253.
16. 102 Wash. 369, 173 Pac. 35 (1918).
17. People ex rel. Ring v. Board of Education, 245 Ill. 344, 92 N.E. 251, 29 L.R.A. (n.s.) 442 (1910), Justices Hand and Cartwright dissenting.
18. State ex rel. Finger v. Weedman, 55 S.D. 343, 226 N.W. 348 (1929), Justices Sherwood and Brown dissenting separately.
19. 226 N.W. at 367–69.
20. 68 So. at 119.
21. 44 N.W. at 973.
22. *Ibid.,* at 972.
23. 68 So. at 121.
24. 92 N.E. at 255.
25. 44 N.W. at 973.
26. 102 Wash. 369, 173 Pac. 35 (1918).
27. Const. of Washington, Art. 1, sec. 2.
28. 102 Wash. at 374.
29. *Ibid.,* at 379.
30. 44. N.W. at 975.
31. 92 N.E. at 253–55.
32. 91 N.W. at 848.

33. *Ibid.,* at 848.
34. 68 So. at 117.
35. 92 N.E. at 255.
36. 226 N.W. at 349–51.
37. 68 So. 116.
38. 44 N.W. at 975.
39. 23 Ohio St. at 244.
40. 92 N.E. at 254.
41. 23 Ohio St. at 248.
42. *Ibid.,* at 248.
43. 91 N.W. at 847.
44. 102 Wash. at 385.
45. 44 N.W. at 976.
46. 226 N.W. at 351.
47. 92 N.E. at 256.
48. *Ibid.,* at 255.
49. 68 So. at 121.
50. 92 N.E. at 257.
51. 76 Wis. 177, 44 N.W. 967 (1890).
52. 44 N.W. at 973.
53. 23 Ohio St. 211 (1872).
54. 102 Wash. 369, 173 Pac. 35 (1918).
55. 159 Wash. 519, 293 Pac. 1000 (1930).
56. 23 Ohio St. at 237.
57. 102 Wash. 369, 173 Pac. 35 (1918).
58. 102 Wash. at 378.
59. 159 Wash. 519, 293 Pac. 1000 (1930).
60. 102 Wash. 369, 173 Pac. 35 (1918).
61. 293 Pac. at 1001–02.
62. 23 Ohio St. at 249–50.
63. 255 Pac. at 618.
64. 44 N.W. at 975.
65. 92 N.E. at 252.
66. *Ibid.,* at 256.
67. State ex rel. Finger v. Weedman, 55 S.D. 343, 226 N.W. 348 (1929).
68. Schempp v. Abington School District, 177 F. Supp. 398 (1959).
69. The Pennsylvania Statute at issue, (24 Pa. Stat. School code 15–1516) specifically provides:

"At least ten verses from the Holy Bible shall be read . . . without comment at the opening of each public school for each school day, by the teachers in charge: provided, that where any teacher has other teachers under and subject to her direction then the teachers exercising such authority shall read the Holy Bible, or cause it to be read as herein directed.

If any school teacher, whose duty it shall be to read the Holy Bible, or cause it to be read, shall fail or omit so to do, said school teacher shall upon charges preferred for such failure or omission and . . . before the board of school directors of the school district be discharged."

70. 177 F. Supp. 398 at 401.
71. The court was especially concerned with this legal concept in light of certain Supreme Court decisions. See: County of Alleganey v. Meshuda Company, 360 U.S. 185 (1959); Harrison v. NAACP, 360 U.S. 167 (1959); Louisiana Power and Light Company v. City of the Thibodaux, 360 U.S. 25 (1959).
72. 347 U.S. 483 (1954).
73. 177 F. Supp. at 405.
74. *Ibid.*, at 406.
75. *Ibid.*, at 407.
76. School District of Abington v. Schempp, 364 U.S. 298 (1960).
77. 201 F. Supp. 815 (1962).
78. *Ibid.*, at 818.
79. *Ibid.*, at 820.
80. School District of Abington v. Schempp and Murray v. Curlett, 374 U.S. 203 (1963).

CHAPTER 5

1. 76 Wis. 177, 44 N.W. 967 ff. (1890).
2. 162 Wis. 482, 156 N.W. 477 ff. (1916).
3. *Ibid.*, at 480.
4. *Ibid.*, at 479.
5. People ex rel. Ring v. Board of Education, 245 Ill. 92 N.W. 259, 29 L.R.A. (n.s.) 442, 19 Ann. Cas. 220 (1910).
6. North v. Trustees of the University of Illinois, 137 Ill. 296, 27 N.E. 54 (1891).
7. 27 N.E. at 55.
8. 28 N.E. at 26.
9. St. Hedwig's Industrial School v. Cook County, 289 Ill. 432, 124 N.E. 629 (1919); Dunn v. Chicago Industrial School, 280 Ill. 613, 117 N.E. 735 (1917).
10. 141 A. 2d. 903 (1961).
11. Knowlton v. Baumhover, 182 Iowa 691, 166 N.W. 202, 5 A.L.R. 841 (1918); Wright v. School District, 151 Kan. 485, 99 P. 2d. 737 (1940); Williams v. Stanton School District, 173 Ky. 708, 191 S.W. 517 (1917); Richter v. Cordes, 100 Mich. 278, 58 N.W. 1110 (1894); Harfst v. Hoegen, 349 Mo. 808, 163 S.W. 2d. 609, 141 A.S.R. 1136 (1942); State ex rel. Public School No. 6 v. Taylor, 122 Neb. 454, 240 N.W. 573 (1932); Dorner v. School District No. 5, 137 Wis. 147, 118 N.W. 353 (1908); Zeller v. Huff, 55 N.M. 501, 236 P. 2d. 949 (1951); Miller v. Cooper, 56 N.M. 355, 244 P. 2d. 520 (1952).
12. 182 Iowa 69, 166 N.W. 202, 5 A.L.R. 841 (1918).
13. 166 N.W. at 212.
14. Iowa Code, 1950, tit. XII, Sec. 280.9.

15. 166 N.W. at 204 ff.
16. 5 A.L.R. 851.
17. Moore v. Monroe, 64 Iowa 367, 20 N.W. 475, 52 Am. St. Rep. 444 (1884).
18. 166 N.W. at 212.
19. Zeller v. Huff, 55 N.M. 501, 236 P. 2d. 949 (1951).
20. Miller v. Cooper, 56 N.M. 355, 244 P. 2d. 520 (1952).
21. 236 P. 2d. at 968.
22. 56 N.M. 355, 244 P. 2d. 520 (1952).
23. 244 P. 2d. at 521.
24. *Ibid.*, at 520.
25. Harfst v. Hoegen, 349 Mo. 808, 163 S.W. 2d. 609, 141 A.L.R. 1136 (1942).
26. 163 S.W. 2d. at 614.
27. *Ibid.*, at 614.
28. Dorner v. School District No. 5, 137 Wis. 147, 118 N.W. 353 (1908).
29. Wisconsin Const. Art. I, Sec. 18.
30. 118 N.W. at 353–54.
31. *Ibid.*, at 354.
32. *Ibid.*, at 354–55.
33. New Haven v. Torrington, 132 Conn. 194, 43 A. 2d. 455 (1945), Millard v. Board of Education, 121 Ill. 297, 10 N.E. 669 (1887); State ex rel. Johnson v. Boyd, 217 Ind. 348, 28 N.E. 2d. 256 (1940); Crain v. Walker, 222 Ky. 828, 2 S.W. 2d. 654 (1928).
34. Millard v. Board of Education, 121 Ill. 297, 10 N.E. 669 ff. (1887).
35. 10 N.E. at 671.
36. New Haven v. Torrington, 132 Conn. 194, 43 A. 2d. 455 (1945).
37. State ex rel. Johnson v. Boyd, 28 N.E. 2d. at 256.
38. State ex rel. Johnson v. Boyd, 217 Ind. 348, 28 N.E. 2d. 256 (1940).
39. Gerhard v. Heid, 66 N.D. 444, 267 N.W. 127 (1936); State ex rel. Johnson v. Boyd, 217 Ind. 348, 28 N.E. 2d. 256 (1940); New Haven v. Torrington, 132 Conn. 194, 43 A. 2d. 455 (1945).
40. Gerhard v. Heid, 66 N.W. at 459, 267 N.W. at 135 (1936).
41. Hysong v. School District, 164 Pa. 629, 30 Atl. 482 (1894).
42. Commonwealth v. Herr, 229 Pa. 132, 78 Atl. 68 (1910).
43. Pennsylvania Acts of 1895, Public Law No. 395.
44. 229 Pa. 132, 78 Atl. 68 (1910).
45. O'Conner v. Hendrick, 184 N.Y. 421, 77 N.E. 612, 7 L.R.A. (n.s.) 402 (1906); Knowlton v. Baumhover, 182 Iowa 691, 166 N.W. 202, 5 A.L.R. 841 (1918); Zeller v. Huff, 55 N.M. 501, 236 P. 2d. 949 (1951).
46. Oreg. Comp. Laws Ann., Sec. 111–2106, 2109 (1940); Neb. Rev. Stat. 79–1403, 1404 (1943).
47. Milwaukee *Journal,* Nov. 23, 1952, State News Section, p. 8. For a thorough discussion of this situation, see William Boyer, Jr., "Religious Education of Wisconsin Public School Pupils," Part I, 1953 (March), *Wis. L. Rev.* 213.

48. Torpey, W. G., *Judicial Doctrines of Religious Rights in America,* (Chapel Hill, N. Car., 1948), p. 260.
49. State ex rel. McCollum v. Board of Education, 333 U.S. 203 (1948).
50. Zorach v. Clauson, 343 U.S. 306 (1952).
51. Nicholas Murray Butler, *Liberty, Equality, Fraternity,* (New York, 1942), pp. 145, 147.
52. A. P. Stokes, *Church and State in the United States,* Vol. II, p. 525.
53. *Ibid.,* at 506–7.
54. From "Report of the Committee of Week Day Religious Education," (m.d.) transmitted by the Reverend C. W. Brown, its Chairman, p. 1, quoted from Stokes, *op. cit.,* Vol. II, p. 506.
55. See Stokes, *op. cit.,* Vol. II, p. 507.
56. A. Johnson, *Legal Status of Church and State Relationships in the United States,* (Minneapolis, 1934), pp. 143, 145.
57. 333 U.S. at 207–9.
58. Stokes, *op. cit.,* Vol. II, p. 516. See also Vashti McCollum, *One Woman's Fight,* (New York, 1951).
59. *Churchman,* Feb. 15, 1946.
60. People ex rel. McCollum v. Board of Education, 396 Ill. 14, 71 N.E. 2d. 161 (1947).
61. People ex rel. Latimer v. Board of Education, 349 Ill. 228, 68 N.E. 2d. 305, 167 A.L.R. 1467 (1946).
62. 71 N.E. 2d. at 168.
63. *Churchman,* Jan. 1, 1948.
64. 333 U.S. at 211, 212.
65. *Ibid.,* at 212.
66. *Ibid.,* at 216.
67. *Ibid.,* at 215.
68. *Ibid.,* at 231.
69. *Ibid.,* at 233–36.
70. *Ibid.,* at 255–56.
71. New York *Times,* Nov. 21, 1948.
72. See J. O'Neill, *Religion and Education Under the Constitution,* (New York, 1949).
73. *Commonweal,* Feb. 18, 1949.
74. Stokes, *op. cit.,* Vol. II, at 522.
75. See in particular, E. S. Corwin, "The Supreme Court as the National School Board," 14 *Law and Contemp. Prob.* 3; Murray, "Law, or Prepossession," 14 *Law and Contemp. Prob.* 23 (1949); Owen, "The McCollum Case," 22 *Temple L. Q.* 159 (1948).
76. See Stokes, *op. cit.,* pp. 504–5.
77. People ex rel. Lewis v. Graves, 245 N.Y. 195, 156 N.E. 663, (1927).
78. Lewis v. Spaulding, 193 Misc. 66, 85 N.Y. Supp. 2d. 682, (Sup. Ct. 1948), *Appeal withdrawn,* 299 N. Y. 564, 85 N.E. 2d. 791 (1949).

79. People ex rel. Latimer v. Board of Education, 394 Ill. 228, 68 N.E. 2d. 305, 167 A.L.R. 1467 (1946).
80. Gordon v. Board of Education, 78 Cal. App. 2d. 464, 178 P. 2d. 488 (1947).
81. The term "released time" here is used synonymously with "dismissed time." The practice complained of in New York is an example of "dismissed time" as was defined earlier.
82. "Constitutionality of the N.Y. Released Time Program," 49, *Col. L. Rev.* 836, 842 (1949).
83. See D. Fellman, "Separation of Church and State," 1950, *Wis. L. Rev.* 426, 473. Defendants' motion to change venue or dismiss was overruled in Zorach v. Clausen, 86 N.Y. Supp. 2d. 17 (S. Ct. 1948), *Aff'g*, 87 N.Y. Supp. 2d. 639 (App. Div. 1949); motion for leave to appeal granted, May 2, 1949, 89 N.Y. Supp. 2d. 232 (App. Div. 1949), In Zorach v. Clausen, 90 N.Y. Supp. 2d. 750 (S. Ct. 1949), the Greater New York Coordinating Committee on Released Time was permitted to intervene.
84. 303 N.Y. 161; 100 N.E. 2d. 463 (1951).
85. 343 U.S. at 306.
86. 100 N.E. at 465.
87. *Ibid.*, at 467.
88. *Ibid.*, at 467–68.
89. Lewis v. Graves 245 N.Y. 195, 156 N.E. 2d. 663 (1927). This case has as one of its major issues, the question of Bible-reading exercises in the public schools.
90. 100 N.E. at 470.
91. *Ibid.*, at 471.
92. Dennis v. U.S. 341, U.S. 494, 508.
93. 100 N.E. at 471. It should be noted that Judge Desmond holds a decided minority view. Our history is replete with multitudinous examples of the exercise of religion being restricted by state and national action. See Torpey, *op. cit.*, Chap. 2, and Stokes, *op. cit.*, Vol. II, pp. 733–40; Vol. III, Chap. XXI, XXII. XXIII.
94. 100 N.E. at 476.
95. *Ibid.*
96. 343 U.S. 306 (1952).
97. *Ibid.*, at 311.
98. *Ibid.*, at 312.
99. *Ibid.*, at 313.
100. *Ibid.*, at 314.
101. *Ibid.*, at 311. It is noteworthy that appellants contended they should have been allowed to prove that this program was actually administered in a coercive manner. The New York Court of Appeals, however, refused to grant trial on this issue. See 306 U.S. 311, Note 7.
102. *Ibid.*, at 316.
103. *Ibid.*, at 319, 320.
104. *Ibid.*, at 320–21.

105. *Ibid.,* at 321–22.
106. *Ibid.,* at 324–25.
107. 82 S. Ct. 1261 (1962).
108. See Chapter 6, pp. 248 ff.
109. See 18 Misc. 2d. 659, 191, N.Y.S. 2d. 453.
110. 268 U.S. 652 (1925).
111. See 10 N.Y. 2d. 174, 218 N.Y.S. 2d. 659; 176 N.E. and 579.
112. 82 S. Ct. 1264.
113. *Ibid.,* at 1266.
114. *Ibid.,* at 1267.
115. *Ibid.,* [Italics mine].
116. *Ibid.,* at 1268.
117. *Ibid.,* at 1269.
118. *Ibid.,* at 1269.
119. *Memorial and Remonstrance against Religious Assessments,* II
     Writing of Madison 183, at 185–86.
120. *Ibid.,* at 1270.
121. 14A 333 U.S. 203.
122. 82 S. Ct. at 1273.
123. 343 U.S. 306.
124. Engel v. Vitale, 82 S. Ct. at 1273.
125. 330 U.S. 1.
126. See 67 S. Ct. at 529–30.
127. 82 S. Ct. at 1274.
128. *Ibid.,* at 1276–77.
129. *Ibid.,* Note 4, at 1276.
130. *Ibid.,* at 1272.
131. The New York *Times,* lead editorial, June 27, 1962; the New
     York *Herald Tribune,* June 27, 1962.
132. The New York *Times,* July 1, 1962.
133. *The Jewish News,* July 6, 1962.
134. The New York *Times,* July 1, 1962.
135. Miami Military Institute v. Leff, 220 N.Y. Supp. 799 (1926).
136. Cincinnati v. Minor, 23 Ohio St., 211, 13 Am. Rep. 233 (1872).
137. 220 N.Y. Supp. at 810.
138. This appears to be a somewhat questionable theory of history,
     particularly if applied to the settlement of New England. See V.
     Parrington, *Main Currents in American Thought,* (New York,
     1930), pp. 16–50, and M. Curti, *The Growth of American
     Thought,* (New York, 1951), pp. 50–55.
139. State ex. rel. Atwood v. Johnson, 170 Wis. 251, 176 N.W. 224
     (1920).
140. 176 N.W. at 228.
141. Watchtower Bible and Tract Soc. v. Los Angeles County, 30 Cal.
     2d. 426, 182 P. 2d. 178 (1947).
142. 182 P. 2d. at 181.
143. *Ibid.,* at 182.
144. Brown v. Orange County Board, 128 So. 2d. 181 (1960).
145. *Ibid.,* at 185.

146. 8 *The Writings of Thomas Jefferson* (Washington ed. 1861) p. 113.
147. Lewis v. Allen, 159 N.Y. Supp. 807 (1957).
148. U.S.C. Title 36, Chapter 10, Sec. 172, 36 U.S.C.A. Sec. 172.
149. N.Y. Laws (1956) Ch. 177, Sec. 802.
150. Article 1, Section 3 of the New York Constitution provides: "The free exercise and enjoyment of religious profession and worship, without discrimination or preference, shall forever be allowed in this state to all mankind; and no person shall be rendered incompetent to be a witness on account of his opinions on matters of religious beliefs; but the liberty of conscience hereby secured shall not be so construed as to excuse acts of licentiousness, or justify practices inconsistent with the peace or safety of this state."
151. Dickman v. School District, 366 Pac. 2d. 533 (1962).

CHAPTER 6

1. Milwaukee *Journal,* December 16, 1952.
2. *Ibid.*
3. *Capital Times,* December 18, 1952.
4. *Ibid.*
5. "The State, Schools and Sects," *Life,* 33 VI:36; Dec. 1, 1952; Protestant critics might contend that this is a somewhat slanted view.
6. W. Herberg, "The Sectarian Conflict Over Church and State," *Commentary,* 14:450, Nov., 1952.
7. Notably H. P. Van Dusen, of Union Theological Seminary. He wrote the tract *God in Education,* (New York, 1951), which attacks secularism in the schools.
8. See the editorial "Christ in American Culture," *Life,* 33 VI:16, Dec. 29, 1952, for a further discussion of religion versus secularism, particularly in American universities. For similar views by Luce publications see, "Argument for the Court," *Time,* 57:55, Mar. 26, 1951; "Replace the Keystone," *Time,* 57:78, May 14, 1951; "Wall Can Be Too High," *Time,* 58:62, July 23, 1951: "Bible in the Schools," *Time,* 56:71, Oct. 30, 1950.
9. A. P. Stokes, *Church and State in the U. S.,* Vol. II, p. 567. This conclusion is bitterly attacked in Wm. McManus' "Church, State and Dr. Stokes," *Commonweal,* 55:41, April 18, 1952. Father McManus, in reviewing these volumes, states "Even in 1774 lay members of the church were not denied their right to read the Bible," p. 44. Note also M. D. Howe, in 64 *Harvard L.R.* 170, criticizing Dr. Stokes for treating the Catholic position too leniently.
10. P. Blanshard, *American Freedom and Catholic Power,* (Boston, 1949), p. 77.
11. *Ibid.,* p. 83. For a most recent work of Blanshard in this field see: *God and Man in Washington,* (Boston, 1960).
12. J. O'Neill, *Catholicism and American Freedom,* (Harper & Brothers, New York, 1952), p. 212.

13. *Ibid.,* pp. 212–13.
14. A. Baer, "On Reading," *Commonweal,* 51:34–36, Oct. 21, 1949.
15. *Ibid.,* p. 36.
16. "U. S. Catholics Honor the Bible," *America,* 88:481, Jan. 31, 1953.
17. See Chapters 3 and 4, *Supra.*
18. H. Beale, *A History of Freedom of Teaching in the Public Schools,* (Charles Scribner's Sons, (New York, 1940), pp. 97–99 and 213–18.
19. R. J. Gabel, *Public Funds for Church and Private Schools,* (Catholic University of America, Washington, D.C., 1937), p. 439.
20. *Ibid.,* p. 442 .
21. See "Statement of Catholic Bishops on Secularism and Schools," N.Y. *Times,* Nov. 16, 1952.
22. "Yale vs. Harvard," *Commonweal,* 56:285, June 27, 1952.
23. Stokes, *op. cit.,* Vol. II, p. 567.
24. *America,* 36:469, Feb. 26, 1927.
25. A. S. Will, *Life of Cardinal Gibbons,* (E. P. Dutton & Co., New York, 1922), Vol. I, p. 478.
26. *America,* 36:78–79, Nov. 6, 1926.
27. *America,* 36:78, Nov. 6, 1926.
28. *America,* 35:366–67, July 31, 1926.
29. See in particular: A. Freemantle, "Either-Or," *Commonweal,* 49:461, Feb. 18, 1949; "Secularism," *Commonweal,* 47:187, Dec. 3, 1948; "Religion and the Schools," *Commonweal,* 54:373, July 27, 1951: "Church-State: A Fresh Approach," *America,* 88:292, Dec. 13, 1952; "A Hymn for a Prayer in Our Schools," *America,* 88:143, Nov. 8, 1952; "That Wall of Separation and the Public School," *Catholic World,* 173:252, Jan. 1951; W. W. Butler, "No Lamb of God in School," *Catholic World,* 167:203–11, June, 1948.
30. See: "Protestants Point at Secularism in Education," *Commonweal,* 49:389, Jan. 28, 1949; "Protestants on Secularism," *Commonweal,* 57:296, Dec. 26, 1952; "Church-State: A Fresh Approach," *America,* 88:292, Dec. 13, 1952; "Sectarian Conflict," *Commonweal,* 57:249, Dec. 12, 1952.
31. See for example: "To Spite His Face," *Commonweal,* 49:435, Feb. 11, 1949, "Sectarian Conflict," *Commonweal,* 57:249, Dec. 12, 1952; "Church-State: A Fresh Approach," *America,* 88:292, Dec. 13, 1952.
32. "To Spite His Face," *Commonweal,* 49:435, Feb. 11, 1949.
33. See, for example: James O'Neill, *Religion and Education Under the Constitution,* (New York, 1949); R. F. Drinan, "The Supreme Court and Religion," *Commonweal,* 56:554, Sept. 12, 1952.
34. R. F. Drinan, "The Supreme Court and Religion," *Commonweal,* 56:554, Sept. 12, 1952; "A Matter of Tradition," *Commonweal,* 56:133, May 16, 1952; "Religion and the Schools," *Commonweal,* 54:373, July 27, 1951.
35. Burstyn v. Wilson, 343 U.S. 493 (1952). See also, "The Miracle Decision," *Commonweal,* 56:235, June 13, 1952.
36. Statement by Catholic Bishops on "Secularism and Schools," New York *Times,* Nov. 16, 1952.

37. New York *Times,* March 17, 1953.
38. Stokes, *op. cit.,* Vol. II, p. 567.
39. *Christian Century,* 43:652, May 20, 1926.
40. "Proposed Bible Reading Legislation in California," *Joint Memorandum of the American Jewish Committee and the Anti-Defamation League of B'nai B'rith,* Feb. 20, 1953.
41. *Ibid.,* p. 1.
42. *Jewish Daily Bulletin,* March 15, 1925.
43. *Churchman,* August, 1947.
44. *The Jewish News,* July 6, 1962.
45. *Ibid.*
46. L. Pfeffer, "Religion and the Public Schools," *Churchman,* Jan. 15, 1948.
47. M. R. Konvitz, "Whittling Away Religious Freedom," *Commentary,* 1:10, June, 1946.
48. Will Herberg, "The Sectarian Conflict Over Church and State," *Commentary,* 14:450, Nov., 1952.
49. See R. A. Billington, *Protestant Crusade,* (New York, 1938) ; and Stokes, *op. cit.,* Vols. I and II.
50. Stokes, *op. cit.,* Vol. II, p. 571.
51. *Forum,* 7:63, March, 1889.
52. J. H. Seelye, *Bibliotheca Sacra,* 13:740, Oct., 1856.
53. Deets Pickett, *Leaflet Number 135,* Board of Temperance, Prohibition and Public Morals of the Methodist Episcopal Church, 100 Maryland Ave. N.E., Washington, D. C. (n.d.) .
54. Milwaukee *Journal,* April 18, 1953.
55. In an interview with the author, June 6, 1953.
56. In an interview with the author, June 6, 1953.
57. C. P. Taft, "Religion and the Public Schools," *Christian Century,* 69:944–46, Aug. 20, 1952.
58. Mr. Taft presents no concrete suggestion as to how this agreement is to be achieved.
59. For similar statements presenting plans for Bible reading and religious exercises in the public schools see: H. E. Fosdick, "Our Religious Illiterates," *Readers Digest,* 42:97–100, Feb., 1949; P. N. Elbein, "Religion in the State Schools," *Christian Century,* 69:1061–63, Sept. 17, 1952; "Denies Public Schools are Irreligious," (Editorial) , *Christian Century,* 70:99, Jan. 28, 1953.
60. "Religion in Public Education," *Christian Century,* 66:231–33, Feb. 23, 1949.
61. Text in New York *Times,* December 13, 1952, p. 17.
62. New York *Times,* December 13, 1952, p. 1.
63. S. T. Spear, *Religion and the State,* (Dodd, Mead & Co., New York, 1876) , p. 384.
64. See Stokes, Vol. II, Ch. XVII, XVIII, and XIX.
65. S. Mathews, *Biblical World,* 27:59–62, Jan., 1906.
66. H. H. Horne, *Biblical World,* 27:58, Jan., 1906.
67. See Stokes, *op. cit.,* Vol. II, p. 569.
68. *Liberty,* Third Quarter, 1942, p. 18–22.

69. For a forceful reiteration of these views, particularly dealing with Catholic attempts to have the public schools engage in religious instruction, see: J. M. Dawson, "Public Schools, Catholic Model," *Christian Century,* 65:627–29, June 23, 1948. Mr. Dawson represents a Southern Baptist group.
70. In an interview with the author, June 8, 1953.
71. "Report From the Capitol," A Bulletin of the Baptist Joint Committee on Public Affairs, June, 1962.
72. *Ibid.,* at p. 6.
73. *The Church and the Public Schools,* Published by the Board of Christian Education, Presbyterian Church of the U.S.A., June, 1957, Part II, p. 11.
74. "Relations Between Church and State," A Report to the 174th General Assembly, May, 1962, p. 5.
75. *Ibid.,* at p. 11.
76. *Doctrines and Disciplines of the Methodist Church,* (1960), p. 707.
77. *Ibid.,* at p. 2029.
78. G. Bromley Oxnam, "Church, State and Schools," *Nation,* 168: 67–70, Jan. 15, 1949.
79. Bishop Oxnam, *op. cit.,* p. 69.
80. "Bishop Corson Comforts Foes of Schools," *Christian Century,* 66:1446, Dec. 7, 1949.
81. *Ibid.*
82. "Prayer in the Public School Opposed," *Christian Century,* 69: 35, Jan. 9, 1952.
83. "Is It Prayer or Patriotism," *Christian Century,* 69:1276–77, Nov. 5, 1952.
84. For other examples of this Protestant journal's criticisms of religious instruction in the public schools, see: "Churches Undermine Public Schools," *Christian Century,* 66:782, June 29, 1949; "Religious Instruction in Public Schools," *Christian Century,* 66: 979, Aug. 24, 1949; "Religious Literature Banned From New Mexico Public Schools," *Christian Century,* 69:660, June 4, 1952; "For Whom This Bell Tolls," *Christian Century,* 67:1287–89, Nov. 1, 1950.
85. C. C. Morrison, "Objectives of Protestants and Other Americans United for the Separation of Church and State," *Christian Century,* 66:236–39, Feb. 23, 1949.
86. New York *Times,* June 18, 1963.
87. *Ibid.,* June 19, 1963.
88. *Ibid.,* June 18, 1963.
89. *Ibid.*
90. Milwaukee *Journal,* June 18, 1963.
91. New York *Times,* June 18, 1963.
92. *Ibid.*
93. Milwaukee *Journal,* June 18, 1963.
94. New York *Times,* June 18, 1963.
95. *Ibid.,* Editorial, June 17, 1963.
96. New York *Times,* June 18, 1963.

97. *Ibid.*
98. *Ibid.*
99. Milwaukee *Journal,* June 18, 1963.
100. *Ibid.*
101. New York *Times,* June 18, 1963.

CHAPTER 7

1. See, in connection with this subject: Beale, *A History of Freedom of Teaching in the Public School,* pp. 95–99, 213–18; Stokes, *op. cit.,* Vol. II, pp. 549–53; R. A. Billington, *Protestant Crusade,* (New York, 1938).
2. See, for example, "Stress Virtue, Not Just Learning, Teachers Told," *Wisconsin State Journal,* Feb. 7, 1953.
3. A. Bierbower, *Report of the U.S. Commissioner of Education for the Year 1888–1889,* Vol. I, pp. 627–28.
4. *Independent,* 55:1841–43, August 6, 1903.
5. A. P. Peabody, *Report of the U.S. Commissioner of Education for the Year 1897–1898,* pp. 1563–64.
6. Peabody, *op. cit.,* p. 1564.
7. New York *Times,* July 1, 1962.
8. For expressions of this opinion see: F. N. Trager, "Religion in Education," *Religious Education,* 46:82, March, 1951; H. V. Williams, "What Can Be Done About Teaching Religion in the Public Schools," *Nation's Schools,* 47:64–66, Sept. 1951; E. M. Creel, "The Legality of Non-Sectarian Bible Instruction in Alabama Public Schools," 10 *Ala. Law,* 86 (1949); L. Goldman, "The Implication of Religious Instruction in Public Schools," *Education,* 59:269, Jan., 1939; M. G. Hunt, "Bible Study and the Public Schools," *Peabody Journal of Education,* 23:156–59, Nov., 1945.
9. For examples of this logic see M. G. Hunt, *op. cit.,* p. 159, and 10 *Ala. Law,* at 87.
10. E. J. Goodwin, *Educational Review,* 35:132–34, Feb., 1908.
11. See, as examples: I. L. Kandel, "The Public Schools and Religious Instruction," *School and Society,* 73:395–96, June 23, 1951; J. Nathanson, "The Foot in the Door," *Nation,* 173:423, Nov. 17, 1951; A. D. Black, "Religious Freedom and the Rights of Children," *Progressive Education,* 25:214–17, April, 1947; H. W. Holmes, "God in the Public Schools," *Atlantic Monthly,* 188:99–105, July, 1940; Sidney Hook, "Moral Values and/or Religion in the Schools," *Progressive Education,* 23:256–57, May, 1946.
12. See Kandel, *op. cit.*
13. See Nathanson, *op. cit.*
14. See A. D. Black, *op. cit.,* and S. Hook, *op. cit.*
15. New York *Times,* May 2, 1925.
16. See also: "Resolution Adopted by the Council of Religious Education Association," March 19, 1920, *Religious Education,* 15:233, Aug., 1920.
17. N. Cousins, "Religion and the Schools," *Saturday Review,* 34 IV: 16, Dec. 29, 1951. For further discussions on this editorial see, *Saturday Review,* 35 I:19, Jan. 23, 1952; 35 I:2, Feb. 24, 1952; 35 I:16, Feb. 26, 1952.

18. *Outlook,* 68:221, May 25, 1901.
19. *Religious Education,* 5:500, Dec., 1910.
20. *Ibid.*
21. N. M. Butler, *Journal of the Proceedings and Addresses of the National Educational Association,* 1902, pp. 71–74.
22. *Independent,* 54:2090, Aug. 28, 1902.
23. *Independent,* 54:2489–90, Oct. 16, 1902.
24. For additional discussion on this point see A. L. Feinberg, "Religion and the Public School," *Congress Weekly,* March 12, 1951, pp. 7–9.
25. For others who feel that a public school teacher's background is inadequate for teaching religion see: W. G. Seaman, *Homiletic Review,* 89:52, Jan., 1925; W. S. Athearn, *Religious Education and American Democracy,* (Boston, 1917), pp. 9–12; Sidney Hook, "Moral Values and/or Religion in the Schools," *Progressive Education,* 23:256–57, May, 1946.
26. *Independent,* 54:2489–90, Oct. 16, 1902. For additional discussion on this point see J. H. Crocker, *Westminster Review,* 144: 203–13, Aug., 1895.
27. *Atlantic Monthly,* 92:298, Sept., 1903.
28. *Ibid.,* at 299.
29. H. H. Horne, *Proceedings of the Second Annual Convention of the Religious Education Association,* 1904, p. 278.
30. See, in particular, E. Bachus, "Shall We Teach the Bible — No," *Teachers College Journal,* 15:51, Jan., 1944; R. Cosway and R. A. Leopfer, "Religion and the Schools," 17 *U. of Cin. L. Rev.* 117 (1948).
31. J. H. Blackhurst, *Education,* 43:383, Feb., 1923.
32. See, for example, W. S. Fleming, "Keep the School Door Open to Religion," *Nation's Schools,* 36:50–51, Dec., 1945; S. M. Amatora, "Educate the Whole Child," *Education,* 72:393–96, Feb., 1951; C. W. Mahoney, *Vital Speeches,* 18:658–63, Aug. 15, 1951; H. V. Williams, *Nation's Schools,* 47:64–66, Sept., 1951.
33. W. S. Fleming, "Keep the School Door Open to Religion," *Nation's Schools,* 36:50–51, Dec., 1945.
34. It might be argued that an increased population and improved police methods could account for the higher arrest rate.
35. Fleming, *op. cit.,* p. 51.
36. New York *Times,* Nov. 13, 1926.
37. See W. F. Buckley, Jr., *God and Man at Yale,* (Chicago, 1951).
38. For the negative side of this question see, J. S. Brubacher, "Public Schools and the Crises in Spiritual Values," *New York State Education,* 34:531–34, April, 1946; J. S. Brubacher, "Why Force Religious Education," *Nation's Schools,* 36:23–24, Nov., 1945; H. Flett, and A. Pittman, "The Public School Builds Moral Character," *Progressive Education,* 27:118–19; Feb., 1949; R. S. Hecks, "Our Schools — Are They Godless?" *California Journal of Secondary Education,* 23:160–63, March, 1948.
39. L. T. Beman, *Religious Teaching in the Public Schools,* (H. W. Wilson Co., New York, 1927), p. 69.

40. J. Lewis, "More Objections to Religion and the Bible in the Public Schools," *Teachers College Journal,* 15:52–53, Jan., 1944.
41. A. N. Franzblau, *Religious Belief and Character Among Jewish Adolescents,* Teachers College Contribution to Education, No. 635, Columbia University, 1934.
42. E. R. Bartlett, "Measuring Moral and Religious Outcomes of Week-day Religious Instruction," *Religious Education,* 29:25–35, Nov., 1934.
43. H. Hartshorne, and M. S. May, *Studies in Deceit, Studies in Service, Studies in the Organization of Character,* discussed in L. S. Cook, *Community Backgrounds of Education,* (New York, 1938), p. 287.
44. *Studies in Deceit,* Vol. II, p. 243.
45. Cook, *op. cit.,* p. 287.
46. "What About Religious Education," *Nation's Schools,* 36:45, Dec., 1945.
47. "Religion in the Public Schools and Bible Reading," *Joint Memorandum of the American Jewish Committee and Anti-Defamation League of B'nai B'rith,* January 27, 1953 (memo).
48. *Ibid.,* p. 21.
49. *Ibid.*
50. *Ibid.,* at p. 4.
51. *Ibid.,* at 5.
52. *Ibid.*
53. New York *Times,* June 18, 1963.
54. Des Moines *Register,* August 8, 1963.
55. *Ibid.,* August 6, 1963.
56. *Ibid.,* August 8, 1963.
57. New York *Times,* June 2, 1964.
58. Des Moines *Register,* August 8, 1963.
59. *Ibid.,* August 15, 1963.
60. *Ibid.,* August 8, 1963.
61. New York *Times,* May 29, 1964.
62. *Religion in the Public Schools,* American Association of School Administrators, 1964.
63. Beman, *op. cit.,* p. 165.
64. Stokes, *op. cit.,* Vol. II, p. 572.
65. *Christian Century,* 59 II:1607, Dec. 23, 1942.
66. Stokes, *op. cit.,* Vol. II, pp. 549 and 572.
67. *Christian Century,* 57 II:1596, Dec. 18, 1940.
68. New York *Times,* April 4, 1927.
69. Bishop Joseph Bucklin, *Theodore Roosevelt and His Time,* (Charles Scribner's Sons, New York, 1951), Vol. I, p. 21.

CHAPTER 8

1. New York *Times,* March 20, 1964.
2. *Ibid.*
3. For a summary see New York *Times* editorial, May 23, 1964.
4. New York *Times,* May 1, 1964.

5. *Ibid.*, March 20, 1964.
6. *Ibid.*, May 23, 1964.
7. *Ibid.*, May 14, 1964.
8. *Ibid.*, May 1, 1964.
9. *Ibid.*, May 2, 1964.
10. School Prayers, Hearings Before the Committee of the Judiciary, House of Representatives, 88th Cong., 2nd Sess., Part I, pp. 566–67.
11. New York *Times*, May 2, 1964.
12. *Ibid.*, May 2, 1964.
13. *Ibid.*
14. New York *Times*, May 29, 1964.
15. *Ibid.*, May 28, 1964.
16. School Prayers, *op. cit.*, Parts I–III.
17. New York *Times*, May 2, 1964.
18. *Ibid.*
19. *Ibid.*, May 14, 1964.
20. *Ibid.*, May 28, 1964.
21. *Ibid.*, May 7, 1964.
22. *Ibid.*, April 30, 1964.
23. *Ibid.*
24. *Ibid.*, May 28, 1964.
25. *Ibid.*, May 7, 1964.
26. School Prayers, *op. cit.*, Part III, p. 2509.
27. *Ibid.*, pp. 2378–79.
28. *Ibid.*, pp. 2368–71.
29. New York *Times*, May 7, 1964.
30. *Ibid.*, May 21, 1964.
31. *Ibid.*, May 14, 1964.
32. School Prayers, *op. cit.*, Part I, pp. 258–59.
33. *Ibid.*, p. 698.
34. School Prayers, *op. cit.*, Part II, pp. 990–95.
35. School Prayers, *op. cit.*, Part I, pp. 922–23.
36. *Ibid.*, p. 449.
37. New York *Times*, May 5, 1964.
38. *Ibid.*, May 2, 1964.
39. School Prayers, *op. cit.*, Part III, pp. 2483–87.
40. New York *Times*, May 9, 1964.
41. Milwaukee *Journal*, June 18, 1963.
42. *Ibid.*
43. *Ibid.*
44. New York *Times*, February 19, 1964.
45. School Prayers, *op. cit.*, Part II, pp. 1326–27.
46. Des Moines *Register*, March 20, 1964.
47. School Prayers, *op. cit.*, Part I, pp. 311–13.
48. New York *Times*, March 20, 1964.
49. *Ibid.*, February 19, 1964.
50. School Prayers, *op. cit.*, Part I, pp. 240–42.
51. School Prayers, *op. cit.*, Part I, p. 266.
52. School Prayers, *op. cit.*, Part I, pp. 266–67.
53. New York *Times*, April 23, 1964.

54. *Ibid.,* May 28, 1964.
55. *Ibid.,* May 1, 1964.
56. *Ibid.*
57. *Ibid.,* May 22, 1964.
58. School Prayers, *op. cit.,* Part III, pp. 2466–71.
59. *Ibid.,* Part II, p. 1305.
60. *Ibid.,* p. 1319.
61. *Ibid.,* pp. 1320–23.
62. *Ibid.,* pp. 1308–9.
63. New York *Times,* May 21, 1964.
64. *Ibid.*
65. *Ibid.*
66. *Ibid.*
67. *Ibid.,* May 29, 1964.

CHAPTER 9

1. For a more thorough discussion, see: L. T. Beman, *Religious Teaching in the Public Schools,* (New York, 1927).

Table of Cases

Hackett v. *Brooksville Graded Dist.*, 120 Ky. 608, 87 S.W. 792, 69 L.R.A. 592, 117 Am. St. Rep. 599 (1905).

Hale v. *Everett*, 53 N.H. 9 (1868).

Hanauer v. *Elkins*, 141 A. 2d. 903 (1961).

Harfst v. *Hoegen*, 349 Mo. 808, 163 S.W. 2d. 609 A.S.R. 1136 (1942).

Hart v. *Board of Education*, 2 Lanc. Law Rev. 351 (1885).

Herold v. *Parish Board*, 136 La. 1034, 68 So. 116 (1915).

Hysong v. *School District*, 164 Pa. 629, 30 A. 482 (1894).

Illinois ex rel. *McCollum* v. *Board of Education*, 333 U.S. 203 (1948).

Kaplan v. *School District*, 171 Minn. 142, 214 N.W. 18, 57 A.L.R. 185 (1927).

Knowlton v. *Baumhover*, 182 Iowa 691, 166 N.W. 202, 5 A.L.R. 841 (1918).

Lewis v. *Allen*, 159 N.Y. Supp. 807 (1957).

Lewis v. *Board of Education*, 157 Misc. 520, 285 N.Y. Supp. 164 (1935), *appeal dismissed*, 276 N.Y. 490, 12 N.E. 2d. 172 (1937).

McGowan v. *Maryland*, 366 U.S. 420 (1961).

Miami Military Institute v. *Leff*, 220 N.Y. Supp. 799 (1926).

Millard v. *Board of Education*, 121 Ill. 297, 10 N.E. 669 (1887).

Miller v. *Cooper*, 56 N.M. 355, 244 P. 2d. 520 (1952).

Moore v. *Monroe*, 64 Iowa 367, 20 N.W. 475, 52 Am. St. Rep. 444 (1884).

Murray v. *Curlett*, 179 A. 2d. 698 (1962).

Nessle v. *Hum*, 1 Ohio N.P. 140 (1894).

New Haven v. *Torrington*, 132 Conn. 194, 43 A. 2d. 455 (1945).

North v. *Trustees of the University of Illinois*, 137 Ill. 296, 27 N.E. 54 (1891).

O'Conner v. *Hendrick*, 184 N.Y. 421, 77 N.E. 612, 7 L.R.A. (n.s.) 402 (1906).

People ex rel. *Latimer* v. *Board of Education*, 349 Ill. 228, 68 N.E. 2d. 305, 167 A.L.R. 1467 (1946).

People ex rel. *Lewis* v. *Graves*, 245 N.Y. 195, 156 N.E. 663 (1927).

People ex rel. *Ring* v. *Board of Education*, 245 Ill. 334, 92 N.E. 251, 29 L.R.A. (n.s.) 442 (1910).

People ex rel. *Vollmar* v. *Stanley*, 81 Col. 276, 255 Pac. 610 (1927).

Permoli v. *New Orleans*, 3 How. (U.S.) 589 (1845).

Pfeiffer v. *Board of Education*, 118 Mich. 560, 77 N.W. 250, 42 L.R.A. 536 (1898).

Richter v. *Cordes*, 100 Mich. 278, 58 N.W. 1110 (1894).

St. Hedwig's Industrial School v. *Cook County*, 289 Ill. 432, 142 N.E. 629 (1919).

Schempp v. *School District of Abington*, 177 Fed. Supp. 398 (1959).

Schempp v. *School District of Abington*, 201 F. Supp. 815 (1962).

School District of Abington v. *Schempp*, 364 U.S. 298 (1960).

School District of Abington v. *Schempp* and *Murray* v. *Curlett*, 374 U.S. 203 (1963).

Spiller v. *Inhabitants of Woburn*, 12 Allen (Mass.) 127 (1866).

State ex rel. *Atwood* v. *Johnson*, 170 Wis. 251, 176 N.W. 224 (1920).

Bibliography

American Association of School Administrators. *Religion and the Schools*, 1964.

ASCH, S. E. *Studies of Independence and Conformity: A Minority of One Against a Unanimous Majority*, 1956.

ATHEARN, W. S. *Religious Education and American Democracy*, 1917.

BAINTON, R. H. *The Travail of Religious Liberty*, 1958.

BARKER, E. *Church, State and Study; Essays*, 1930.

BATES, M. S. *Religious Liberty: An Inquiry*, 1945.

BEALE, H. K. *Are American Teachers Free?* 1936.

———. *A History of Freedom of Teaching*, 1941.

BEARD, C. AND M. *The Rise of American Civilization*, 1933.

BELL, S. *The Church, the State and Education in Virginia*, 1930.

BEMAN, L. T. *Religious Teaching in the Public Schools*, 1927.

BERENDA, R. W. *The Influence of the Group on the Judgements of Children*, 1950.

BETH, L. P. *The American Theory of Church and State*, 1958.

BILLINGTON, R. A. *The Protestant Crusade, 1800–1860*, 1938.

BLANSHARD, P. *American Freedom and Catholic Power*, 1949.

———. *Communism, Democracy and Catholic Power*, 1951.

———. *God and Man in Washington*, 1960.

BLANSHARD, P. *Religion and the Schools,* 1963.

BLAU, J. L. *Cornerstones of Religious Freedom in America,* 1949.

BOORSTIN, D. *The Americans: The Colonial Experience,* 1958.

BOWERS, C. *The Young Jefferson,* 1945.

BRANT, I. *James Madison: Nationalist, 1780–1787,* 1948.

BROWN, E. E. *The Making of Our Middle Schools,* 1903.

BUCKLEY, W. F., JR. *God and Man at Yale,* 1951.

BUCKLIN, J. *Theodore Roosevelt and His Times,* Vol. I, 1951.

BURY, J. B. *A History of Freedom of Thought,* 1952.

BUTLER, N. M. *Liberty, Equality and Fraternity,* 1942.

BUTTS, R. F. *American Tradition in Religion and Education,* 1950.

CHITWOOD, O. P. *A History of Colonial America,* 1961.

COBB, S. H. *The Rise of Religious Liberty in America,* 1902.

CONFREY, B. *Secularism in American Education, Its History,* 1931.

COOK, L. A. *Community Backgrounds of Education,* 1938.

COOLEY, T. M. *A Treatise on Constitutional Limitations,* 8th ed. Vol. II, Ch. XIII, 1927.

CORWIN, E. S. *A Constitution of Powers in a Secular State,* 1951.

COUSINS, N. *In God We Trust,* 1958.

CUBBERLEY, E. P. *Public Education in the United States,* 1934.

CULVER, R. B. *Horace Mann and Religion in the Massachusetts Public Schools,* 1929.

CURTI, M. *The Growth of American Thought,* 1951.

CUSHMAN, R. E. *Civil Liberties in the United States,* 1956.

DAWSON, J. M. *America's Way in Church, State and Society,* 1953.

DEARDEN, R. JR., AND WATSON, D. *The Bible of the Revolution,* 1931.

DODD, C. H. *The Authority of the Bible,* 1958.

DUNN, W. K. *What Happened to Religious Education?* 1958.

ECKENRODE, H. J. *Separation of Church and State in Virginia,* 1910.

FELLMAN, D. *The Limits of Freedom,* 1959.

———. *The Supreme Court and Education,* 1960.

FRANZBLAU, A. N. *Religious Belief and Character Among Jewish Adolescents,* Teachers College Contribution to Education, No. 635, Columbia University, 1934.

FRIEDMAN, L. M. *Early American Jews,* 1934.

GABEL, R. J. *Public Funds for Church and Private Schools,* 1937.

GREENE, E. B. *Religion and the State,* 1941.

HAMILTON, O. T. *The Courts and the Curriculum,* 1927.

HARE, A. P. *Handbook of Small Group Research,* 1962.

HARNER, N. C. *Religion's Place in General Education,* 1949.

HARTFORD, E. F. *Moral Values in Public Education,* 1958.

HEALEY, R. M. *Jefferson on Religion and Public Education,* 1962.

HENRY, V. *The Place of Religion in the Public Schools,* 1950.

HONEYWELL, R. J. *The Educational Works of Thomas Jefferson,* 1931.

JOHNSON, A. W. *Legal Status of Church and State Relationships in the United States,* 1934.

———— AND YOST, F. H. *Separation of Church and State in the United States,* 1948.

KILPATRICK, W. H. *The Dutch Schools of New Netherland and Colonial New York,* 1912.

KINNEY, C. B., JR. *Church and State, the Struggle for Separation in New Hampshire, 1630–1900,* 1955.

KURLAND, P. B. *Religion and the Law,* 1962.

LERNER, M. *America as a Civilization,* 1957.

LOCKE, J. *A Letter Concerning Toleration.* Reprinted from *Great Books of the Western World,* Vol. 45, 1952.

MANWARING, F. *Render Unto Caesar: The Flag-Salute Controversy,* 1962.

MARTIN, R. H. *Our Public Schools — Christian or Secular,* 1952.

MASON, R. E. *Moral Values and Secular Education,* 1950.

McCOLLUM, V. *One Woman's Fight,* 1951.

Methodist Church. *Church-State Issues in Religion and Public Education,* 1953.

MEYER, J. C. *Church and State in Massachusetts, 1740–1833,* 1930.

MILLER, P. *The New England Mind,* 1939.

————. *Roger Williams: His Contribution to the American Tradition,* 1953.

MODE, P. G. *Source Book and Bibliographical Guide for American Church History,* 1921.

MOEHLMAN, C. H. *School and Church,* 1944.

MOEHLMAN, C. H. *The Wall of Separation Between Church and State,* 1951.

MORISON, S. E. *Harvard College in the Seventeenth Century,* 2 Vols., 1936.

———. *The Puritan* Pronaos, 1936.

MORTON, R. K. *God in the Constitution,* 1933.

NICHOLAS, R. F. *Religion and American Democracy,* 1959.

O'NEILL, J. *Catholicism and American Freedom,* 1952.

———. *Religion and Education Under the Constitution,* 1949.

PADOVER, S. *The Complete Jefferson,* 1943.

PARRINGTON, V. *Main Currents in American Thought,* 1930.

PFEFFER, L. *Church, State and Freedom,* 1953.

RAY, M. A. *American Opinion of Roman Catholicism in the Eighteenth Century,* 1936.

READ, C. *The Constitution Reconsidered,* 1938.

"Religion and the State — a Symposium," *Law and Contemporary Problems,* Vol. 14, Winter, 1949.

RICHARDSON, J. D. *Messages and Papers of the Presidents,* 1896.

SCHACHNER, N. *Church, State and Education.* Reprinted from the *American Jewish Year Book,* Vol. 49, (1947–48), 1947.

SCHLESINGER, A., JR. *The Age of Jackson,* 1949.

SEBALY, A. L. *Teacher Education and Religion,* 1959.

SMITH, S. *The Relation of the State to Religious Education,* 1926.

SPARKS, J. *The Works of Benjamin Franklin,* 1844.

SPEAR, S. T. *Religion and the State,* 1876.

STEWART, G., JR. *A History of Religious Education in Connecticut,* 1924.

STOKES, A. P. *Church and State in the United States,* 3 Vols., 1950.

SWEET, W. S. *The Story of Religion in America,* 1950.

THAYER, V. T. *The Role of the Schools in American Society,* 1960.

THORPE, F. N. *The Federal and State Constitutions, Colonial Charters, and Other Organic Laws of the States,* Vols. I–VII, 1909.

TORPEY, W. G. *Judicial Doctrines of Religious Rights in America,* 1948.

VAN DUSEN, H. P. *God in Education,* 1951.

WALSH, J. J. *Education of the Founding Fathers of the Republic: Scholasticism in the Colonial Colleges,* 1935.

WARD, N. *The Simple Cobler of Aggawam,* 1647.

WHIPPLE, L. *Our Ancient Liberties,* 1927.

————. *The Story of Civil Liberty in the United States,* 1927.

WIERNIK, P. *History of the Jews in America,* 1930.

WILL, A. S. *Life of Cardinal Gibbons,* 1922.

WILSTACH, P. *Adams-Jefferson Letters,* 1925.

WOODBRIDGE, F. J. E. *Nature and Mind,* 1937.

WRIGHT, T. G. *Literary Culture in Early New England, 1620–1730,* 1920.

ZOLLMAN, C. F. *American Civil Church Law,* 1917.

————. *Church and School in the American Law,* 1918.

Index